D1458413

Oxford and the Evangelical Succession

Oxford and the Evangelical Succession

Sir Marcus Loane

ISBN 1-84550-245-0
ISBN 978-1-84550-245-4

10 9 8 7 6 5 4 3 2 1

First published in 1950
This edition published in 2007
by
Christian Focus Publications Ltd.,
Geanies House, Fearn, Ross-shire,
IV20 1TW, Scotland

www.christianfocus.com

Cover design by Danie Van Straaten

Printed and bound by WS Bookwell, Finland

Contents

To my wife, true and willing helpmate
in home and ministry, with gratitude
and affection this book is inscribed.

Foreword

I feel honoured that Canon Marcus Loane has asked me to write a foreword to this timely and valuable book, not only because anyone who is associated in any way with the great men it portrays is highly favoured, but because their example and specific message are desperately needed today. Indeed it is not too much to say that therein lies the solution to our present-day problems.

Canon Loane's book is a worthy successor to Bishop Ryle's Christian Leaders of the Eighteenth Century. To bring back to our memory their lives, to recall to our mind their teaching, and to reveal afresh the secret of their power, is a signal service to our own and to future generations.

One cannot read the story of these men, so fascinatingly told in these pages, without receiving one indelible impression, namely, that of their supreme devotion to Jesus Christ and utter loyalty to the doctrines of Grace.

Lecky says of the Evangelicals of the eighteenth century, 'They gradually changed the whole spirit of the English Church. They infused into it new fire and a passion of devotion, kindled a spirit of fervent philanthropy, raised the standard of clerical duty and completely altered the whole tone and tendency of the ministers.

Through the ministry of such men as these whose story is told in this book, there was established in the centre of the national life a redeemed community, exhilaratingly conscious of their debt to grace and therefore of their love for the Christ who was its author. It was also a worshipping community, indifferent to surroundings and to the refinements and technique of worship, because its adoring spirit transcended all those human things and found satisfaction in a personal adoration of the Lord of Glory. Thus we, who have lost something of their ecstasy, think their worship dull. The core of their gospel was the grace of God which redeems helpless sinners. This aroused a missionary dynamic which had no need of the constant flagellations which today keep alive our missionary interest. Their love was creative and had to find some expression, some outlet, in action. They found it in the Societies which are a monument to their care for both the physical and spiritual welfare of all mankind.

Today, the world is frantically searching for security and looking more and more to material philosophy personified in human dictatorship. A Church which hopes to transform our civilization as the Evangelicals transformed the face of England will not do it by deifying its leaders or magnifying its priesthood, but by magnifying its Lord and demonstrating His power to bring peace and security.

The progressive regimentation of the individual which is a characteristic of our age does nothing to check the drift. Centralization and controls help to produce the type of person who is content to leave others to think and plan for him and to decide the mould which his religious life shall take. The increasing power of diocesan organization, reinforced by recent legislation and necessitating ever-mounting financial demands, is gradually eliminating the type of initiative which was the glory of our Church and was manifest in the great missionary societies. The preaching of the Church no longer sets forth in all its grandeur the doctrine of grace, which glorifies Christ and which is the mainspring of our worship and the motive power of our organization, but rather the ethical exhortation which is an appropriate accompaniment of the 'Welfare Church', and is only Christian in that it offers Christ as an example.

I can conceive of nothing better than that we should recover that single-minded devotion to the Lord and to the grace which the heroes of this book exalted and proclaimed, and thus prepare the way for the revival and renewal which accompanied their preaching.

If this book should lead us to proclaim its message afresh, how immeasurably great will be its service to our day and our generation.

The author, nurtured in the happy tradition of the diocese of Sydney, has presented his heroes in a most attractive setting. His gracious style and the ease and often beauty of his language, make reading a delight. May this book be the means of pointing the way to spiritual revival without which the future seems to offer only the atom bomb and its devastating possibilities.

T. G. Mohan, M.A.,
Secretary, Church Pastoral Aid Society.

Author's Preface

This short series of biographical studies bears the title of Oxford and the Evangelical Succession, and this may need some kind of explanation. It is not a study of Oxford as the nursing-ground of Evangelical thought and scholarship, but of men who passed through Oxford to prove themselves on the field of Evangelical life and leadership. As a matter of fact, two of the five were not Oxford men at all; John Newton and Thomas Scott had little school and no university education to fit them for their place in life. But both have a claim on our interest as we trace the succession of Oxford Evangelicals; their conversion was so decisively linked up with the story of others that the narrative cannot be thought complete apart from them.

My aim has been to tell in broad outline the main story of these five lives so as to bring out their character and their particular contribution to the Evangelical Movement. As far as possible, I have endeavoured to do this in the light of their own words or the words of their contemporaries. I have tried to show the remarkable line of descent from one generation to another as God raised up spiritual sons to carry on the work age by age. And I have tried to show how these honoured fathers of the

Evangelical Party were used, each in turn, to help and influence many others whose praise is now in all the churches.

Some would dispute the claim for George Whitefield to stand at the head of the Church Evangelicals; but such a man as John Charles Ryle dared to place him first and foremost among all the leaders of the eighteenth century. It is not an easy task to compress the vast mass of material on the life of Whitefield, in public and private, into so brief a space, but I trust that I have made out the claim. The torch passed from his hand to that of John Newton in the second generation, and his life is full of romance and surprise. He was like a spiritual father both to Scott and Cecil in the third generation, and great was their value in the age which saw the steady development of the Evangelical cause as a vital and lasting factor in the life of the Church of England. Scott and Cecil were in turn the spiritual guides of Daniel Wilson, whose great gifts as a missionary statesman have never perhaps been fully recognized.

Thus we see how God used each generation to beget and quicken another so as to maintain the succession of these remarkable men. It is right to stress the fact that they were all strong Churchmen. They loved the Church of England, and refused to leave her in spite of scorn and contempt. They were devoted to the form of doctrine in her Articles and the form of worship in her Liturgy, and they thought that there were none to compare with the Reformation formularies which are the pride of the Church of England. They were all moderate Calvinists in an age when feeling and controversy ran high; they were all practical Christians in an age when slackness and stupidity lay like a dead hand on the Church. They were earnest students of the Bible, and were as much at home on their knees as a priest of old before the Mercy Seat. They preached in order to get souls saved, and their ministries were richly owned by God. Are not all these the marks of true worth and greatness in the Kingdom of which Jesus is Lord and King?

I have tried to trace the inner story of their spiritual development, and where material has been wanting I have tried to show what manner of men they were from their written works and their public ministry. If we would know what kind of trust is ours as heirs of the Evangelical Movement, let us study the lives of these noble men and seek to share the secret of their devotion. Their deeds are part of the inheritance of the saints on earth; their names are the glory of the Evangelical party. Let us reverence their memory; let us emulate their example.

I have appended a bibliography to each of the five studies. Any obscurity in the shortened footnote references will, it is hoped, be made clear by a glance at the appropriate bibliography.

The illuminating extract from *Rogue Herries* on pp. 54–9 is quoted by permission of Sir Hugh Walpole's executors and Macmillan & Co. Ltd.

1

George Whitefield
1714–70

George whitefield was born on December 14, 1714 in the Bell Inn at Gloucester, the city where Hooper had sealed a true witness by his death at the stake. He was the youngest of seven children, and he came of good stock; but his parents had met with the sorry fruits of fallen fortune, and he had to do battle with poverty while still in his childhood. His father died when he was only two years of age, and his mother married for the second time when he was ten years old. His residence in Gloucester made it possible for him to receive a good education at the Free Grammar School of that city, and this at least paved the way for his later career at Oxford. He became a day scholar at the Grammar School at the age of twelve, and he soon won a name for himself through his prowess in elocution and recitation. But much against his own desire, he was compelled to leave school at the age of fifteen in order to assist in the duties of the Bell Inn. He donned the blue apron and took his place behind the bar for nigh a year and a half, drawing and serving for the tipsters and tradesmen who loved to haunt the Bell. But this state of things did not last more than eighteen months, for business did not flourish and his mother gave it up in the end altogether. It was about twelve months later that he paid a visit to an elder brother at Bristol, when he heard the sermon which first awoke his soul to serious thought for God. His old life and habits soon became distasteful in the extreme; he gave up the reading of plays, and lost his desire to go on the stage. He began to try his hand at sermon making, and was filled with desire to be ordained as a minister of the Church of England.

He was still a stranger to the comfort of the Gospel in a saving knowledge of Christ; but God had made him an earnest seeker for truth, and he strove to live up to such light as he had. He once recalled:

> When I was sixteen years of age, I began to fast twice a week for thirty-six hours together, prayed many times a day, received the Sacrament every Lord's Day, fasting myself almost to death all the forty days of Lent, during which I made it a point of duty never to go less than three times a day to public worship, besides seven times a day to my private prayers; yet I knew no more that I was to be born again in God, born a new creature in Christ Jesus, than if I were never born at all.[1]

Then an old school fellow revived in his mind the idea of going to Oxford, and he went back to his old schoolmaster at St. Mary de Crypt in order to prepare himself for undergraduate life. The Gloucester Grammar School held two exhibitions at Pembroke College, and friends were raised up to support his claims for one of these. Success crowned their efforts, and his mother borrowed the ten pounds which custom required for the enrolment of his name as a servitor at Pembroke. It was towards the end of 1732, while not yet eighteen years of age, that he took his place at Oxford, 'a shy, retiring, shabbily dressed lad, with dark blue eyes and a singularly beautiful face'.[2] He found himself at last on the first rung of that ladder which he was so anxious to climb, and he gladly engaged in the menial tasks that fell to a servitor to pay for the education for which he longed. Above all, his eager desire for a saving knowledge of truth kept pace with his progress as a student, and soon began to ripen fast into a clear and decided conversion.

Oxford perhaps had never sunk to so low an ebb of academic thought or spiritual life as at the time when Whitefield took his place in Pembroke. There were few lectures, and still less learning; the chief centres of life and interest were the cockpit and the tavern. Gentlemen-commoners in powdered wigs lounged in Lyne's Coffee House, or made love to tradesmen's daughters in the Merton Walks.[3] Yet it was just in the darkness of these years that a new movement took its rise which was soon to shake England from end to end. In November 1729, when John Wesley returned to take up his duties as a Fellow of Lincoln, he found a small group of students gathered round his brother Charles. He placed himself at the head of this little band, and they began to meet nightly in his rooms outside which the famous Lincoln vine twines round the windows. They read the Greek text of the New Testament together, and pledged themselves to live by rule. Thus they reviewed what each had done in the day which had passed, and they planned what steps each should take on the morrow at hand. They took the Sacrament once each month, a custom which had fallen into sad neglect, and they addressed themselves to the needs of the sick and poor. They set out to visit prisoners in the Castle gaol, reading and praying with them in spite of smells and fever; and they set up a little school in the slums, paying the mistress and clothing the children. Loose and careless students looked on, and made them the butt for endless jibes and nicknames. They were laughed at as Bible Moths and Bigots; they were dubbed as the Holy Club or Supererogation Men. Many other names were coined, but at length someone hit on an old soubriquet and hailed them as a new sect of Methodists.

This name came into vogue at once, although no one could have guessed that it would one day become a name of great and lasting honour. But none of these men had yet attained a clear knowledge of the way of salvation; they were in dead earnest, but they were still vaguely groping their way towards the light. 'They were all…tenacious of order to the last degree, and observant for conscience' sake of every rule of the Church and every statute both of the university and of their respective Colleges,' wrote John Wesley in 1777, some fifty years later; 'they were all orthodox in every point, firmly believing not only the three creeds, but whatsoever they judged to be the doctrine of the Church of England.'[4] They were in fact all too rigid in self-discipline and too rabid in church ritual; and such were the hall-marks, not of cheerful Christians, but of morose ascetics. For a time they followed much the same line as did the men of the Oxford Movement under Newman and Pusey a hundred years later, and an outburst of mild persecution ensued in university circles. Their numbers fell away until there were only seven still in the field: the two Wesleys and James Hervey, Morgan and Ingham, Broughton and Clayton. Morgan died a few weeks before Whitefield came to Pembroke, and it was commonly said that John Wesley had killed him with fasting. The Oxford Methodists were facing their darkest hour when they suddenly gained their most famous recruit. They were in general disfavour when George Whitefield began life at Pembroke, but he admired them from the first. Twelve months passed by while he admired them in secret, and then came an opportunity to make the acquaintance of Charles Wesley. It was a notable incident for both men, and George Whitefield soon stood in the midst of that small Oxford circle, on fire for God and for glory.

Whitefield seems to have been the first of that little band at Oxford to get a clear grasp of the Gospel, and not one of them held it more tenaciously than he did to the end. In 1740, he published *A Short Account of God's Dealings* with him up to the year of his ordination, and this tells us how the turning point was reached when Charles Wesley lent him a little book called *The Life of God in the Soul of Man*. 'I never knew what true religion was', he wrote, 'till God sent me that excellent treatise.'[5] He saw for the first time that man must be born again, or perish. He took the book in his hand and prayed that if he were not yet a Christian, God would show him what true Christianity was. Then he read on and discovered that true religion means a vital union of the soul with God; that is, Christ formed within the heart. This was like a ray of divine light which shone clear on his soul and put darkness to flight. He wrote letters forthwith to all his kith and kin, and spoke to the students who came into his room, telling them that there was such a thing as the new birth until they thought that he was beside himself. But he was not beside himself; he had grasped the secret of everlasting life. 'It may be superstitious perhaps,' he once confessed, 'but whenever I go to Oxford, I cannot help running to that place where Jesus Christ first revealed Himself to me and gave me the new birth.'[6] He was now determined to live like a saint and to work like a slave, putting away all trifles and living by rule lest a moment should be misspent. Thus he began to care for the sick and read to the poor, and he allied himself with the Methodists in all their charities.

But from the first he felt a particular longing for the humility of the Lord Jesus Christ, and for a time he seems to have been in danger of laying too much weight on self-discipline and self-denial. He began to practise the most rigorous forms of austerity and to live like an ascetic, as though he thought that holiness could be attained by a kind of legalism or mysticism. He writes in *A Short Account:*

> I always chose the worst sort of food, though my place furnished me with variety. I fasted twice a week. My apparel was mean. I thought it unbecoming a penitent to have his hair powdered. I wore woollen gloves, a patched gown, and dirty shoes; and though I was then convinced that the Kingdom of God did not consist in meats and drinks, yet I resolutely persisted in these voluntary acts of self-denial because I found them great promoters of the spiritual life.[7]

At length he shut himself up for six weeks in his study, and cut himself off from all his old friends. Then Charles Wesley sought him out and took him to see John, who advised him to resume all known duties, but to rely upon none of them for inward peace or holiness.[8] But he could not escape the penalty of this ascetic life with its long-continued abstinence, for his health had been so impaired that a day soon came when he found himself unable to creep up the college stairs. He was ill for seven weeks, but he learned to think of those weeks not long before Easter in the year 1735, as 'a glorious visitation'.[9] All the uncertainties of the past twelve months, all the despondencies of a long, lone fight, were laid at rest, and he saw that the way of holiness no less than the Way of salvation was through faith in the name of Immanuel. Never again did he pursue the vain path of the legalist or the ascetic; never again did he turn aside to strange views of Christian perfection. The long night of darkness and desertion had passed away, and the Bright and Morning Star had begun to shine with never fading beauty in the sky of his soul.[10]

By the end of May 1735, he had kept no less than nine terms at Oxford without a break; but then, on the advice of friends, he left Pembroke for a time to recruit his health and to visit his family at Gloucester. He now had far clearer views of the way of salvation, and his home-folk were much surprised to find him so cheerful and content. He was soon made instrumental in the awakening of souls to the reality of things unseen, and a little band of brethren was formed in his native city on the model of the group at Oxford. He also gave himself up at this time to an intense study of the Bible, and all other books were laid aside while he pondered the Word of God. 'When God was pleased to shine with power upon my soul,' he said, 'I could no longer be contented to feed on husks or what the swine did eat; the Bible then was my food; there, and there only, I took delight.'[11] He read it on his knees, and tried to pray over every line and every word. 'I got more true knowledge from reading the Book of God in one month', he wrote, 'than I could ever have acquired from all the writings of men!'[12] 'Oh, what sweet communion had I daily vouchsafed with God in prayer!' he wrote again. 'How often have I been carried out beyond myself when sweetly meditating in the fields!'[13] He had received more light on the doctrines of grace as one result of his long and bitter conflict; they were firmly grasped, and his hold was never loosed. Nine months later, in March 1736, he went back to Oxford, his heart full of the pangs and the pleasures of the new birth. But his position as a servitor had not been lost to sight by his fellow-students, and he had to suffer many indignities for the sake of his hard-won convictions. The Master of Pembroke used to chide him and once threatened to expel him if he continued to visit the sick and poor, while a handful of the students used to throw dirt at him or take their pay away from him because his life was a rebuke to them.[14]

But while he was in Gloucester, he had met Lady Selwyn, who told Bishop Benson of his desire to take Orders in the Church of England. A few days later, as he was returning from the cathedral service, one of the vergers asked him to wait on the bishop who was anxious to speak with him. The good bishop met him at the head of the palace stairs, and led him by the hand into a private room. He said that he had heard of his character, and had marked his behaviour in church; and that notwithstanding the fact that he had said that he would not ordain a man under three and twenty years of age, he would take it as his duty to ordain Whitefield as soon as he was ready. He then drew out his purse, and made him a welcome present of five guineas. But this unexpected offer came to him just at a time when he was full of scruples about his own fitness for the ministry. 'God knows how deep a concern entering into the ministry and preaching was to me,' he declared in after years; 'I have prayed a thousand times till the sweat has dropped from my face like rain, that God of His infinite mercy would not let me enter the Church before He called me to and thrust me forth in His work.'[15] He wrote to all his friends in town and country to ask them to pray against the step, but they all with one voice urged him to close with the bishop's offer. This cut the knot, and brought him to the point of decision. 'I began to think myself', he wrote, 'that if I held out any longer, I should fight against God.'[16] Thus on Trinity

Sunday in June 1736, at the age of twenty-one, he was ordained in Gloucester Cathedral. 'I could think of nothing', he said, 'but Samuel's standing, a little child before the Lord.'[17] He preached his first sermon the next Sunday to a crowded congregation in St. Mary de Crypt, and a complaint was lodged at once with the bishop that he had driven fifteen people out of their wits. The good bishop merely hoped that their madness would not be forgotten before the next Sunday.[18]

'Thou, O God, knowest that when the bishop put his hand upon my head', exclaimed Whitefield, 'I looked for no other preferment than publicly to suffer for the Lamb of God.'[19] Bishop Benson had set aside two small livings for him, and treated him with the utmost kindness; but the Wesleys had now gone to Georgia, and he resolved to return to Oxford. He soon took his degree, and his time was spent in daily visits to the gaol and in the oversight of the Methodist schools. In August 1736, he took duty for two months at Tower Hill in the heart of London, and a tremendous sensation broke out under the spell of his youthful preaching. Then he moved on to spend two months more at Dummer, a small Hampshire village, where he received a pressing call from the Wesley brothers to throw in his lot with them in Georgia. Charles had come home to seek more labourers, and now wrote beseeching him to go. Then John also wrote to urge the claims of Georgia in moving words: 'What if thou art the man, Mr Whitefield? Do you ask what you shall have? Why, all you desire: food to eat, raiment to put on; a place where to lay your head, such as your Lord had not; and a crown of life that fadeth not away.'[20] Such an appeal Whitefield could not resist; he felt his heart leap as it were for joy. On January 1, 1737, he set out for Gloucester, and found that the bishop approved his plans. Then in March, he went to London, and was kindly received by the Trustees of the Colony. Potter and Gibson, the Primate and the Bishop of London, gave him a cordial interview, and his only want was a ship to sail without delay. But no vessel was to be had, and months were to slip past before he could cross the ocean.

The next twelve months were spent in an unbroken succession of preaching engagements, partly in Wessex, partly in London, and the course of labour on which he thus embarked was to form the ruling bias of his future career. From the very outset he was heard and hailed with applause such as few, if any, before or since, have ever known, and his popularity grew by leaps and bounds until the whole land rang with the fame of his doings. Thousands and tens of thousands crowded to hear him on Sundays and weekdays alike, and his name ran like wild-fire throughout the length and breadth of a startled realm. Hearers who were inclined to scoff at first sight of his youth were taken by surprise and carried by storm. Thus at Stonehouse, people crowded the church until it could not contain, and in Bristol, many clung to the rails of the organ loft in order to hear. Lordly offers were held out to induce him to remain, now here, now there, but no power on earth could confine him now to a single church or parish. He gave up most of the year to London, preaching nine times a week to men who heard like those who hear for eternity. Weekdays found him at Wapping Chapel or Tower Hill, at Ludgate or Newgate, and in many other churches as well; Sundays found him starting out at six in the morning at Cripplegate or Forster Lane, and then going on to preach three or four times elsewhere in the course of the day besides walking ten or twelve miles to and fro in order to keep his various appointments. Long before daybreak on Sundays, the streets were to be seen in a bustle as men hurried along to get a seat in church, with their lanterns in hand and their converse on the things that are above; so great were the crowds who came that constables had to be placed at the church doors to keep order and to prevent accidents, and yet thousands were often turned away from the largest churches for want of room.[21] 'The plain truth is', says Ryle, 'that a really eloquent extempore preacher, preaching the pure gospel with most uncommon gifts of voice and manner, was at that time an entire novelty in London.'[22] He might have been ruined by such limelight, but the grace of God preserved him; and many a time at midnight or at one in the morning, after he had been wearied almost to death in preaching all day, God gave new life to his soul as he knelt in prayer and praise with a few loving and faithful friends.[23]

At length, on December 30, 1737, he went on board a ship moored at Purfleet, and set out on the long voyage to Georgia. This was the first of no less than thirteen transatlantic journeys upon which he embarked, for his life from this time forward was to be divided between England and the New World. His ship still lay in the Downs, one day out from Deal, on the morning when John Wesley arrived home in England, and it was not until early in May that Charles Delamotte bade him welcome to the town of Savannah. He at once began to tour and visit the farms and homes of the early settlers, preaching a score of times week by week to little handfuls of scattered souls. There was still no regular ministry in the infant colony, and he was urged to let his name stand for nomination; and this meant an early voyage home to England for Priest's Orders and for approval of the appointment. He had also become absorbed with the idea of an orphan house to be built on the model of Francke's Orphanage at Halle in Germany. It was a well-meant scheme which he hoped would demonstrate the practical character of the Evangel, and it was to occupy a large share of his time and attention to the end of his life. But it seems to have been a design of rather doubtful wisdom from some view-points, and it was to load him with a world of care and responsibility. At all events, with this in view, after a stay of only a few months, he set sail in September 1738, and a perilous voyage of three months and more brought him to London in December. The Primate and the Bishop of London agreed to his appointment to Savannah, and approved of his plans for an orphanage in Georgia. In January 1739 he went up to Oxford where he received his full Orders at the hands of Bishop Benson; then he returned to raise funds in London before he set out once more for the New World.[24]

It was hardly more than twelve months since his preaching had been acclaimed as the most popular in all England, but he had been away just long enough for the whole aspect of things to undergo a drastic change. Signs of opposition from some quarters had not been wanting even twelve months before. The crowds who had followed him had emptied other church pews so freely that the clergy had grown angry; parishioners had been prone to complain that there was no room for the regular congregation when he was the preacher, and the wardens had put a stop to the weekday lectures from many church pulpits. But he now found that the great bulk of the clergy had grown hostile, and that almost all church pulpits were closed to him. He was looked at askance as a fanatic or an enthusiast, and this feeling had been aggravated by the fact that the Wesleys had begun to imitate him. He had published a sermon on the Nature and Necessity of the New Birth, which had been the means of the great awakening in Bristol and London, and the clergy were scandalized by a doctrine of Regeneration which did not coincide with their views of Baptismal Grace. But the thing which gave most offence was his violation of Church order in his visits from house to house among his friends to expound and exhort; this was an infringement of all true decorum which the clergy could by no means tolerate! Within three weeks after his return from Oxford, he preached more than twenty sermons and spoke nearly fifty times in private; but there were not more than half a dozen pulpits where he was still welcome. He was asked to preach in Great St. Helen's by his old friend Broughton, who held the afternoon lectureship; but Broughton was promptly dismissed from his office, and one more church was closed. In February, he went down to Bristol, the scene of his early triumphs, but within a fortnight not one pulpit in that city was still open to him. His great problem was thus how to get pulpits and how to collect funds, for his sphere of useful opportunity in the Church of England had begun to contract on every side.

It was at this juncture that he took the step which gave a new turn to the whole course of his ministry; he turned away from the closed pulpits of Bristol and took to the open air as a field preacher. He saw that there were thousands who would never attend a place of worship, and who always spent the Lord's Day in idleness and sin; and he resolved to go out in the spirit of a holy crusade and compel them to come in.[25] He thought of the Kingswood colliers who gave Bristol its coal and fuel, but who lived in a poor and neglected district without church or school. Their drunken savagery made them at times a public menace, and more than once troops had been called out to save the city from loot and plunder. After much prayer, he walked out on Saturday afternoon, February 17, 1739, and preached to some two hundred colliers on Hannam Mount. 'I thought it might be doing service to my Creator', he wrote in a manuscript narrative of the event, 'who had a mountain for His pulpit, and the heavens for His sounding-board.'[26] The news soon spread, and though it was in the depth of winter, the crowds grew each time he returned; the two hundred on February 17 had swollen to ten thousand by February 25, and that ten thousand had grown to more than twenty thousand by March 18! The fields and lanes were packed with men whose cheeks and clothes were black as the pits where they toiled; but all were hushed to hear him preach, rapt in silent awe and wonder. 'Having no righteousness of their own to renounce,' he wrote, 'they were glad to hear of a Jesus who…came not to call the righteous, but sinners to repentance.'[27] His first discovery of their response was when he saw the white gutters made by the tears which coursed down their soiled cheeks. Hundreds were brought under strong conviction, and the future proved that this led to a sound and thorough conversion.

The Rose Green and the Fish Ponds as well as Hannam Mount were soon chosen as stands for preaching, and the fields of Kingswood were thus the first rough cradle in which a new movement was rocked and nurtured. Many came on horseback or by carriage from a distance, and twenty or thirty coaches were to be seen drawn up on the edge of the crowd. The open sky above, the spreading fields around, with the sight of those vast numbers, some on horseback, some in coaches, and so many thousands standing for an hour or more at a stretch, all wrapped in deep silence or drenched with tears, made up a scene such as England has seldom known. He could never forget the thrill with which he heard the long echo of their singing as it travelled from end to end of those vast crowds. He was as much amazed at the result of his own field preaching as any one; but he saw at once that it met a need and had a power which should not be confined to a single city. He wrote to John Wesley with an urgent summons to come and take his place in Bristol so that he might be free to visit other centres. 'March 22, 1739: I am but a novice; you are acquainted with the great things of God. Come, I beseech you; come quickly.'[28] Wesley felt most reluctant at first, but came eight days later to join him in the fields. He then settled down to constant preaching in the open air in Bristol and its environs, while Whitefield moved to Gloucester where he daily addressed many thousands in his brother's field or in the county 'boothall'. He then made a short tour through South Wales with Howell Harris, the one preaching in English and the other in Welsh to many thousands. They were denied the use of church pulpits, and they invariably turned elsewhere: to a horse-block or a churchyard on fine days; to a large room or an ale-house in bad weather. On his return from this circuit as he loved to call these short tours, he set his face towards the east and preached his way through town and country until at the end of April he was back in London. Whitefield had found his great life's sphere, and he never faltered from that day when he made up his mind to do or die at Kingswood.

One church was still open to him in the metropolis, and on Friday, April 27, he went to preach at Islington. But the wardens asked him for his licence, and then denied his right to the pulpit. Rather than cause a disturbance, he held his peace until the service was over and then preached his sermon to the congregation in the churchyard. This he did again the next day, and went that night to a friend's place at Dowgate Hill. There he found two or three thousand gathered in the street, and he was obliged to preach from the windowsill. 'Surely it is high time', was his pungent comment, 'to take to the field!'[29] This decisive step he took on the morrow, the last Sunday in that stirring month of April, when he went to Moorfields in the morning and Kennington Common in the evening. He was warned that he would never escape from the crowd at Moorfields alive, but they fell back and let him pass right through to the very midst of its gravelled walks and grass-laid plots. Thus the last thread was cast, and from then on, he spoke in the open air in all weathers and at all seasons. The next Sunday, May 6, there were some twenty thousand in 'the city mall' at Moorfields in the morning, and near fifty thousand in the riff-raff park at Kennington Common in the evening. 'There was an awful silence among the people,' he wrote; 'I continued my discourse for an hour and a half.'[30] He went on preaching at these two centres Sunday by Sunday throughout his stay in London; but he also began to lift up his voice in many other parts of the city, such as Hackney and Mayfair, Smithfields and Blackheath. The crowds often numbered more than twenty thousand, and more than a hundred coaches could be counted at times; his voice could be heard near a mile, and their singing two miles away.[31]

All this meant that, within a few months of his first attempt at field preaching, he had borne his witness from all sorts of pulpits; he had preached in bowling greens and glasshouse-yards, from market cross and cudgel stage; on windmill steps, in open fields, with horse-block or table or nothing at all on which to take his stand. 'I hope I shall learn more and more every day', he wrote, 'that no place is amiss for preaching the Gospel.'[32] He had been sought after with amazing avidity two years before when the churches were still open to him, but he became far more popular from the moment when he took to the fields. It is difficult for the modern world to recapture the thrill, the sensation, which field preaching inspired, for it had been wholly unknown in Great Britain before, apart from the field preaching of the Scotch Covenanters. It was a new experiment in the eighteenth century, but it was much too bold for the Church as a whole. There was nothing in his conduct to compromise his position as a minister of the Church of England, but it was condemned out of hand by the clergy who drank, and diced, and swanked, and swore, and failed to preach the Gospel. There were a few honourable exceptions throughout England, but the great bulk of the clergy turned him out of church and pulpit once and for all. He loved the Church in which he was ordained; he gloried in her Articles, and used her Liturgy with delight.[33] But he found himself disowned and despised, and his pulpit ministrations in the Church of England were brought to all but a fullstop.[34] But if ever a love for souls burned with pure and lambent flame in man's heart, that man was George Whitefield. There were thousands who would never hear a sermon inside a church, yet who would listen greedily when he preached in the open air. Hundreds began to wait on him in deep concern, and he often spent half the night with troubled souls, clearing up their questions or smoothing out their problems. 'Brethren,' he cried, 'my heart's desire and prayer to God is that you may be saved; for this cause I follow my Master without the camp. I care not how much of His sacred reproach I bear, so that some of you be converted from the error of your ways.'[35]

In August 1739 he sailed once more for America, and the cool sea air soon braced up his health. He soon changed his mind with regard to the Savannah appointment, partly no doubt as a result of his success in field preaching. He was not the man to remain long in one fixed centre, and his whole character was far too expansive to let him take up the settled duties of a tiny parish in an out-of-the-way corner of the New World. He knew that he had dropped out of favour with the clergy at home, and he still felt with real pain the low tone to which the Church as a whole had succumbed. 'Oh pity, pity the Church of England!' he wrote; 'see how too, too many of her sons are fallen from her *Articles*, and preach themselves, not Christ Jesus the Lord!'[36] But he knew where blame was to be ascribed, and he could not conceal his grief for the criminal folly which seemed to rule so much of the clerical conduct: 'These, these are the men', he cried,

'...that hang out false lights, and so shipwreck unthinking souls in their voyage to the haven of eternity!'[37] But he had felt, too, the fascination of a free and itinerant calling, and he longed to rove through woods and fields as a huntsman of souls. 'I am, I profess, a member of the Church of England,' he said; 'but if they will not let me preach in the church, I will preach anywhere; all the world is my parish, and I will preach wherever God gives me opportunity.'[38] The prime result of such feelings was that the course of his life from this time on to the day of his death was governed by a single pattern; he was engaged in one uniform employment which served to make each new year much the same as all the others.

On October 30, he went ashore at Lewis Town and set out to ride through one hundred and fifty miles of seemingly endless forest to Philadelphia. The dead hand of hostility had not as yet fallen across the sea on the New World, and he was made gladly welcome by the clergy; but their churches were too small to house the numbers who flocked to hear, and he soon had recourse to more irregular avenues of preaching. He went on to New York, where he encountered the first serious opposition; he was disowned by his own Church, but he preached to huge crowds both in the fields and in friendly chapels. He was soon on his way back to Philadelphia, but that brief tour was the first step to an itinerant ministry in America. On November 29, 1739, he set out on the long journey south through Virginia and Carolina, and on January 11, 1740, he reached Savannah after a hard journey through primeval woods and miasmal swamps for at least six hundred miles. He soon obtained a grant of five hundred acres some ten miles from Savannah as a site for his orphanage for which he had chosen the name of Bethesda; he had it cleared and fenced at once, and the first brick of the main building was laid by the end of March. He then set out by sea for a two month tour of Pennsylvania, and found that church and pulpit were no longer free to him in Philadelphia; but he took to the fields and the crowds soon grew to ten and twenty thousand.

On his return in June he was engaged in preaching and tending the sick in Savannah, while he watched the buildings rise at Bethesda. At the end of August he went north once more by sea to escape the summer heat, and was away until near the end of the year. He spent most of his time in New England, and was heard by many thousands with great delight on the famous Boston Common. We catch a glimpse of his inner life in letters written while this tour was still in progress: 'Lean thou on His sacred bosom night and day,' he wrote in November; 'keep close to Him, and be what I long to be—a little child.. The more the Lord honours me, the more I feel my unworthiness. I am sometimes sick of love, and often, often sick of self.'[39] On December 13, he arrived once more at Savannah, and found his orphanage in full swing with a resident family of some eighty persons. But he soon felt the need to find someone who could introduce order and system to Bethesda, and the cloud which seemed to set for home and England was watched with the steady interest of a foregone conclusion.[40]

In March 1741, Whitefield arrived in London to face a trying time. 'Old and valued friends who had stood by and encouraged him through the storm of ecclesiastical hostility during his last visit…were now…scattered, or divided into Arminian and Calvinistic sectarianism.'[41] This marked the public outbreak of the great controversy which drove a wedge between Whitefield and the Wesleys, and which split the Evangelical Movement of the Eighteenth Century from top to bottom. Whitefield owed much to the Wesleys while at Oxford; they owed perhaps still more to him in their after career. He felt drawn by ties of peculiar affection to Charles Wesley, who was his senior by six years and who had introduced him to the Methodists at Oxford. Charles was the link between Whitefield and John Wesley, and his gentle nature helped to form a bond of union among them all their days. But a sad breach with John Wesley occurred at the close of 1740 when he began to preach in a strong Arminian strain. Whitefield loved and honoured him as his friend, 'but he would not part with a grain of sacred truth for the brother of his heart'.[42] He felt that he could not remain silent, and at length he wrote to him in the month of May:

> I can not entertain prejudices against your conduct and principles any longer without informing you. The more I examine the writings of the most experienced men and the experience; of the most established Christians, the more I differ from your notion about not committing sin, and your denying the doctrines of election and final perseverance of the saints. I dread coming to England, unless you are resolved to oppose these truths with less warmth than when I was there last.[43]

He wrote again in June in a yet more urgent strain to check, if possible, the drift to division: 'For Christ's sake, if possible, dear Sir, never speak against election in your sermons…For Christ's sake, let us not be divided amongst ourselves.'[44] But the time of healing was still far off, for the publication of John Wesley's sermon on Free Grace provoked a frank and open rupture. 'What a fond conceit is it to cry up perfection, and yet cry down the doctrine of final perseverance,' he wrote in September after he had read this sermon; 'O that you would not be too rash and precipitate! If you go on thus, honoured Sir, how can I concur with you?'[45]

Further letters which passed between the two men were full of earnest solicitude for the peace of Israel, but the outspoken prejudice of the Wesleys drove him at last to write an Open Letter in defence of the Doctrines of Grace. On his return to London in March 1741, Charles Wesley saw this Letter in manuscript, and begged him to sheathe his sword. But the Letter was soon in print, and the breach was complete. He had one interview with John Wesley, who summed it up in his Journal with real regret: 'March 28, 1741. He told me, he and I preached two different Gospels; and therefore, he not only would not join with me or give me the right hand of fellowship, but was resolved publicly to preach against me and my brother, wheresoever he preached at all.'[46] But the warm Welsh heart of Howell Harris was grieved by this quarrel, and scarce six months had passed before the breach was healed. Whitefield was easily moved in the way of Christian love, and in October, he wrote in a new strain to Wesley: 'May God remove all obstacles that now prevent our union! Though I hold particular election, yet I offer Jesus freely to every individual soul.'[47] He grieved to think that his friends and fellow-pilgrims should fall out by the way, and the end of the year saw them knit once more in the bonds of love. The breach was healed because they agreed to differ, and we only catch a distant echo of that ugly year of strife in the after days. Thus on September 11, 1747, Whitefield put John Wesley once more in mind of their compact:

> As for universal redemption, if we omit on each side the talking for or against reprobation, which we may do fairly, and agree as we already do in giving an universal offer to all poor sinners that will come and taste of the water of life, I think we may manage very well…I long to owe no man anything but love. This is a debt, Reverend Sir, I shall never be able to discharge to you or your brother. Jesus will pay you all. For His sake, I love and honour you very much, and rejoice as much in your success as in my own.[48]

Whitefield clung fast to the doctrines of grace right to the end, but he never ceased to proclaim a full and free gospel invitation for all who were willing to hear. 'I believe Christ's redemption will be applied to all that shall believe,' he wrote on June 29, 1750; 'who these are, we know not, and therefore we are to give a general offer and invitation; convinced of this, that every man's damnation is of himself, and every man's salvation all of God.'[49]

Whitefield found that his old hearers had all scattered in his absence, and two or three hundred were all that now gathered where there had been thousands before. But the Moorfields Tabernacle was set on foot, and his popularity steadily returned. He was much cheered by two short tours, first to Bristol, then in Essex, and in July he set out on his first visit to Scotland. He was given a great welcome both in Edinburgh and in Glasgow, and he preached both in kirk and field to ever-growing crowds. He travelled as far north as Aberdeen, and preached in at least thirty towns before he set out for London again at the end of October.[50] The winter months of 1741 were spent in London, and the early spring of 1742 saw a fresh visit to the west. Then he resolved to take the bold step of preaching at Moorfields on the great annual Whitsuntide holiday, the season of all others, he said, 'when, if ever, Satan's children keep up their rendezvous'.[51] He set out at six o'clock on Whit Monday, and chose a site for his wayside pulpit. A crowd of ten thousand heard him in hushed and solemn awe, and he was glad to find that for once, as it were, he had got the start of the devil. On his return at noon he found a crowd of twenty thousand or more, but all was noise and confusion. They were what he would have called 'the devil's castaways', the scum of the London slums, clad in rags and labelled with the telltale marks of vicious living. He felt that the fields were white for the harvest of Beelzebub rather than of Emmanuel, but the crowds soon left the merry-andrews and the puppet-players to hear him with reverent attention. He came back yet again at six o'clock in the evening, to the acute chagrin of the puppet masters. They flung rotten eggs, dead cats, and stones at him, until he felt that his soul was indeed among the lions. But he was left in possession of the field, and carried home a pocket full of notes from people in deep concern for their soul's salvation.[52]

He then set sail for Leith, and reached Scotland early in June at the time when the great Cambuslang Revival was in full swing. He preached three times, at two, at six, and at nine, on the day of his arrival to the thousands who had gathered on the heath-clad hill-sides. All night in the fields could be heard the voice of prayer and praise, and the next day the Lord's Supper was administered to upwards of twenty thousand in the open air. He was astonished at these days of the Son of Man: 'God seems to awaken scores together,' he wrote; 'I never was enabled to preach so before.'[53] One week's itinerary in the month of August on leaving Cambuslang gives an idea of his labours: 'On Thursday, August 19, I preached twice at Greenock; on Friday, three times at Kilbride, and again on Saturday, once; and twice at Stevenson. On Sunday, August 22, four times at Irvine; on Monday, once at Irvine, and three times at Kilmarnock; on Tuesday, once at Kilmarnock, and four times at Stewarton; on Wednesday, once at Stewarton, and twice at the Mearnes; and yesterday, twice at this place,' that is, at Cambuslang.[54] That meant twenty-six sermons within eight days at as many different centres; nor was this at all exceptional. 'I never preached with so much apparent success before,' he wrote of this circuit; 'I must cry out continually, Why me, Lord? Why me? Oh for a passive, tender, truly broken, child-like heart!'[55] He left Scotland at length in November and rode to London in five days. He spent the winter months in London, and the Moorfields Tabernacle had to be enlarged to hold the congregations. In the spring of 1743, he went on a preaching circuit in the West of England, where his labours were once more on the scale of his work in Scotland the year before. It was past one in the morning before he could lie down to rest at Gloucester; yet at five o'clock he was up and away to preach to another vast multitude at Stonehouse. He preached again at ten o'clock, and then rode on to Stroud to preach with uncommon power and freedom to some twelve thousand in the fields. At six in the evening he preached to a vast crowd at Minchinhampton, and closed the day with a love-feast for the United Societies. It was midnight before he went to bed, but the next day began with a similar programme.[56] The whole year was thus shared in ceaseless toil between London and the western counties, until in January 1744, we find him in Plymouth, preaching to dockers and seamen, and waiting for a fair wind to carry him back to the New World.

He sailed with a convoy in August 1744, on a voyage which took eleven weeks and which was not without adventure. This was to prove the longest of all his transatlantic visits, for it was spread over nearly four years of constant toil. But he had now discontinued his *Journals*, and his *Letters* are comparatively few in number for these years. Thus we lose that insight into the life of his own soul, which the journal would have supplied, while his letters contain less of historical value than those of any other period in his life. His *Journals* were a copious narrative of his trials and labours from December 28, 1737, to March 11, 1741, and they had been published in parts from time to time in England. James Hervey wrote to tell him what they had meant for him: 'Your Journals, dear Sir, were a means of bringing me to a knowledge of the truth.'[57] Henry Martyn was one day to record his sense of gratitude: 'July 20, 1805: Read some of Whitefield's journal, and found it a greater spur than any I have received a long time.'[58] But the *Journals* contained much that ought not to have been staged before the public eye, and they had at once been assailed by friends as well as foes. Bishop Warburton angrily declared that they proved him to be quite as mad as George Fox had been; Gilbert Tennent wrote in friendly strain to urge him to be more cautious. 'I thank you for your kind caution,' he replied; ' my mistakes often humble me. Never did Jesus send out a more weak and worthless wretch. I have not freedom now to continue writing a Journal.'[59] He was very sorry he had let so many details appear in print, and at length he felt obliged to bring out a new and expurgated edition. He wrote in June 1748:

> Alas! Alas! In how many things have I judged and acted wrong! I have been too rash and hasty in giving characters both of places and persons. Being fond of Scripture language, I have often used a style too apostolical, and at the same time I have been too bitter in my zeal. Wild-fire has been mixed with it, and I find that I frequently wrote and spoke in my own spirit when I thought I was writing and speaking by the assistance of the Spirit of God. I have likewise too much made inward impressions my rule of acting, and too soon and too explicitly published what had been better kept in longer or told after my death. By these things, I have given some wrong touches to God's Ark, and hurt the blessed cause I would defend.[60]

But the storm which brought his journals to an end was forgotten in the joy which met him as soon as he reached Boston, for he found that a great Revival had broken out in New England as a result of his own earlier ministry and the preaching of the Tennents. Two and three thousand people soon thronged the largest churches to hear his daily lectures at six o'clock in the morning, and on one occasion at least the crowd was so large that he was obliged to climb in through the window.[61] It is impossible through lack of the materials to trace his course in the twelve months which then ensued; but the first three months of 1746 were spent at Bethesda. He then embarked on a preaching campaign which took him far afield for months on end, but the close of the year found him back once more at the orphanage after a long horseback journey through the immense forests of Virginia and Carolina. It was now his settled resolve to range far and wide, more and more, hunting for souls in the strength of Jesus, and the spring of 1747 found him at Charlestown en route for Maryland by sea. 'According to the present temper of my mind', he wrote from Maryland in May; 'I could be content that the name of George Whitefield should die if thereby the Name of my dear Redeemer could be exalted.'[62] He then travelled on through Pennsylvania to New England, though his health was showing signs of strain which slowed him down in progress. In September he turned his face once more to Bethesda in the south, but the long lonely ride through the woods and swamps of South Carolina laid him so low that he could no longer preach with wonted energy. He reached the Orphanage at the end of October, and remained there until the new year. The financial affairs of the Orphanage had caused him great anxiety throughout the whole of this visit, and the constant necessity to make appeals on its behalf irked him not a little. But he would be sold as a slave to toil at the galleys rather than leave his orphan wards to starve,[63] and he affirmed time and again that he would stand by them, cost what it might: 'Poor, yet making others rich, shall be my motto still.'[64] But in March 1748, ill-health led him to make a voyage to Bermuda, whence an unexpected opportunity occurred for a free passage to England.

He reached London in July 1748, and was welcomed by thousands with a joy which almost overcame him. It was on this visit that he entered upon a new phase of his ministry through the active friendship of the Countess of Huntingdon. This good lady had met him as early as the year 1736, when she had taken a deep interest in his ordination.[65] Then in 1742, with her husband, she had been in constant attendance on his winter ministry in the Moorfields Tabernacle.[66] Now she formed the plan of inviting the nobility to hear him preach in her home at Chelsea, and he gladly concurred 'A word in the Lesson when I was last at your Ladyship's struck me,' he wrote; 'Paul preached privately to them which were of reputation (Gal. 2: 2). This must be the way I presume of dealing with the nobility who yet know not the Lord.'[67] Hitherto his opportunities for reaching the upper classes had been few, and he had no special footing with the aristocracy at all apart from two or three noble families in Scotland. But the Countess now made him one of her chaplains, and he began to preach to crowded and brilliant assemblies week after week in her Chelsea mansion. Peers like Chesterfield and Lord Bolingbroke, noble ladies like the Duchess of Somerset and the Duchess of Montague, heard him with rapt attention; and who can tell how much so many of England's leading statesmen and famous houses owed to his faithful preaching? The close relationship which now grew up between the great evangelist and the Countess of Huntingdon had a far-flung significance which is only in part disclosed by the subsequent history of the Lady Huntingdon Connection and of Calvinistic Methodism. In September 1748, he paid his third visit to Scotland, but on his return he began to preach twice a week in her house. This new field of labour made him weigh up the need to drop his work either in Great Britain or in New England: 'I find it is a trial', he wrote, 'to be thus divided between the work on this and the other side of the water.'[68] But his introduction to the wealthy classes brought new friends to his aid, and the pecuniary embarrassments of the Orphanage which had so much harassed him in recent years were largely allayed by their support.

Thus he could give himself with a free mind to the claims of England, and in February 1749 he set out on a tour of the west in which he believed that the sound of his Master's footsteps was behind him. But he observed that awakening times were like spring-times; there were often many blossoms, but not always very much fruit.[69] In the summer he paid a fresh visit to Bristol and Plymouth, the cities where, above all others, he seems to have met with success on the grand scale. 'God has given me a glorious season at the dock, where I preached to a great multitude,' he wrote from Plymouth; 'this morning, the King of kings showed Himself in the gallery of His Ordinances indeed, and this evening I preached to many thousands in Plymouth fields.'[70] He is next heard of in the north, having ridden through the Midlands as far as Newcastle. 'Thus do I lead a pilgrim life,' he cried; 'God give me a pilgrim heart, and enable me to speak of redeeming love to a lost world till I can speak no more!'[71] He was back in London for the winter, and the vast crowds that thronged the morning lecture at six o'clock thrilled his whole soul with joy and praise. 'Our Lord is pleased to bow the heavens, and come down amongst His people,' he wrote; 'His glory fills the Tabernacle, and the shout of a King is heard in our camp.'[72] It was near his birthday, and we hear his comment: 'O what a blessed Master is Jesus Christ! I am just now come to my thirty-fifth year of age. I blush and am confounded when I think for what little purpose I have lived. It is time now to begin to do something for Him who has done and suffered so much for me.'[73] In February 1750, he set out on a spring campaign in the west, though often exposed to rain and hail. In June, he was 'beating up for recruits' in Lancashire,[74] and in July he was preaching twice a day to greater crowds than ever in Scotland. The long winter months in London tried his patience, and made him yearn for spring when he could launch a fresh campaign.[75] In May 1751, he paid his first visit to Ireland, where God blessed him both in Dublin and in Belfast; then in July, he crossed over to Scotland, where he was followed more than ever. 'O Edinburgh! Edinburgh!' he cried, on his departure a month later; 'surely thou must never be forgotten by me! The longer I stayed, the more eagerly both rich and poor attended on the Word preached. Perhaps for near twenty-eight days together in Glasgow and Edinburgh, I preached to near ten thousand souls every day.'[76] But he was in London by mid-August, and had sailed for America by the end of the month.

He reached Savannah at the end of October 1751, but it was only for a very brief stay. His time was spent chiefly in Georgia and South Carolina, but he set sail once more in April and was back in London by May 1752. 'The Lord help me to hold on and hold out unto the end,' he cried; 'I dread the thoughts of flagging in the latter stages of my road. Jesus is able to keep me from being either weary or faint in my mind; in Him, and in Him alone, is all my strength found.'[77] At the end of August he left for Scotland where he preached twice a day to immense numbers. 'I wondered they were not wearied,' he wrote; 'but the more they heard, the more they seemed desirous of hearing.'[78] By mid-November he was back in London; he had travelled about a thousand miles in the past ten weeks, and had preached twice and thrice a day to many thousands.[79] He was now in winter quarters with a ministry to thousands, but with a longing for spring that he might take the road again. 'Humility must be taught us as Gideon taught the men of Succoth, with briars and thorns,' he said; 'these will frequently fetch blood from the old man. O that we may be made willing to have him bleed to death. Away with him! Away with him! Crucify him! Crucify him! May this be the language of your heart and mine!'[80] In June 1753, he was back once more in Scotland, and worked his way south through the north and west, preaching in the fields right down to the end of November when his hands and feet were often numb with piercing cold.[81] The winter months were spent in London, and in April 1754 he set out on his fifth visit to America. He at once took up an itinerant life and found an open door on all sides. At length, late in November, after a five-month tour of the northern provinces, in the course of which he preached from New York to Boston, he set out on the long fourteen hundred mile ride to Georgia. 'Oh, what days of the Son of Man have I seen!' he wrote, just after he had turned forty; 'God be merciful to me, an ungrateful sinner.'[82]

He set sail for England in March 1755, and the outbreak of the Seven Years War kept him at home for the longest single period of his ministry. The summer of 1755 saw him in the west and in the north, while the winter found him back in London, where John Newton first heard and met him. Newton loved to recall how he had seen Moorfields as full of lanterns at four and five in the morning while working men were on their way to the Tabernacle as the Haymarket was of flambeaux at eight and nine in the evening when social fops were on their way to the opera.[83] In the summer months of 1756 he paid a fresh visit to Scotland and then returned to London in time to open his new chapel in Tottenham Court Road. In 1757, he went north once more to Scotland and then crossed over to Ireland. Hitherto his health had suffered but little from the constant wear and tear of so much travel and field preaching; but the fatigue of long journeys by land and sea, the strain of speaking to vast multitudes in the open air, and the ceaseless labours by night and day, at last began to tell. He was ill in February 1758, and his summer campaign did not begin until the month of May; horseback was exchanged for a chaise, and then the chaise for a carriage. But one year was still much the same as another, and he was in Scotland for the tenth time in the summer; in 1760 he held a summer campaign in the west and an autumn circuit in the north. He had reached the zenith of his fame and usefulness, but his health was now much broken. Thus, in 1761, illness laid him aside for some months, though he journeyed as far as Scotland in November; but, in 1762, he was once more in the west for the spring, and in Scotland for the summer. Then, in 1763, he preached his way north to Scotland and then embarked at the port of Greenock in June on his sixth visit to the colonies overseas. He was hampered by illness and could not move about in the New World with his wonted freedom; but field preaching was still his 'grand catholicon', and he could not bear an enforced silence.[84] Thus, in June 1765, he set sail once more for England and, in July, he was at work again in his London chapels.

Whitefield was a Churchman both by profession and by conviction; he loved the Articles and the Liturgy of the Church of England, and he never lost an opportunity to reaffirm his loyalty to the Church and her formularies. 'My constant way of preaching is first to prove my propositions by Scripture,' he told the Bishop of London, 'and then to illustrate them by the Articles and Collects of the Church of England.'[85] He could not bear the thought of separation, and frowned with all his might against all plans to break away from the Church of England. 'No, my lord, unless thrust out, I shall never leave,' he told the Bishop of Bangor; 'and even then I shall still continue to adhere to her doctrines and pray for the restoration of her discipline, even to my dying day.'[86] He took to pen and print time and again to deny that the Methodists had gone outside the pale of the Established Church: 'The Methodists are no sect, no separatists from the Established Church,' he cried; 'neither do they call people from her communion.'[87] Whitefield and the Countess of Huntingdon longed to reform the Church itself, not to create new sects outside the Church; they thought that if they could only put the pulpits right, the pews would soon improve. His part was to raise up converted men for the ministry, while hers was to secure Orders and build chapels for them; it was a grand vision and it placed him at the very head of the Church Evangelicals in the eighteenth century. But he also maintained his right to take the world for his parish and to preach in the fields in the teeth of opposition from bishops and clergy alike; there was no law by which he stood condemned, and he gladly bore the reproach of men and went without the camp when church and chapel were denied to him. The fields were the 'airy pluralities' which he loved best of all.[88] His *cri du coeur* may still be heard by all who will: 'Oh that I may die in the field!'[89]

His labours and travels in this work were almost unparalleled and would appear incredible if they were not confirmed by irrefragable proof; but the more he laboured, the more he longed to spend and be spent for his Lord. He was always on the move by land or water, and he moved with astonishing rapidity when we recall the narrow, muddy roads and the clumsy sailing brigs which were his sole means of transport. Twice he made a tour of Ireland and fifteen times he went to Scotland; he paid seven visits to the New World and he crossed the Atlantic no less than thirteen times. As for England and Wales, he rode from the Channel to the border time and again; there was hardly a single town of size or note in north or south, in east or west, where he failed to lift up his voice like a silver trumpet with the Gospel message. 'May the Lord give me a pilgrim heart for my pilgrim life', he cried, 'and then, all will be well.'[90] He was not a man of brave and fearless soul by nature, but he faced great risks with calm and steady courage. He was attacked by violent hands and maligned by vicious tongues, but he held on his way undeterred. He was pelted with eggs at Moorfields[91] and was battered with stones in Dublin.[92] He was bruised by a clod of earth in Staffordshire[93] and was scarred by a chunk of stone in Devonshire.[94] He was beaten with a cudgel at Basingstoke and was basted with a walking-stick at Plymouth. He was reviled as a sleek scoundrel who made fabulous sums from his appeals; he was assailed as an anarchist who was paving the way for a bloody revolution.[95] He was lampooned on the stage in a blasphemous farce; he was maligned by the press in a scandalous style. More than once he was in peril of life, but he never wavered. His London engagements in the winter season when field preaching was in abeyance were just as prodigious as his country circuits in the spring and summer; he was preaching fifteen times a week at the time when his chapel at Tottenham Court Road was opened.[96] In summer and winter alike he carried on a correspondence with a host of people on both sides of the Atlantic; in a single day at one time he received a thousand notes from people who were under concern.[97] That his human frame could so long endure all the demands which he imposed on it was wonderful, for the strain and fatigue to mind and body must have been enormous. Henry Venn could not but marvel that he could use his voice for between forty and sixty hours in a single week to address thousands, and that week in and week out for year after year; and then remain up till midnight in prayer and praise with his friends or his hosts, as his custom was wherever he stayed.[98] His friends would often entreat him to spare himself, but he would always return the same reply: 'Oh this pilgrim way of life! To me it is life indeed. No nestling, no nestling on this side eternity!'[99] He was in truth immortal until his work was done.

Whitefield and John Wesley were the two chief agents in God's hand for the great spiritual movement which saved England from the horror of a political revolution such as broke out in France; but it is a striking fact that there were other remarkable movements in the eighteenth century, both in Great Britain and in New England, and that Whitefield was just as prominent in them all. He was the leading figure in the Welsh Revival and in the Scottish Revival, and he inspired men like Howell Harris with the fire of his own radiant enthusiasm; he was the moving spirit in the great awakening that shook New England, and he enthused men like Gilbert Tennent with the zeal of his own glorious evangelism. There have been few since the age of St. Paul who, with less of selfish motive or with more of holy passion have bent all the faculties of mind and soul, all the resources of voice and health, to such lifelong perseverance in the winning of souls. No one saw as soon as he did just what the times required, and no one was so bold in the great work of spiritual aggression. He was among the first to see that the one way to meet the assaults of sceptics and infidels was to preach a living Gospel, and the preaching of Whitefield and Wesley did far more to roll back the flood of unbelief than all the writings of men like Butler and Paley. He was among the first to fix men's minds once more on the old truths which lay at the bed-rock of the Reformation, for his noble assertion of the great doctrines taught by the Reformers and his constant reference to the Articles and the Homilies and to the best English divines shook men from their torpor and stirred them to re-think the facts of truth. He was the first in all England, except perhaps Richard Baxter, who grasped the need for an all-out attack to take captive those who were in bondage to the powers of darkness, and he set on foot a course of action which was almost unknown before his time. The rise and progress of the Evangelical Movement within the Church received a mighty impulse from his labours; his decisive influence on men like James Hervey and John Newton, and his intimate fellowship with men like Romaine and Grimshaw, placed him at the very head of the stream of blessing. It is hard to assess the full value of his life and labours by the scales of human judgment; but though the records be few and meagre here on earth, they will be found full and entire in the Lamb's Book of Life.

But all this was in the way of the indirect good which he did to souls; he brought light and blessing to thousands who never saw or heard him. The direct good which he did to immortal souls was enormous. 'I will go further,' Ryle boldly says; 'I believe it is incalculable.'[100] No preacher in England has ever so seized and held the attention of such vast multitudes as he constantly addressed; no preacher in England has ever so kept his hold on the common people in town and country for a full third of the century. We have but to think of the crowds of near fifty thousand who stood to hear him at Moorfields at a time when London's population was not more than one tenth of the present census; and what is more, credible witnesses have set it down as their judgment that his converts could be numbered by the thousand. John Newton was a man of shrewd mind and wide knowledge, and he said:

> That which finished his character as a shining light and is now his crown of rejoicing was the singular success which the Lord was pleased to give him in winning souls.…It seemed as if he never preached in vain. Perhaps there is hardly a place in all the extensive compass of his labours where some may not yet be found who thankfully acknowledge him as their spiritual father.[101]

Henry Venn was a man of strong sense and ripe judgment, and he said: 'If the greatness, extent, success, and disinterestedness of a man's labour can give him distinction amongst the children of Christ, we are warranted to affirm that scarce any of His ministers since the Apostles' days has exceeded, scarce anyone has equalled, Mr Whitefield.'[102] John Wesley knew him from his Oxford days, and he bore witness in his funeral oration:

> What an honour hath it pleased God to put upon His faithful servant! Have we read or heard of any person since the Apostles...who called so many thousands...to repentance? Above all, have we read or heard of any who has been a blessed instrument in His hand of bringing so many sinners from darkness to light and from the power of Satan unto God?'[103]

And Ryle frankly affirms: 'I place him first in the order of merit without any hesitation. Of all the spiritual heroes of a hundred years ago...I should think I committed an act of injustice if I placed any name before his.'[104]

Whitefield was the evangelist *par excellence* of the Evangelical Revival, and he must rank as one of the greatest preachers of the Gospel England has ever known. He came at a time when congregations slept through sermons with dull morals and cold ethics which left the heart untouched, and he came with all the force and vigour of a fresh and mighty message. He was blessed by nature with some of the choicest gifts a preacher can ever possess, and he was endowed by grace with all the life and fire the Gospel can ever impart. His slender figure and handsome features gave him a pleasing appearance; his graceful manner and perfect action won him a ready acceptance. His voice was an instrument of singular power and beauty,[105] and the music of its rich and varied tones could always silence every ruder sound.[106] It was like a deep and well-tuned organ, full of charm and pathos, rich in sweet expression, and with carrying properties rarely excelled. It was managed with the greatest effect, and he could use it to express every emotion; yet this was the result of feeling and instinct rather than of study or design, as its ever changing melodies passed from simple narrative to measured argument, or from yearning admonition to tender consolation. Franklin declared as the result of an experiment that it could be heard in the open air without effort by a crowd of thirty thousand.[107] Plymouth people used to say that he was often distinctly heard at the distance of a full mile across the stretch of water which lies between Tor Point and New Passage. Tradition says that when he preached at Bristol, his voice was heard on Staincliffe Hill, a mile and a half from where he stood, crying: 'O earth, earth, earth, hear the Word of the Lord!'[108] He had a most vivid sense of drama, and could describe a scene or illustrate a point in such graphic style that it seemed to live before men's eyes. His great picture of the ship caught in a storm at sea, with masts gone and hull down, came to a thrilling climax when his voice rang out with a bewildered cry, as though he were at a loss to know what next to do; and the sailors in the vast crowd thundered as one man in reply: 'The long-boat! Man the long-boat!'[109] Or his famous picture of the blind man skirting the edge of a precipice, decrepit with age and deserted by his dog, moved on in breathless suspense when the staff slipped through his nerveless fingers and he stooped down to retrieve it, bending all unaware over the cliff, and then stumbling forward; and Lord Chesterfield sprang from his seat in Lady Huntingdon's chapel with the cry: 'Good God! He's gone!'[110] Oratory like this might easily seem melodramatic and intolerable on the lips of a lesser man, but with Whitefield's tremendous earnestness, it never palled. His great command of words and his fluent ease in speech were never at fault, and he spoke with a kind of holy violence that carried all before him. The thrilling and spontaneous bursts of impassioned eloquence were the highlights of his oratory, but they were backed with an overwhelming sincerity which made people feel that his whole heart and soul were bent on making them believe that what he said was true. There was an element of pure pathos in all his preaching, and men could not mistake the note of yearning which made him sob aloud. He felt such an intense love and longing for those whom he addressed that his feelings found an outlet in tears. One who knew him well and often heard him preach said that he hardly ever knew him to preach without weeping; his voice would be choked with sobs and his flow of words interrupted with involuntary tears.[111] This forced weeping silence on the preacher's part was at times most effective; few could withstand the sight. It woke up affections and touched the hidden springs of the heart as nothing else could ever do; men could not hate one who loved and wept for their souls.[112] There could be no doubt as to his sincerity; all who ever heard him were unanimous on the point. His flashing eyes and trembling lips, his weeping silence and thrilling appeals were the outward signs of a large and loving heart, for no sermon ever left him content that failed to bring men to the feet of Christ. 'If anyone were to ask me who was the second preacher I ever heard, I should be at some loss to answer,' said good old John Newton; 'but in regard to the first, Mr Whitefield exceeded so far every other man of my time that I should be at none.'[113] He was of the same opinion still when in old age he was the breakfast guest of William Wilberforce, whose diary records the one brief comment: 'He talked in the highest terms of Whitefield, as by far the greatest preacher he had ever known.'[114]

Whitefield never set apart a special time for study, but a notebook which he compiled shows, that he preached more than eighteen thousand sermons in a little less than thirty-five years.[115] He would prepare himself for the pulpit in the early morning and then would spend an hour or so if he could with Henry or Cruden beside him. Eighty-one of his sermons in all found their way into print, and seventy-five of these were produced in due course in one large volume. But the student who turns to them without warning will find himself keenly disappointed; he will wonder where the secret of his preaching power really lay, for he will not find it in these printed sermons. There are few marks of genius, scant signs of eloquence, and no gems of intellect in these sermons; they are not profound in thought or fancy, do not excel in style or culture, and are meagre in learning and language. But we must consider that the first forty-six at least were in the press before he was twenty-five years of age; and we must remember that the last eighteen at least were taken down in shorthand and were published with no revision and no correction at all.[116] Ryle says that his scribes were equally ignorant of grammar and Gospel, and the preacher himself cried out time and again when he read their loose and inaccurate reports.[117] 'I wish you had advertised against the publisher of my last sermon; it is not verbatim as I delivered it,' he complained in 1769; 'in some place he makes me to speak false concord, and even nonsense; in others, the sense and connection are destroyed by the injudicious, disjointed paragraphs, and the whole is entirely unfit for the public review.'[118] Yet, with all their faults, these sermons will well repay a close reading, and they do throw some light on the technique and quality of his preaching. His language was plain and lucid to a degree; no one could fail to grasp its meaning, whether or not they liked it. He seldom vexed his hearers with abstruse questions or involved reasons; he saw his mark and shot at it with direct and unerring aim. A conversational style of speaking with spontaneous flights of oratory, simple statements of truth and apt illustrations, were his common weapons.

And then, 'Whitefield preached a singularly pure Gospel; few men perhaps ever gave their hearers so much wheat and so little chaff.'[119] He saw that man is guilty, but may be forgiven; he saw, too, that man is immortal, and must ripen now either for endless weal or for endless woe.[120] Thus his two great themes were the necessity for regeneration by the Holy Ghost and for righteousness by faith in Jesus Christ; there are indeed but few sermons in which these themes fail to occur. 'O the righteousness of Christ!' we can still hear him cry; 'it so comforts my soul that I must be excused if I mention it in almost all my discourses. I would not if I could help it, have one sermon without it!'[121] 'His righteousness', he told a friend, 'is the only rock on which you can build any solid comfort.'[122] He was endowed to a remarkable degree with the art of speaking to each individual soul in a vast congregation, and his hearers were never let alone. He was very bold and very direct, and the call on his lips was an urgent summons to repent and believe: 'Believe me, I am willing to go to prison or death for you, but I am not willing to go to heaven without you!' he cried; 'The love of Jesus Christ constrains me.. My heart is now full.. And I could now not only continue my discourse until midnight, but I could speak till I could speak no more!'[123] 'Though the sun is going down, though the shadow of the evening is coming on,' so he would press home his appeal, 'God is willing, O Man, God is willing, O Woman, to be a sinner's God; He has found out a way whereby He can be reconciled to you!'[124] When we reflect that this tender passion for souls found voice through an unrivalled exercise of the finest gifts a preacher could possess, we can sense the tremendous impression it would create. The more truly he preached, the more really did he whet and sharpen the edge of men's desire to hear him again. London had flocked to hear him at the age of two and twenty, until one might as it were walk on the people's heads.[125] Boston had thronged to hear him at the age of five and twenty, until hundreds used to drop their tools and leave their trades at his approach.[126] Critics and sceptics like Bolingbroke and Chesterfield gladly sat at his feet; nobles and ladies like the Earl of Dartmouth and the Countess of Huntingdon gladly drank in his words. Franklin spoke in unqualified praise of his manner; Garrick spoke in superlative terms of his action. The poor heard him just as gladly and used to rise at four o'clock on the coldest mornings to stream in their thousands to the place where he was to preach. 'Nothing like it had been seen in Christendom since the days of Peter the Hermit,'[127] and the Holy Ghost made use of that golden voice to rouse Great Britain and New England from the sleep of death to light and life immortal.

Whitefield had the manners and address of a gentleman, with a pleasing absence of all that was stiff and formal; he was the soul of kindness and courtesy, and loved to have things round him clean and neat. His style of living was plain and frugal, and his moderation at the table was almost a byword.[128] He was married at the age of six and twenty to a widow in her thirty-sixth year, but he never allowed the claims of wife or home to interfere with his calling as an evangelist. 'I would often have nestled,' he wrote in September 1749; 'but God always put a thorn in my nest.'[129] He had one child who died in early infancy; 'but he left a name far better than that of sons and daughters.'[130] He was strict in later life in retiring from all company at ten o'clock, while in summer and winter alike he used to rise at four in the morning. He would often get up during the night to pray; sometimes whole nights were spent in prayer and devotion. 'O prayer! prayer!' he cried; 'it brings and keeps God and man together. It raises man up to God and brings God down to man. If you would…keep up your walk with God, pray, pray without ceasing.'[131] He was a man of singularly open and transparent character; there was little about him that required apology or explanation. His faults and his virtues were all as plain as the sun at high noon, and the former were as trivial as the latter were glorious.[132] He was prone to err in judgment, and was often hasty with lip and pen; he used to draw rash conclusions with regard to providence, and he often mistook his own feelings for the leading of God's Spirit.[133] He was guilty of rank self-exposure in his journals and of frank adulation in his Letters to Lady Huntingdon; but these very defects in their context help to reveal the one great end for which he lived. He saw no wrong in the social system which was based on the use of slave labour, but he flayed the brutal customs which were then so common and he strove to win the negro no less earnestly than his owner. Sir James Stephen felt that the current of devout and holy thought which filled his soul when he stood on what he loved to call his throne was not free from some sense of human exaltation, and that he did not move with enough of silent awe as he strode among the infinities and eternities of the invisible world.[134] But he was a man of deep and unfeigned humility, a man of true and unmeasured self-denial. 'Oh this self-love, this self-will!' he cried in 1755; 'it is the devil of devils! Lord Jesus, may Thy blessed Spirit purge it out of all our hearts!'[135] He spoke with a noble sense of freedom when he had to do with men; he knelt with a lowly sense of worship when he had to do with God.

He never ceased to cultivate the life of God in his own soul and not even Wesley could have asked for more than he was able humbly to claim. 'Thanks be to His great Name,' he declared in 1753, 'I can truly say that for these many years past, no sin hath had dominion over me; neither have I slept with the guilt of any known, unrepented sin lying upon my heart.'[136] He kept up a bright and cheerful spirit all through his life, and it stood him in good stead in the midst of many cares. Tried and vexed as he was, despised by the Church and maligned by the world, betrayed by false brethren and disowned by cold clergy, harried by money matters and worried by controversies, this elasticity never failed him. Wonderful singleness of eye and amazing detachment from self marked him out as a man without guile who lived for one thing only. 'O for a disinterested spirit!' he cried, as he began the New Year in 1750; 'O to be willing to be poor that others may be rich! O to be nothing that Jesus may be all!'[137] This love for Christ breathes and burns through all his letters; that is the Name which gleams and shines through all his correspondence. He would have *aliquid Christi* in all that he wrote,[138] and, like fragrant ointment, it gave charm to his words. He seemed to live only for the glory of God and the rescue of souls; his own favourite expression hits this off as nothing else can: 'Let the name of George Whitefield perish if Christ be glorified!'[139] John Wesley bore noble witness to his large and loving spirit: 'He had a heart susceptible of the most generous and the most tender friendship.'[140] He felt keenly the defection of friends from time to time, and he always thought the contradiction of saints harder to bear than that of sinners.[141] 'I think I can say that I am willing to be forgotten even by my friends if Jesus Christ may thereby be exalted,' he wrote to one wavering friend in 1748; 'but then, I would not have my friends act an inconsistent part towards that Friend of all, the glorious Emmanuel.'[142] We feel that we understand what James Hervey meant when he said that he had never seen so fair a copy, so true an image, of the Saviour.[143] We feel that we comprehend what John Newton meant when he blessed God that he had lived in his time.[144] The quarterings of George Whitefield have been deeply engraved on the Evangelical scutcheon, and we are proud of the blazonry.[145]

On his return to England, in 1765, a long struggle set in between impaired health and the lure of field preaching. He had possessed such high tension of soul that for years there had been no room for weariness or lassitude; but now nervous fatigue had begun to make itself felt, and it levied a serious toll on his mind and body. On October 28, Wesley had breakfast with him and spoke of him as 'an old, old man, fairly worn out in his Master's service, though he has hardly seen fifty years.'[146] For two years he could do little in the way of preaching at all; he paid brief visits to the west, but soon returned to his London quarters. But the winter months of 1766 found him preaching at the Moorfields Tabernacle and the Tottenham Court Chapel on alternate Sundays, and he rejoiced to know that the shout of the King was still to be heard in their midst. The spring and summer of 1767 found him once more in the field, both in the western counties and in Yorkshire. They were golden seasons for him and he wrote with an air of triumph: 'Field and street preaching hath rather bettered than hurt my bodily health.'[147] The summer of 1768 saw his fifteenth and final visit to Scotland, where the sun of his popularity knew no decline. In the spring of 1769 he paid a final visit to the scene of his early triumphs at Kingswood, and the colliers who first gave him a hearing in the open air were thus among the last who heard his voice in England. In September 1769, he embarked on his seventh visit to America, where he at once arranged to place the affairs of the Orphanage in the hands of trustees. He was soon in better health than he had been for some years, and he began to preach in his old style almost daily. In May 1770, he set out for Philadelphia where he spent a month; then he went on to New England where he engaged in what was to prove his final circuit.

His strength and energies seemed once more to be in their full vigour, until he fell ill in the month of September. It was in the mercy of God that his life moved towards its close just before the outbreak of the War of American Independence, and the subsequent destruction of his beloved Bethesda; either event, had he lived to see it, would have gone near to break his heart.

As it was, he went on preaching daily in spite of fresh illness until the morning of September 29, when he set out from Portsmouth on horseback to keep an engagement to preach at Newbury Park. But on the way he was earnestly entreated to preach at a place called Exeter and, though he felt ill, he had not the heart to refuse. A friend remarked that he looked far from well, more fit indeed for bed than for the pulpit. 'True, Sir,' Whitefield replied, and then he turned aside, clasped his hands, looked up, and said: 'Lord Jesus, I am weary in Thy work, but not of Thy work; if I have not yet finished my course, let me go and speak for Thee once more in the fields, seal Thy truth, and come home, and die.'[148] He then went out to preach in the open air to a vast multitude; it proved to be his last sermon, and it was a fitting close to his whole career. When he stood up to preach, thin with illness, pale as death, he remained for some minutes quite unable to speak. 'I will wait for the gracious assistance of God,' he said at last, 'for He will, I am certain, assist me once more to speak in His Name.'[149] Then he found his voice and preached for nigh on two hours on Faith and Works in a strain of highest rapture: 'Works! Works! A man get to heaven by works!' he cried, in a voice of thunder; 'I would as soon think of climbing to the moon on a rope of sand!'[150] But the sound of his voice in the open fields had scarce died away when the call came, and the wish that his pilgrim life should close while still in harness was fully gratified. He dined with a friend and then rode on to Newbury Port where he supped and retired early. It is said that as he climbed the stairs he could not resist the desire to turn round and speak once more to his friends below. But as he spoke, the fire kindled within, and he did not finish until the light of the candle had burned right down and gone out in its socket.[151] He then withdrew to his own room, but was soon seized by a violent attack of spasmodic asthma. He fought for breath between intervals of broken sleep until soon after four o'clock the next morning. But a fit of coughing then woke him up and he knew that death was not far away. He could hardly speak for choking, but he went on fighting for breath by the open window until the day began to break and the shadows fled away. Then, just at six o'clock on the morning of September 30, he fetched one gasp and breathed no more. At the age of fifty-five, the Prince of English preachers was dead, a prince that hath no peer; that voice whose charm had so often reached the remotest hearer in the assembled thousands had joined at last in the endless chorus of the angel host, of the Church of the First-born, who stand before the Throne and praise the Lamb night and day for ever.

The Field Preacher

'As they drew near to the town, along the path and across the watery meadows, people were walking and riding. In the Town Square there was a thick pressing multitude. He asked a fellow what the matter was, and some one told him it was the Methodists, and then another fellow volunteered that it was George Whitefield, the most remarkable preacher of them all.

Herries was interested in all that he had heard of the Methodists, who had now for a number of years been strengthening their position in the country, and especially of this Whitefield, concerning whom and his extraordinary preaching he had had, like everyone else at this time, many reports.

He knew that this was a courageous man who was ready, for his religion, to meet any form of contempt, abuse, and danger. He knew that he was sincere, of deep piety, of constant energy, of selfless industry. Against these things he weighed what he had heard of his emotionalism, theatricality, and fanaticism, all qualities to which Herries, by his own reserved and private mind, was deeply hostile.

He had heard that Whitefield had but one desire, to save souls for God, that often he preached fifty or sixty hours in the one week, and that his journeys, involving as they did at that time so much physical discomfort, were ceaseless.

He knew, too, that he was a man free of all meanness; his bitterest adversary did not attribute to him small ambitions, petty jealousies, sly revenges. He appeared to Herries, from what he had heard of him, to be feminine in his hysteria, weak-nerved, histrionic, ill-balanced; but he was, even because of these defects, exactly suited to move great masses of people by impassioned appeals, passing from place to place like a torch of fire.

When he heard that it was Whitefield who was here, he decided that he must listen to him. He backed his horse out of the crowd and, dismounting, took the horse by the bridle, …finding some higher ground where he could watch what was going forward..

Very soon he was aware of a voice coming to him very clearly over the heads of the people. He could see, only indistinctly, any figure. The crowd, of every type and order of person, was packed tightly across the square; they seemed to press against the houses behind them as though they would bend them back. It was an intent and silent crowd, so intent that the urgency seemed to spread to the distant line of hills, Causey and Cat Bells and Maiden Moor, beyond the roofs, so that they, too, were listening.

The figure was indistinct, someone lit with the pale February sun, a body of grace and good proportion, but it was the voice that came straight to Herries, as though it were to him alone that it was appealing. He realized then that every man and woman in that crowd felt as he did, that it was to him or her alone that the voice was speaking. At once, hostile though he was to public emotion and theatrical display, he yielded to the beauty of the voice. It was, beyond any sort of argument, by far and far the most moving and lovely voice that he had ever heard. Every word was distinct and clear, running to him with a separate and special urgency, and the words were bound into a general rhythm most melodious and musical; yes, it was like music, the perfect and rounded notes following one after another, to make, at the fitting moment, a completed harmony. So lovely was the voice that for a little while he did not listen to the words; then they were forced upon his attention with a pressing gentleness, as though someone, very gracious and kindly, were at his elbow, saying, 'You must hear this; this is for you and for you alone. It has great importance for you.'

He listened then with the utmost attention.

'It is simply as an occasional preacher that I am come to preach the Gospel to all that wish to hear me, of whatever denomination. I have nothing to do with denominations, for it is the righteousness of Jesus Christ that I am preaching, and that righteousness has no denominations. You have heard many times of the righteousness of Jesus Christ, and at every time you have been wearied or indifferent to Him or busied with affairs. It may be that this is the last time you will hear of Him and the last time that I shall preach of Him. Here into this town He has come, knowing that it is for the last time; but you do not know. The clouds have circled over your heads, the sun is about to set, and, setting to-night, it will not come again. You are returning to your homes, your candles are lit, your children are at your knee, and distantly from over the hills there is the faint sound of a trumpet. The sound is distant, for the hills cover it, and your many daily businesses, the food for gossip, the food for the belly, the food for pride and vanity, these make a babel in your ears and blot out the distant call. But soon', and here the voice rose to a high bright summoning call, 'the trumpeters have crossed the hills! The trumpeters have crossed the hills! The trumpeters have crossed the hills!'

He paused as though he were listening. It seemed that everyone else was listening too. The crowd was tense and concrete, as though its eager attention had moulded it into one man. Across the silence there struck stray sounds, the crowing of a cock, the sharp bark of a dog, the stamping of some horse's hoofs against cobbles. These emphasized the stillness. They could see the hills where the trumpeters were. They could name them Skiddaw and Saddleback, Helvellyn and Fairfield, Langdale Pike and the Gavel, Seatallan and Haycock, and through that circle of grey listening hills they could see the trumpeters moving.

The voice took a personal colour. 'The Trumpeters come first, moving down the valleys, and after them the cohorts of the Saints in their shining armour, and after them the Priests and Prophets with judgement in their hands, and after them'—the voice sank to a whisper, and through the crowd there ran a little rustle of apprehension—'after them the Great Judge Himself.'

There was silence again. A stout countrywoman near Herries began to sob.

'Who in this valley shall be ready for that awful army? Now, outside your door, there is one summoning blast. No time for preparation, for hiding the things that should not be seen. THY JUDGE IS THERE...THY JUDGE IS THERE...And He is just, and He is merciful. Yes, but He is just. Think not only of the mercy; think also of the Justice.' And then, with a sudden agonizing, beseeching cry: 'Oh, my hearers, the Wrath to come, the Wrath to come!'

There was a terror and imminent fearful apprehension in that last cry that even a man like Herries, steeled against every sentimental appeal, could not resist. He started as though someone at that instant came running to him, crying out that the end of the world was upon him. He looked hastily around him, as though a wild animal or flaming fire were at his back. And on the crowd the effect of that cry was immediate and tremendous. Superstitious, ignorant, simply and often savagely moved, cut off as they had been for many centuries from all contact with a larger world, they were ready to be seized by any swift emotion, ready and eager. Here Whitefield, however, had won his hardest victory, for these North Country people were not Celts as the Cornish and Welsh were. They were neither dreamers nor fanatics. As Herries knew, five years before they had stoned the Methodist preacher almost to death, and the whole district from Kendal to Carlisle had a name of great danger for the sect.

But they would not stone Whitefield now. He himself began to be moved with the crowd; his body swayed, his arms rose and fell, his voice was torn with distress and urgency. Tears, they said afterwards, were pouring down his cheeks. He picked out men and women from the crowd. 'Oh, sir, are you indeed ready? Have you your garments packed for the journey, your horse harnessed, and your conscience clear? For Heaven and Hell, Death and Judgement, are not names only for you. They are real, they are present. Eternity is a true word, and Everlasting Punishment is no lie. Can you be led to the Judgement Seat before that awful crowd of Witnesses and not tremble? Your deeds are behind you. There is no hope now that they may be altered, for they are written in the book. There is the pause. You have made your plea. You are waiting for the sentence, and even as you stand here now, so it is certain that you will stand before your God. Eternal Damnation! Damnation for ever and ever more, suffering and torment and the agony of a repentance that is out of time!'

His voice sank again to a pleading whisper, while now his utterance could be heard to be broken with sobs. 'O God, where is Thy mercy? O God, whither shall I turn?' Then, with a great cry that rang, glittering, resonant through the air: 'In Christ Jesus! In Christ Jesus only is there any hope! But even He is just.' His voice was now of an awful solemnity: 'Sinner, I must do it. I must pronounce sentence upon you.' Again there was a terrible silence, and then, in a voice of thunder as though the very cobbles of the town must rock:

'Depart from me, ye cursed, into everlasting fire!' The crowd began to cry out: 'O Christ, save me!' 'Christ be kind to me!' God have mercy upon me!' Men were pushing against one another to reach nearer to the preacher, tears fell from many eyes, and suddenly, with a great burst of sound that had in it something gloriously strong and victorious, the hymn 'Oh God, our help in ages past' broke out and was carried, it must seem, far beyond the confines of the town.'

Hugh Walpole, *Rogue Herries*
(Vol. I of The Herries Chronicle, 1930), 223–6.

Bibliography

Works by the Rev. George Whitefield, M.A.

Works, Vol. I, Letters i to ccccxcvii.

Works, Vol. II, Letters ccccxcviii to dccccl xiv.

Works, Vol. III, Letters dccccl xv to mccccl xv.

Works, Vol. IV. Tracts and other writings.

Works, Vol. V, Sermons i to xxxi.

Works, Vol. VI, Sermons xxxii to lix (1771).

A Short Account of God's Dealings with the Rev. George Whiteftfeld from his Infancy to the time of his entering Holy Orders. (Published by the Committee of the General Assembly of the Free Church of Scotland; 1st ed. 1740. Revised, 1756.)

Seventy five Sermons on Important Subjects (edited by Samuel Drew, 1864).

Biographies of George Whitefield and Other Works Quoted

John Gillies, *The Life of the Rev. George Whitefield* (New Ed., 1838).

Laurence Tyerman, *The Life of the Rev. George Whitefield* (2nd Ed., 1890).

J. R. Andrews, *George Whitefeld* (John Ritchie Ltd., 6th ed.).

J. C. Ryle, *Christian Leaders of the Last Century*, Chapter iii, 'George Whitefield and His Ministry' (New Ed., 1880).

A. R. Buckland, *Selected Sermons of George Whitefield*, Introduction (R.T.S., 1904).

'A Member of the Houses of Shirley and Hastings', *The Life and Times of Selina, Countess of Huntingdon* (1839).

John Wesley, *The Journal of the Rev. John Wesley, A.M.* (Ed. Nehemiah Curnock, Bicentenary Issue, 1938).

John Wesley, *The Letters of the Rev. John Wesley, A.M.* (Ed. John Telford, Standard Edition, 1931).

James Stephen, *Essays in Ecclesiastical Biography* (New Ed., 1875).

G. R. Balleine, *A History of the Evangelical Party* (New Ed., 1933).

2

John Newton
1725–1807

John Newton was born on July 24, 1725, in London, the child of a very peculiar providence and the heir of a truly romantic destiny. His mother's chief aim in life was to bring him up in the fear of the Lord, and she watched over him with the tenderest solicitude. She stored his memory with whole chapters of Holy Writ and poured out her heart for him in ceaseless prayer. She taught him so well that he could read with ease by the age of four and he began to learn Latin in his sixth year. But God's design for him went far beyond the aims of an earthly parent, for he was to become a rare example of divine grace and patience. All his mother's plans were cut short by her death less than a fortnight before his seventh birthday in July 1732; but who can doubt that by her prayers and tears she won for him at last all that the saintly Monica had once won for the mighty Augustine? She had married a man of clear common sense and firm moral code, who was in charge of a vessel engaged in Mediterranean trade; but she died while he was away at sea and he knew not how to take her place in the life of the motherless child. He had been brought up in Seville, where his early training had given him an air of cold and stern reserve; this made his son hold him in awe rather than love, though in the course of time he learnt to love as well as revere him.[1] But he married again a year later and sent his son to school as a boarder for two years in Essex. Newton's life was far from happy at school; it only served to foster in him a dark and rebellious temper. He reached and held the first place in the Latin class; but he was pushed too fast, and soon forgot what he had learnt. The imprudent severity of the master almost broke his spirit and quite destroyed his first relish for books.

Newton left school in his tenth year and went to sea with his father at the age of eleven. He was away five times in all up to the year 1742 and, at one stage, he spent a few brief months in Spain. But by the age of twelve he had learnt to curse and blaspheme when out of his father's sight or hearing, and thus he took his first stride down the road of prejudice and profanity. He was often disturbed by his religious convictions, but they would pass away like the morning cloud or the early dew. He had more than one narrow escape from death and he tried to reform himself several times in vain; he would read and pray until he grew weary and then he would give up the attempt. 'In brief,' he said, 'I took up and laid aside a religious profession three or four different times before I was sixteen years of age. But all this while my heart was insincere…I loved sin and was unwilling to forsake it.'[2] At length he came upon the second volume of Shaftesbury's Characteristics in a little shop in Holland, and 'The Rhapsody' just seemed to suit his turn of mind. It was always in his hand and he almost knew it by heart; 'it operated like a slow poison and prepared the way for all that followed.'[3] Thus, in December 1742, in his eighteenth year, when his father was planning to settle him in Jamaica, he had no real heart for business and knew very little of grace or truth. He was a strange medley of religion and sentiment, of false philosophy and downright indolence; his mind and heart were ripe for the seed of all kinds of evil and mischief.

In December 1742, he was sent down to Kent on an errand for his father and a journey which was to change the whole course of his life. He was only meant to fill in the time before he sailed for the sugar plantations of Jamaica; instead, he was now to stumble upon the path of destiny in a way which no one could have foreseen. His route lay within half a mile of the house in which his mother had died and he felt a desire to lodge beneath the same roof on his way. He knew that a coolness had crept between her friends and his father on his second marriage, and he had not heard from them for many a year. But his father gave his consent for him to pay them a visit and he received a most kindly welcome both from the parents and their two daughters. He knew not then that the older of these had been thought of by both mothers as his future bride while they were still mere children, but he fell in love with Mary Catlett as soon as he saw her. He was only a lad of seventeen and she only a child of thirteen; but his love for her never abated or lost its influence on his heart from that hour. 'December 12, 1742,' he fondly recalled long years afterwards, 'was the memorable day on the event of which my future life was to turn.'[4] He was ere long to lose all sense of conscience and prudence in other things, but his love for her still shone like one solitary star in the dark night of sin and senselessness. 'I may perhaps venture to say', so he wrote, 'that none of the scenes of misery and wickedness I afterwards experienced ever banished her a single hour together from my waking thoughts.'[5] He could not speak of his affection to her family or to his own father; he had to keep it like a dark fire locked up in his own breast. But he could no longer bear the prospect of four or five years of comparative exile in far-off Jamaica, and he prolonged his stay for three weeks instead of for three days to make sure that his ship set sail without him.

On his return he was sent to Venice as a common sailor and he began to relax the sobriety which he had more or less preserved for two years past. He made a few feeble efforts to call a halt, but soon took fresh and yet worse strides towards what must have seemed hopeless apostasy. He was back in London twelve months later in December 1743, and at once went down to his friends in Kent, but he stayed so long that his father was almost provoked to disown him. Then he was seized by a naval press-gang and was sent on board the H.M.S. Harwich while she lay off the Nore. He had to put up with a month of great hardship; then his father got him posted as a midshipman on the quarter-deck. This would have brought him ease and respect if it had not been for his own unsettled mind and conduct. But he began to sink slowly in the mire of unbelief and to throw overboard all restraint and goodness. 'Thus like an unwary sailor who quits his port just before a rising storm,' he wrote, 'I renounced the hopes and comforts of the Gospel at the very time when every other comfort was about to fail me.'[6] Twelve months later, in December 1744, his ship was in the Downs, bound for the East Indies. He was given a day's shore leave and, careless of consequence, he rode to Kent in order to take a last leave of her he loved. His late return cost him the captain's favour and it was never regained. They sailed from the Spithead with a large fleet, but storms forced them back to Plymouth after the loss of several ships off the coast of Cornwall. Here he made up his mind to desert in an attempt to join his father who had come down on business to Torbay. He walked for the better part of two days, but then fell in with a band of soldiers. They brought him back to Plymouth under guard and marched him through the streets like a felon. Two days were spent in the guard-house; then he was sent on board in irons. He was stripped and flogged in public; then he was degraded from office and was boycotted by command. Shame and fear filled his heart and his love for Mary Catlett was the only restraint he now had left; for he could not bear to reflect that she might think meanly of him when he was dead.

The next three years were to yield an almost incredible story; it leaves us in a whirl as we watch the course of events which they entailed. He could never express with what wistful regret he saw the coast of England fade from before his eyes, and he was a prey to all the most gloomy thoughts on the long voyage out to Madeira. 'Whether I looked inward or outward', he confessed, 'I could perceive nothing but darkness and misery; I think no case except that of a conscience wounded by the wrath of God could be more dreadful than mine.'[7] But at Madeira, by an act of providence, he was transferred from the Indies Fleet to a ship which was bound for Sierra Leone. This gave him a new lease of hope and life, but it was soon abused worse than ever. He was among strangers and he felt that he could behave without the least disguise. 'I not only sinned with a high hand myself,' he wrote, 'but made it my study to tempt and seduce others upon every occasion; nay, I eagerly sought occasion sometimes to my own hazard and hurt.'[8] Six months passed by and then he heard that the ship was about to sail for the West Indies; this filled him with fresh dread lest he should be transferred once more to some naval command, for that was a prospect which he thought more hateful than death. But he gained his release from the ship's crew the day before they sailed for the Indies on condition that he joined the service of a certain merchant who dealt in slaves. Thus he landed on the Island of Benanoes with little more than the clothes that were on his back; it was for all the world as though he had made his escape from a shipwreck.

His new master lived on one of the islands known as the Plantanes, seven leagues to the south and close to the mouth of the River Sherbro. This man was completely under the thumb of the negro mistress with whom he lived as his wife and to whom he owed his rise in the slave trade. She soon conceived a fierce dislike for John Newton and he was crushed with a load of scorn and hardship beyond the lot of the meanest of her own poor black slaves. Sometimes, in his master's absence, it was only with the utmost difficulty that he could get a draught of cold water to slake his thirst in the heat of burning fever; sometimes she would send him scraps of food on her own unwashed plate after she had dined, or would leave him to be relieved by the slaves of the chain from their wretched pittance. He was almost as harshly used when he went abroad with his master on his trading journeys; he was often chained to the deck and he would have starved but for the fish which he caught with the entrails of the poultry flung out to him from his master's table.

Life went on like this for nearly twelve months, for the truth was that the negro mistress took a kind of savage delight in making a white man miserable. 'Almost naked and famished, a burden to myself and to all around me, helpless and hopeless,' he wrote, 'I dragged through almost a year.'[9] Bullied by a negro mistress, pitied by the poorest of her black slaves, destitute of food and clothing, depressed and abased in a state of the most abject misery, he had reached the lowest depths of social degradation and moral humiliation. 'My haughty heart was now brought down,' he owned; 'not to a wholesome repentance, not to the language of the prodigal; this was far from me; but my spirits were sunk; I lost all resolution, and almost all reflection.'[10] But there were still two links with a higher life which remained and, strange as it may seem, one was a love for books. In spite of all, he could sometimes collect his mind for the study of the one chance volume which he possessed, a battered copy of Barrow's *Euclid*, and he mastered the first six books with no other aid than a stick with which to draw diagrams in the sand. But when he came to feel that he had made shipwreck of faith and hope and conscience, it was only his love for one far-away friend and the well-nigh hopeless hope that he might live to see her again that kept his soul from sinking into the unplumbed depths of darkness and despair.

After twelve months his lot improved with a change of masters, and he obtained a share in the management of a slave depot on the banks of an inland river. It was not long before a ship arrived at Sierra Leone with orders to inquire for him and bring him home; but the captain heard that he had gone far inland and gave him no more thought. But just at that time the hand of God brought him to a point within a mile of the sea and the ship hove in sight while his partner was walking on the beach. This man at once sent up a smoke signal to stop the ship for trade and then went on board by canoe. One of the first questions he was asked by the ship's captain was with regard to John Newton, and when he heard that he was close at hand, he went ashore at once to bring him off. It was the memory of one fair face in Kent and the hope that he might see that face again that turned the scales and won Newton over, and he embarked in February 1751, after fifteen months of terrible enslavement. The ship was on a cruise for gold and ivory, bees-wax and dyer's wood, and it took twelve months more to collect a full cargo. Newton was housed in the captain's cabin and dined at his table; he had nothing to occupy his time and idleness completed his moral ruin. He was never lustful and seldom drunken; but he gave himself up to the most horrid forms of blasphemy and unbelief. 'I know not that I have ever met so daring a blasphemer,' he confessed; 'not content with common oaths and imprecations I daily invented new ones.'[11] His favourite kind of wit took the form of blasphemous parodies of the Cross and Passion, and the extremes to which he went were so grave that they shocked and scandalized men who had long been hardened in sin and unbelief.

Thus month after month slipped away while he ignored the warnings of conscience and its voice grew faint and silent. The goodness and mercy of God failed to lead him to repentance; the dangers and terrors of sin failed to stir him to decision. Breathless escapes from death were all like lost lessons to him in his blindness, and the social degradation of the past seemed to be outstripped by the moral obliquity in which he now revelled.

> The admonitions of conscience, which from successive repulses had grown weaker and weaker, at length entirely ceased; and for a space of many months, if not for some years, I cannot recollect that I had a single check of that sort…I seemed to have every mark of final impenitence and rejection; neither judgments nor mercies made the least impression on me.[12]

Such was his frame of mind while the crew ranged right down the coast as far as Cape Lopez; but in January 1747, they set their sails for home. The long voyage and hot climate had left the ship in bad repair; sails and cordage were worn out and she was quite unfit for a stormy passage. At first they sailed due west to the coast of Brazil and then north to the banks of Newfoundland;

but on March 1, they left these banks and pushed homewards with a hard gale right behind them. Nine days out, on March 9, a thought flashed through his mind to which he had long been impervious, and his system of crude unbelief sustained its first real shock. He found a copy of Stanhope's *Thomas a Kempis* and picked it up to while away an hour or two. He was reading it with as much indifference as if it had been a penny romance; he had read it in like manner often enough before. But ere long an involuntary suggestion sprang up in his mind: What if these things were true? He could not bear the force of that inference and flung the book aside to escape its challenge. But God's hour and God's hand were nigh, and he was now nearing the grand crisis of his strangely colourful life. The conviction he was so unwilling to receive was to be impressed on his soul at last by a truly awful dispensation.

That night he fell asleep with his usual unconcern, but soon woke up in violent alarm. The ship was in the throes of a tremendous storm; the sea had burst on board with a disastrous shock. It had torn away the timbers of the upper poop and had swept along the cabins on the lower deck. Wreck and ruin seemed inevitable, and the ship would certainly have sunk with a common cargo on board. But the crew manned the pumps and began to bale, and she was kept afloat by her freight of porous wood and bees-wax. Day broke an hour or so later and the wind eased and dropped. They choked the leaks with clothes and bedding, and the water began to abate. Newton remained at the pumps from three in the morning till near noon, lashed to his post with ropes lest he should be swept out to sea by the waves which broke over his head. Near nine o'clock in the morning, spent with cold and labour, he had been struck with a thought in a way he had not known for years. If all their pains did not avail, then let the Lord have mercy upon them! But what mercy, he began to wonder, could there be for a man like him? This made him dread the thought of death and he began to fear that the ship would sink in the trough of each new wave. But that ninth day of March 1748 was to prove a day that he would remember as long as he lived; the Lord had sent from on high to deliver him from darker waters than those on which he was sailing.

He could do no more by noon and he went below for an hour's rest; then he was called to the helm, where he stayed until midnight. Steering gave him leisure for a calm retrospect of the past, and all God's warnings and rescues, all his own follies and failures, swept through his mind. 'I thought…there never was nor could be such a sinner as myself; and then…I concluded… that my sins were too great to be forgiven.'[13] The ship was at last baled out by sunset and a new gleam of hope sprang up. He thought he saw the hand of God displayed in their favour and he began to pray; he thought of Jesus and His death, 'a death for sins not His own, but as I remembered, for the sake of those who in their distress should put their trust in Him'.[14] He saw at least a peradventure of hope on the Gospel scheme, while elsewhere he saw nothing but blank despair. The storm blew itself out, but their food stores were lost and their sails were torn to threads. The vessel was almost a wreck and adverse winds carried them still farther out of their course. Their provisions sank to half a salted cod for twelve men each day; they had no bread, few clothes, bitter cold, and constant toil at the pumps. The captain took Newton for a Jonah and was half inclined to throw him overboard. Newton himself thought it very probable that all their calamities were due to him, and the captain's threats were grimly endorsed by his conscience. 'I was at last found out by the powerful hand of God', he said, 'and condemned in my own breast.'[15] But at length, on April 8, four weeks after the storm, while their last victuals were on the boil, they dropped anchor in an Irish port near Derry. Two hours later a fresh wind sprang up with a violence which would without doubt have sent their shattered vessel to the bottom had they still been at sea. 'About this time', Newton observed, 'I began to know that there is a God that hears and answers prayer.'[16]

No news had been heard of his ship for eighteen months and he had long since been given up for lost. But he wrote from Ireland just in time to reach his father before he set out from

England to take up his post as Governor of York Fort in Hudson Bay. Newton arrived in Liverpool at the end of May 1748 on the day that his father sailed from the Nore; they were never to meet again for his father was drowned in the icy waters of Hudson Bay three years later. But the letters which passed between them were full of thankful goodwill, and the returning prodigal found that his old father had bespoken the interest of a well-to-do Liverpool merchant on his behalf. Thus he received the most timely offer of a command, but he chose to sail as ship's mate for one voyage at least so that he could learn to obey. He paid one brief visit to London before the voyage began, but he only saw Mary Catlett once in all too brief an interview. But he knew that his father had been to see her parents in Kent and had given his consent for their union in marriage if he could win her heart and hand. He was tongue-tied at their meeting in London, but he wrote to her from Liverpool to bring matters to a head. He hardly dared to open the letter when her reply at length arrived; but he found that it was written in terms that were cautious, but kind. 'I knew it was much in my favour that you would write at all and that you designed I should understand it so,' he recalled long after. '...Then, my dearest Mary, on that very day I began to live indeed, and to act in all my concerns with a spirit and firmness to which I before was a stranger.'[17] He felt that he could set out on his long voyage with a light heart, for she had told him that she was willing to wait for his return.

He soon found himself once more at Sierra Leone and the Plantanes, and the scenes of his early disgrace and misery served to remind him with peculiar force of his former ingratitude. He had been delivered from the curse of blasphemy and unbelief, and he was in many ways a new man in a new world. He could no more make a mock at sin or jest with holy things; he could no more doubt the truth of Scripture, or slight the voice of conscience. He knew that this change, as far as it prevailed, had been wrought by the Spirit and power of God, but he felt that he still stood in need of a work of grace in his soul if he were to be saved. Yet it was the Lord who had stretched out His arm thus far to save him and he could not resist the hope that He would yet do more. 'Therefore,' he wrote, 'I consider this as the beginning of my return to God, or rather of His return to me.'[18] The work of grace begun in storm at sea was now to reach its climax on the coast of Africa. He was stricken with a raging fever and all his fears revived as life ran low. His great perils and many mercies, his solemn prayers and earnest vows, his ungrateful returns for God's goodness, all pressed upon his mind at once. He thought for a while that the door of hope had shut; then he began to seek God's face again. Weak and almost delirious he rose up from his bed and crept away to a lonely spot where he could pour out his heart in prayer. He durst make no more resolves in his own strength, but cast himself in naked need before the Lord. Then he tells us how he was able to believe in a crucified Saviour; the load of guilt rolled away from heart and conscience, and he found that he was at peace with God. 'And from that time, I trust,' he wrote long years after, 'I have been delivered from the power and dominion of sin.'[19] The prayers and longings of his mother's heart were crowned with their reward at last, and the story of his conversion is a romance of grace which stands side by side with that of the great Augustine.

John Newton could never forget how God had put forth His arm to save him when he seemed past saving; he felt that he was like a pattern meant to shew forth the mercy and forbearance of God.

> Many a time when sickness had brought me, as we say, to death's door, I was as easy and insensible as the sailor who in the height of the storm should presume to sleep upon the top of the mast, quite regardless that the next tossing wave might plunge him into the raging ocean beyond all possibility of relief. But at length a day came, which though the most terrible day I ever saw, I can now look back upon with thankfulness and pleasure; I say, the time came when, in such a helpless extremity and under the expectation of immediate death, it pleased God to command the veil from my eyes, and I saw things in some measure as they really were.

> Believe me, it was not a whim or a dream which changed my sentiments and conduct, but a powerful conviction which will not admit the least doubt; an evidence, which like that I have of my own existence, I cannot call in question without contradicting all my senses. And though my case was in some respects uncommon, yet something like it is known by one and another every day, and I have myself conversed with many who…have been like me brought to glory in the Cross of Christ, and to live by that faith which they had before slighted and opposed.'[20]

This long and important paragraph, with its nautical metaphor and its personal assurance, was the fruit of diligent reflection in after years; but it plainly shows that when he thought on the way by which God had led him, he felt that he was a trophy of grace such as no man could deny.

It was in the power of this faith that he rejoined his ship and lived through a long and trying voyage. His task was to sail here and there in the long-boat for the purchase of slaves, and he had his share of perils both by land and by sea. He was exposed to heat and chills, to winds and rains, in an open boat and in the broken surf; he was engaged in perilous journeys through the jungle and in dangerous missions with the natives. He was in deaths oft, for he could not swim; his boat often capsized in troubled seas and he was more or less half-drowned before strong arms could snatch him to safety. More than once he had been restrained at the last moment from some fresh venture which cost the life of the man who was sent to take his place; the full story of his risks and rescues leaves us with a sense of awe and wonderment. Eight months passed by and then they sailed for the West Indies and for Charlestown. Almost daily he would retire into the woods or fields for prayer; they were his favourite oratories, and he began to taste the joy of communion with God. His relish for the world was growing weaker as he grew in grace and he was kept from all that he now knew to be sinful. 'I had for the most part peace of conscience,' he wrote, 'and my strongest desires were towards the things of God.'[21] At length they made their way home to Liverpool and he immediately set out for London and Kent. Seven years and more had now elapsed since his first memorable visit to that home; the one constant anchor which had mercifully preserved his soul from final self-abandonment had been his passionate affection for that fair Kentish maiden. All the old obstacles which had once barred his way were now removed and it only remained for him to win her full and free consent. Once and again she would not hear; but he thought that she was not quite so peremptory on his second attempt. In a little while she heard him without interruption, and he began to promise himself success. He pressed his suit still more warmly and, at last, she put her hand in his in token of her consent.[22] The story of that human love is interwoven in a unique romance with the story of love divine, and on February 1, 1750, their hands were joined and their hearts were sealed in a marriage union of rare grace and gladness.

Between August 1750 and August 1754 Newton made three more expeditions to Africa and the Indies, but he sailed as his own captain. He felt the wrench from his wife with acute distress, but he kept up a voluminous correspondence with her while at sea. He wrote two or three times each week, even when there was no homeward packet for six or eight months at a stretch; sometimes two hundred sheets of paper were despatched in a single packet! Many of these letters were published some forty years later in 1793, and they provide us with a clear account of each voyage. He sailed on his first command in August 1750; he had a crew of thirty and he wanted a cargo of two hundred slaves. For fourteen months he was away in varied scenes of danger and difficulty, but he reached home at length in November 1751. He did not set out on his next voyage until July 1752; then he sailed with a new ship and had to meet fresh perils. There were close and constant shaves with death and danger, both on board and ashore; he had to deal now with a plot by the crew to turn to piracy, and now with a plot by the slaves to stir up mutiny. He reached home once more in peace and safety in August 1753, but he only enjoyed a brief respite of some six weeks before he sailed again. He was away on this voyage for nigh on twelve long months, but he berthed in Liverpool at last in August 1754. 'I had the pleasure of returning thanks in all the churches', so he wrote to his wife, 'for an African voyage performed without any disaster or the loss of a single man. This was much noticed and spoken of in the town, and I believe it is the first instance of the kind.'[23]

The long days at sea had been spent in diligent self-improvement and he had taught himself Latin in his cabin on the slave-ship just as once he had taught himself Euclid on the dry sands of the seashore. He had no grammar or lexicon when he began, but he made Horace and Juvenal his first study; then by slow degrees and hard labour, by indomitable pains and perseverance, by almost incredible efforts in the teeth of difficulty and disadvantage, he made himself at home with all the great Latin classics. But as time wore on he began to feel that the remnant of life for him was too short to spend on learned trifles, for neither Virgil nor Livy could tell him one word of Jesus. 'The classics were at first restrained to one morning in the week', he wrote, 'and, at length, were quite laid aside.'[24] Nothing is more striking in his *Letters to a Wife* than the rich development of the work of grace in his own soul. His light on the things of God at the time of his marriage was as the first faint streak of dawn; 'and I believe', he wrote, 'it was not yet daybreak with my dear wife.'[25] But his letters assumed a more tender insight as light increased and, in due time, God made the truth shine on her heart in the same glorious way as on his. He found that he could not live without prayer and he pored over the sacred text of Holy Writ day by day. The ship's bell rang twice each Sunday to call his crew to the upper deck, and he led them in the forms of worship laid down by the Book of Common Prayer. He kept a Diary from the beginning of his second voyage and it began with the entry: 'December 22, 1751: I dedicate unto Thee, Most Blessed God, this clean unsullied book; and at the same time, renew my tender of a foul, blotted, corrupt heart.'[26] His last two voyages taught him more of communion with God than he had ever known, though thus far he had walked the path of life without an earthly guide. For some six years, from 1748 to 1754, he had not met a single friend who could help him; but at length at St. Kitt's, on his third voyage, he met a fellow-captain by the name of Clunie who was well versed in the things of God. For near a month they spent night after night in each other's company, and they often sat up on deck until daybreak. That good old captain of the sea brought new light to John Newton in a thousand ways; 'he not only informed my understanding, but his discourse inflamed my heart.'[27] He grew clearer and more Evangelical in doctrine, bolder and more experimental in witness; he learnt the joy of social prayer and sailed for home at last with the names of many honoured servants of the Gospel in his pocket. 'I had much comfort and freedom during those seven weeks,' he recalled 'and my sun was seldom clouded.'[28]

Thus John Newton was the master of a vessel engaged in the slave-trade, and as yet he felt no sense of scruple at this wretched traffic in human life; he was the child of an age which saw no scandal in that hateful market of murder and man-stealing. He had only been a new man in Christ for six short years, and those years in the main had been spent far away in loneliness and solitude. No voice had yet reached his conscience to condemn the horrors of the slave trade, and it was not till years had passed away that he learnt to hate the whole great evil. Then, in 1787, he published his *Thoughts on the African Slave-Trade*, a most terrible exposure of that raw and festering wound. It was a plain record of facts, for he could quote from the log-book of his own adventures:

> The ship in which I was mate left the coast with two hundred and eighteen slaves on board…I find by my journal of that voyage…that we buried sixty-two on our passage to South Carolina, exclusive of those which died before we left the coast, of which I have no account.[29]

On February 28, 1794, he preached a fast-day sermon in St. Mary Woolnoth, in which he bared the naked truth:

> I should be inexcusable, considering the share I have formerly had in that unhappy business, if…I should omit to mention the African slave trade. There is a cry of blood against us; a cry accumulated by the accession of fresh victims, of thousands, of scores of thousands, I had almost said of hundreds of thousands, from year to year.[30]

Again, on December 19, 1797, he laid bare his own heart in the same church: 'I have more than once confessed with shame in this pulpit the concern I too long had in the African slave trade.'[31] He thought that the purchase of slaves year by year could hardly be less than one hundred thousand men and women, and that not less than an equal number lost their lives long before they reached the place of sale.[32] He was summoned in his old age as a witness to the bar of the House of Lords, and he pronounced judgment without reserve on the crime of the whole vile trade.

But all this still belonged to the future on his return home in 1754, for he thought then that it was a lawful calling. 'I considered it as the line of life which God in His providence had allotted me, and as a cross which I ought to bear with patience…till He should be pleased to deliver me from it.'[33] The one duty which his conscience required was that he should treat the slaves in his care with as much of humanity as the safety of all on board, black as well as white, would admit, and it may be safely affirmed that there were few more kindly masters of slave-ships than John Newton. But his heart was not in it, and in a half-conscious kind of way he was ill at ease. The voice of prayer and praise on the deck above was so pitifully incongruous with the irons and groans of men packed like books on a shelf in the hold below. Newton felt that he was like a gaoler, even though he thought it lawful, and he was shocked with a calling which for ever had to do with bolts and chains and shackles. It drove him at length to be much in prayer that God would be pleased to fix him in some more humane way of life; and God was pleased to hear his cry, though in a way he had little thought.[34] He meant to put to sea again in November 1754, and he seemed to be in full health and vigour. But a sudden illness seized him when he was within two days of sailing and he was forced to resign his command the day before the ship slipped its moorings. This cut the knot which bound him to that vile commerce in heartsick and stifled men and women, than which few things were more iniquitous, more cruel, more oppressive, or more destructive.[35] But it solved a second problem as well, for it put an end to the long separations from his wife and his home. His heart had long been in England, and each new departure wrung all his feelings with fresh and poignant distress. But now his life as a sea captain and a slave-trader was at an end and a new sphere of work and interest was about to unfold itself before his eyes.

The ten years from 1754 to 1764 were designed in the providence of God to prepare him for the ministry, though he was led by a way he knew not. For the better part of twelve months he stayed on in Kent and London, but in August 1755 he was installed in a well paid post as a Surveyor of Tides for the Port of Liverpool. In Kent he passed some hours each day when the weather was fine in the thickest woods or on the highest hills: 'I always find these rural scenes', he wrote, 'have some tendency both to refresh and to compose my spirits.'[36] But in London he found himself at the very well-head of spiritual life and activity, and he had soon heard and met George Whitefield who was then at the height of his career. He was up one morning at four o'clock to hear him preach at five, and he was so impressed by the sermon that he lost all relish for food or company that day. Four weeks after he took up his appointment in Liverpool, Whitefield paid his first visit to the great city on the banks of the Mersey. 'Most of my leisure this week will be taken up with Mr Whitefield,' he wrote to his wife; '...he warms my heart, makes me more indifferent to cares and crosses, and strengthens my faith.'[37] Four days later he wrote again:

> Mr Whitefield left us yesterday morning; I accompanied him on foot a little way out of town till the chaise overtook us. I have had more of his company than would have come to my share at London in a twelve-month. I heard him preach nine times, supped with him three times, and dined with him once…and on Sunday he dined with me. I cannot say how much I esteem him and hope to my dying day I shall have reason to bless God in his behalf.[38]

Newton did not lack in moral courage, and stood up for the great preacher so well that he was soon dubbed as 'a young Whitefield!'[39] He came to know Wesley in April 1757 and he blessed God for him almost as much as for Whitefield; he went to see Grimshaw two months later and he preached in his house to an assembly of one hundred and fifty people. So then in these years his Evangelical associations sprang up and grew, and he was linked with the great and honoured leaders of the Revival.

He had now set himself to the pursuit of the highest knowledge, a choice which soon divorced him as much from Classics as it had from Euclid. His first task was to learn enough Greek to read the New Testament and the Septuagint; then he took up Hebrew and even Syriac with such success that he learnt to read the Psalms and the historical books with comparative ease. He kept up a course of reading in the best divines, both English and Latin, and thus slowly acquired the learning and attainments requisite for a clergyman. His first thoughts of ordination had sprung up round the words of St. Paul: 'But they had heard only that he which persecuted us in times past now preacheth the faith which once he destroyed' (Gal. 1: 23). He thought that there could be none so fit as he to proclaim the truth that Christ came to save the chief of sinners; but his early desires for the ministry were long beset with difficulty and perplexity. He was distressed about what was or was not a proper call to the ministry, while he sometimes felt that he must preach, though it were only in the streets.[40] Thus, in 1757, he took a day from six in the morning till five in the evening to fast and pray, and to offer himself in an unreserved surrender for God's service.[41] But the seven years of waiting before he won his bride were now to be matched by seven years of waiting before this goal could be achieved. His first leanings were all towards Dissent, for he did not feel that he could subscribe to the Articles of the Established Church. But his overtures to the Dissenters broke down and the delay led him to see that he could conform with a good conscience.[42] In December 1758, he applied to the Archbishop of York for ordination, but was met with a refusal. His patience and humility all through these trying years were of the first order, but he found silence hard to bear. 'I fear it must be wrong,' he wrote to his wife in 1762, 'after having so solemnly devoted myself to the Lord for His service, to wear away my time and bury my talents in silence…after all the great things He has done for me.'[43] But at length on April 29, 1764, this long trial came to an end and he was ordained by the Bishop of Lincoln as the curate of Olney. He wrote:

> I received ordination in the Church of England with a πληροφορία, with wind and tide, if I may so speak, in my favour, with the most pleasing disposition of outward events and the most assured persuasion in my own mind that I was following the call and doing the will of God; of which I had at that time little more doubt than if an angel had been sent from heaven to tell me so.[44]

Newton was installed at Olney as the substitute for an absentee vicar on the pittance of £60 per annum and, for fifteen years, from May 1764 to December 1779, it was the centre of his life and ministry. Olney was a fair sized country town, but it was inhabited 'chiefly by the half-starved and ragged of the earth.'[45] Two thousand people were trying to wring a livelihood from the doomed trade of lace-making, and were sullenly fighting a stern battle with starvation. But the Earl of Dartmouth and John Thornton gave him funds to relieve the poor and he was then able to give himself to the care of their souls. Thornton promised him a stated sum of £200 each year as a supplement to his salary and gave him upwards of £3,000 in all over the years. 'Be hospitable', he wrote, 'and keep an open house for such as are worthy of entertainment.'[46] Newton found a band of praying people in the Church at Olney, men and women who had long walked in the light and comfort of the Gospel. 'The Lord has led me by a way that I little expected', he wrote on September 14, 1765, 'to a pleasant lot where the Gospel has been many years known and is highly valued by many.'[47] He threw himself at once into the work of his parish and organized a round of meetings which leaves us frankly surprised. There were daily meetings for prayer or for Bible study in a large house near the church, and cottage meetings were often held in the most remote corners of the parish. The congregations grew and galleries were built; yet 'there seemed no more room in the body of the church than before'.[48] He refused the invitations which came ere long to go elsewhere; preferment was not necessary to his peace or usefulness. He would not itinerate like Whitefield or Grimshaw, fast friends though they all were; he made the parish his world while others made the world their parish.

Thus 'the rebellious forces of his unregenerate youth, seized, tempered, harmonized by the grace of God, had taken a new direction in the form of a persistent diligence, an unpretentious courage in face of opposition or contempt, and a never dying glow of love for the souls of men.'[49] The bluff old sea captain soon became known to all in his blue sea jacket; he could hardly ever be persuaded to change his dress for clerical attire. He knew that dress could not make a minister; that was a work for grace alone. 'I have long since learned that if I was ever to be a minister,' he wrote, 'faith and prayer must make me one.'[50] He was a faithful preacher and a most diligent visitor, but his chief gifts lay in private dealing with troubled souls. Fletcher of Madeley was deeply impressed with his sober insight and wrote of him to Whitefield as early as May 1767: 'I think I hardly ever met his fellow for a judicious spirit.'[51] This was high praise from such a quarter, but it was fully borne out in the life of his parish. Men came in a constant stream to his door in Olney, men who were in the grip of sin and who felt the need of salvation. 'They found in him one who had been a worse sinner than themselves, ...one who was able to speak with authority as to the way of salvation.'[52] He had made a study of the human heart, with all its workings and counter-workings in nature and in grace, for this was the favourite interest of his pastoral ministry. [53] Thus his knowledge of the lure of sin was drawn from the deep moral disorder of his own early life, and his knowledge of the power of grace was drawn from the great inner renewal of his own worthless soul. Over the mantelpiece in his study at the top of the house, he had painted words which would keep these facts ever in view: 'But thou shalt remember that thou wast a bondman in the land of Egypt, and the Lord thy God hath redeemed thee' (Deut. 15: 15). It taught him to walk by the light of that wisdom which is from above and to lean upon the arm of an almighty Friend.[54] The result is described in a beautiful tribute from the pen of Richard Cecil: 'There was a gentleness, a candour, and a forbearance in him that I do not recollect to have seen in an equal degree among his brethren and which had so conciliating an effect that even the enemies of truth often spoke loudly in praise of his character.'[55] Newton did not appear to the best advantage in the pulpit; his utterance was imperfect and his attitude was ungraceful. But his parent-like tenderness and deep affection for his people made such defects of small account in their judgment, and they preferred him to the most popular orators of the day. 'At first my chief solicitude used to be what I should find to say,' he told a friend; 'I hope it is now rather that I may not speak in vain.'[56] He chose his texts like a servant who holds a key which will only unlock one particular drawer; he felt that he could not expect to be helped to more than one text at a time.[57] He wrote out his sermons in more or less detail, but preached without notes or manuscript. 'When we read to the people', he said, 'they think themselves less concerned in what is offered than when we speak to them point-blank.'[58] He found it an easy task to preach if he were in the right frame of trustful prayer: 'A written sermon is something to lean upon,' he wrote; 'but it is best for a preacher to lean wholly upon the Lord.'[59] Richard Cecil tells us that his hearers were often delighted with the most felicitous illustrations, and that these were expressed with so much grace on his part that they could not fail to move and enlarge their hearts also.[60] Newton himself thought that the best and most useful part of his sermons occurred to him *de novo* while he was preaching.[61] His grand aim, as he loved to say, was to break the hard heart and to heal the broken in heart.[62] 'A faithful minister will account a single instance of success a rich recompense for the labour of a life,' so he feared not to say; 'may this joy be mine!'[63]

The doctrinal views which he urged on heart and conscience were strictly those of the Church of England as set forth by the Reformers in her Articles and Formularies. He was convinced that there could be nothing in the English language, apart from the Bible, which would compare with the Prayer Book in simplicity, energy, and comprehensive fullness of expression.[64] He felt rather like a speckled bird where parties were concerned, for he had been a debtor to all and was a member of none. Thus he described himself in playful mood to a Dissenter whom he counted amongst his closest friends: 'Church and Meeting, Methodists and Moravian, may all perceive something in my coat taken from them.'[65] He was a moderate and clear-sighted Calvinist in an age when controversy ran high. 'Of all people who engage in controversy,' he wrote, 'we who are called Calvinists are most expressly bound by our own principles to the exercise of gentleness and moderation.'[66] He saw that no doctrine can be an infallible token of a humble mind, and his own moderation exposed him to sharp stricture on the part of many. 'I hope,' he said to Cecil with a smile, 'I hope I am upon the whole a Scriptural preacher; for I find I am considered as an Arminian among the High Calvinists, and as a Calvinist among the strenuous Arminians.'[67] Scriptural he was in doctrine, in preaching, and in appeal; he desired no other touch-stone for his faith and message. He exclaimed in a sermon on Justifying Faith:

> I account it my honour and happiness that I preach to a free people, who have the Bible in their hands; to your Bibles I appeal! I entreat, I charge you, to receive nothing upon my word any farther than I prove it from the Word of God; and bring every preacher and every sermon that you hear to the same standard. If this is the truth, you had need to be well established in it; for it is not the current and fashionable doctrine of the times.[68]

Newton's residence at Olney is famous in the annals of English literature for his friendship with William Cowper. He was a son of the rectory at Berkhampstead, a descendant through his mother of the great Dean of St. Paul's, John Donne. His early years in a clergyman's home brought him into automatic contact with many sides of common life, not least with the life of the poor. His mother's death when he was six years old overwhelmed him with an agonizing sense of loss which only seemed to grow with the years. Now and then, in early manhood, he was the prey of a mysterious despondency which proved to be the sad prelude of a tragic future. The first attack occurred in 1752 when he was in chambers at the Temple, and it came like some dark crisis for heart and mind. Ten years then passed away without horror of soul, but without purpose in life. Then, in 1763, his sensitive mind gave way afresh and he tried repeatedly to do away with himself. This awful delusion took the form of a strange certainty that he was doomed to lose his soul. His friends placed him in a private asylum at St. Alban's, and here at length the dark cloud broke. The pure sweet light of peace and hope burst out from the shadows as he was reading the text of Holy Writ (Romans 3: 25). From St. Alban's he went to live with the Unwins at Huntingdon, where he shared the simple culture and gentle habits of a holy home. It was here that he met Newton, not long before Unwin's death in 1767, and the upshot was that with Mrs Unwin he came to settle at Olney. Cowper had made up his mind to move to Olney for the sake of Newton's friendship as much as for that of his ministry, and their friendship was deep and real, whether it moved on hills of sunny light or in vales of awful gloom. 'The Lord who had brought us together so knit our hearts and affections', wrote Newton, 'that for nearly twelve years we were seldom separated for twelve hours at a time, when we were awake and at home. The first six I passed in daily admiring and trying to imitate him; during the second six I walked pensively with him in the valley of the shadow of death.'[69] There was only a field and a garden between Orchard Side and the Vicarage, and they talked away many a summer hour beneath the trees on themes as high as God and as wide as man.[70] The homely pastor and the gentle poet worked hand in hand for the relief of the sick and the poor, and Cowper was remembered in the village as the Squire long years after his death. The constant round of duty and devotion may have imposed some kind of strain on Cowper's mental ease; it may at times have probed his inner life with a touch too profound for the delicate poise of his sensitive soul. But we never read that he felt it to be so, and it is a baseless slander to suggest that Newton was his evil genius. On January 2, 1773, six years after their first friendship, he was attacked again by his old and terrible malady, and it left him with an unreasonable, but quite immovable conviction that he was doomed to be a castaway. There was a horror, a darkness in that cloud, almost unique in degree; the symptoms were at times visibly terrible. 'I can hardly conceive that anyone in a state of grace and favour with God can be in greater distress,' Newton declared; 'and yet no one walked more closely with Him, or was more simply devoted to Him in all things.'[71] One fair day in April, he fled from his own house as from fiends incarnate to find refuge in the Vicarage, and he refused to leave for twelve full months while he remained in this state of profound distress. Within that gloom of black despair, Newton watched and prayed, with superb and unfailing patience; beneath that load of dark distress, Cowper clung to the friend who loved him as to an angel of light. Then that stage of acute horror passed off, though its pains never wholly left his soul. It is common enough to find among men of letters many who prize Cowper and slight Newton; but to ascribe Cowper's state of mind to Newton's views of truth is either a lie or a mistake which cannot be tolerated. Cowper never knew the meaning of settled peace apart from Christ; it brought him the only rays of sunshine which he ever enjoyed. Newton's strong and cheerful faith was the best comfort he could have asked in his mental sorrows, and the intimacy of those years at Olney was still maintained by pen and ink as long as Cowper lived.

It is pleasant to think of that friendship between the homely and rugged sailor on the one hand and the gentle and troubled Templar on the other hand. The whole friendship was all for good, for the differences between the two men were mainly on the surface. Cowper was reserved and sensitive towards the outside world, but beneath his exterior, his powers of thought were as true and virile as those of a giant; Newton was forceful and vigorous amongst his fellow-men, but behind this exterior his warmth of heart was as soft and tender as that of a child. Cowper's mysterious illusion on one great subject ran parallel with his luminous good sense on every other; Newton's moderate Calvinism in one great matter was consistent with a generous optimism in every other. It may be that Newton could have done more to encourage Cowper in his literary activities; but Cowper himself had yet to discover where his real genius in these things lay. At all events, it was to his friendship with Newton that we owe the Olney Hymns; it was this that awoke his dormant gifts and gave his mind the bias and impulse which were so largely to guide his future activities. These hymns were meant for the use of Newton's people in their mid-week meetings and were gladly sung in church and cottage as they appeared from week to week. For two years they flowed in a steady stream from Orchard Side and the Vicarage; then came Cowper's illness and the whole scheme was dropped. But in due time Newton resumed the task alone, and the full collection of three hundred and forty-eight hymns was published in 1779.

Newton's Preface reveals at once his own humility and his deep sense of Cowper's worth: 'A desire of promoting the faith and comfort of sincere Christians, though the principal, was not the only motive to this undertaking; it was likewise intended as a monument to perpetuate the remembrance of an intimate and endeared friendship.'[72] The two friends had laid themselves out to serve the Church of God, and they paid scant enough regard to the demands of a nice ear or an accurate reviewer. They chose a style that was neat and clear, but made sparing use of colour or imagination. Many of the hymns are far from poetry at all, but some of them have earned a place in all the most permanent treasuries of sacred song. 'If the Lord whom I serve has been pleased to favour me', so wrote Newton with disarming frankness in his Preface, 'with that mediocrity of talent which may qualify me for usefulness to the weak and the poor of His flock…I have reason to be satisfied.'[73] Only sixty-eight of the hymns came from Cowper; the much larger number of two hundred and eighty from Newton was due to the illness which laid Cowper aside. Cowper touched the highest notes of poetry and devotion in his best hymns: 'Hark, my soul, it is the Lord'; 'Oh for a closer walk with God'; 'God moves in a mysterious way'; 'There is a Fountain filled with blood'; 'Jesus, where'er Thy people meet'. But we are bound to recognize that, with all their beauty, they are not more beautiful than the best of Newton's hymns: 'How sweet the Name of Jesus sounds'; 'Approach my soul the Mercy Seat'; 'Come my soul, thy suit prepare'; 'Great Shepherd of Thy people hear'; 'For mercies countless as the sands'. Newton is not one whit behind, even as to English diction, in hymns like these; his voice is as pure and strong as the faith of which he sings. And he is the author of the one outstanding hymn of a thoroughly objective character in the whole collection: 'Glorious things of thee are spoken'. Hymns were still a new thing in the worship of the English Church at the time when the work of Newton and Cowper appeared, and the Olney Hymns must ever hold an honoured place side by side with those of Watts and the Wesleys in the early development of our national hymnody.

Newton's residence at Olney is hardly less famous for his friendship with Thomas Scott. He had received Orders as a deacon in September 1772 and had become curate to the nearby parish of Ravenstone and Weston Underwood. He was almost a Socinian in Theology, and he loved to ridicule what he did not understand in the way of Evangelical truth. In May 1775 he met Newton at a visitation and at once set out to engage him in controversy in a room full of clergy. Newton refused to be drawn, but a day or two later sent him a short note and a copy of *Omicron*. Scott seized the chance which now seemed to offer for an elaborate controversy, and wrote him a long and provocative letter. On June 23, Newton sent a friendly reply in which he carefully avoided all that was contentious: 'You may see…what is the desire of my heart for you; but I am not impatient…I have travelled the path before you, I see what you yet want; I cannot impart it to you, but He can and I trust He will.'[74] July and August saw a second and a third letter on their way to Scott, in which Newton parried his blows with his own experience: 'Your objections neither displease nor weary me… for I have formerly made the like objections myself,' so he wrote on August 11; 'I have stood upon your ground and I continue to hope you will one day stand upon mine.'[75] Scott was nettled and soon showed it; but he could not move Newton. A fourth and fifth letter followed in September and October, and Scott was told that the Lord alone could give light to the soul and that Newton's part was only to throw in a word here and there as a witness: 'From your letters and sermons I am encouraged to address you in our Lord's words, Thou art not far from the Kingdom of God,' he wrote on October 21; 'I am persuaded the views you have received will not suffer you to remain where you are. But fidelity obliges me to add, Yet one thing thou lackest. That one thing I trust the Lord will both show you and bestow upon you in His due time.'[76]

This was not all to Scott's liking and the next three letters from Newton met with no reply. Newton felt that he had done enough to discharge his conscience, though he could not discharge his affection: 'It remains with you whether our correspondence continues or not,' he wrote on December 8, 'as this is the third letter I have written since I heard from you, and therefore must be the last till I do.'[77] This broke off their friendship for the time being, but there is an entry in his journal which shows that Newton was still mindful of him: 'December 22, 1775: He has sincerity, if I mistake not, in such a sense as he could not have if the Lord had not in some degree visited his heart. May He be pleased to lead him gently on and to reveal His salvation to him.'[78] But they seldom met for a long time and few words were exchanged when they did. 'Yet', Scott admits, 'he all along persevered in telling me to my no small offence that I should accede one day to his religious principles; that he had stood on my ground and that I should stand on his; and he constantly informed his friends that though slowly, I was surely feeling my way to the knowledge of the truth.'[79] At length, in April 1777, discouragement drove Scott to call upon Newton and his gracious converse quite won his heart. He was now glad to think of him as a friend, though he would not call him so. He still refused his doctrinal views and was ashamed to be seen in his company; 'but', he confessed, 'I sometimes stole away to spend an hour with him.'[80] On September 2, Newton noted the silent change in his journal: 'A visit from Mr Scott yesterday morning. O my Lord, I thank thee for Thy goodness to him; I think he gets forward in the light of Thy truth.'[81] In January 1778, he began to attend Newton's preaching and was surprised to find the secrets of his own heart so clearly exposed. He was driven to take up the study of the Bible with greater care, and day after day he walked up and down the beautiful park at Weston with his Greek Testament in hand. 'Thus', he tells us, 'I began experimentally to perceive our Lord's meaning when He says, Except ye receive the Kingdom of God as a little child, ye shall in no wise enter therein.'[82] Newton had won his man at last; he had won him by a rare display of gentleness and tolerance, of tactful sympathy and fearless loyalty. He blessed God as he watched him grow and prayed for him more than ever: 'December 11, 1778: Breakfasted with Mr Scott…I think I can see that he has got before me already. Lord, if I have been useful to him, do Thou I beseech Thee make him now useful to me.'[83]

Newton's letters to Scott were but a part of the wide and varied correspondence which flowed in a ceaseless stream from the Vicarage at Olney. He found time and opportunity to ply his pen in a fruitful round of literary toil, and there was a steady output from his labours for many years. In 1767, he published his *Olney Sermons*, and in 1786 his *Sermons on the Messiah*; in 1769, he published his *Review of Ecclesiastical History* and, in 1779, his *Olney Hymns*. The *Review of Ecclesiastical History* set out to trace the work of the Spirit of God from age to age rather than the movements of men and politics. It had been laid aside after the first two books, but enough was written to put Joseph Milner on the track. 'He got the hint from me,' Newton told a friend when his great Church History appeared.[84] But it was in the now obsolete toil of careful loving letter-writing that John Newton excelled, and he used his pen for this purpose with remarkable success. He was the letter-writer *par excellence* of the Evangelical Revival; this was his distinctive contribution to that great movement. He was not unconscious of his gifts in this direction: 'It is the Lord's will' he said that I should do most by my letters.'[85] Balleine describes, him as 'the St. Francis de Sales of the Evangelical Movement, the great spiritual director of souls through the post.'[86] All his Letters would have made up several folios, and he was urged by his friends to put them in print for the world at large. He chose many for this purpose in the belief that this would best avoid mistakes in the future and he fondly hoped that no liberties would be taken with the unpublished residue. His *Omicron* and *Vigil* in 1774 and his *Letters to a Wife* in 1793 were his first and last efforts in this direction. But the *Narrative of his Life* in 1764 and his *Apologia* in 1784 were both cast into the form of letters to a friend, and they derive much of their piquancy from this epistolary style.

But by far the best-known of his works was *Cardiphonia, The Utterance of the Heart in the Course of a Real Correspondence,* which was given to the world early in the year 1781. It was William Cowper who thus christened the book and the title was one fitly chosen. It took its place at once as an English classic of the highest value, and it will be read as long as devotional literature is in demand. There are one hundred and fifty-six letters, addressed to twenty-four correspondents, and they were written on and off during the two and twenty years between 1757 and 1779. Newton wrote to the recipients and asked for their permission to publish the correspondence, but he withheld names and circumstances from the public. But, in 1868, Bull made it known that the Earl of Dartmouth and Thomas Scott, Mrs Thornton and Mrs Wilberforce, were among the recipients. Newton's Letters are in the realm of devotional life very much what Cowper's Letters are in the sphere of pure literature. 'They are the best draught of his own mind,' Richard Cecil declared;[87] they make up 'a volume of the purest apostolical and evangelical truth,' said Alexander Whyte.[88] They are rich in paragraphs which have seldom been surpassed in their quiet beauty, and they possess the rare flavour of true originality. They are written in a neat and natural style, with plain idiom and strong emphasis, in level English and easy language, and they abound in a wise and kindly tone of instruction, and with a shrewd and racy turn of expression. They are rich in the unction of Christian charity and strong in the secret of genuine sympathy. 'His eye is upon me while I write, His eye will be upon you when you read,' so runs a letter in the year 1783; 'may He touch my heart and yours, and give a happy issue!'[89] The two ever-recurring themes are the depravity of the sinner's heart and the sufficiency of the Saviour's grace, and they combine such kindly feeling with such manly counsel, such friendly, earnest love with such sturdy, common sense, that we can well believe that he was a friend in whom it was indeed good to confide. *Omicron* and *Cardiphonia* are both in that class of books which is by far the best in the whole world of books.

At the close of the year 1779, Newton received a call to the united Cure of St. Mary Woolnoth and St. Mary Woolchurch

Haw in London, as a result of the kindly intervention of his friend, John Thornton. There had been a time when he would have looked askance at the very idea of a city parish; he used to speak of London Grace and Country Grace, and he felt a decided preference for the country. He had written in 1769:

> By London Grace, when genuine, I understand grace in a very advanced degree, the favoured few who are kept alive to God, simple-hearted and spiritually-minded…in the midst of such snares and temptations, appear to me to be the first-rate Christians of the land. I adore the power of the Lord in them and compare them to the young men who walked unhurt in the midst of the fire.[90]

Again, in 1778, he wrote in the same strain to another friend: 'I honour the grace of God in those few, comparatively few I fear, who preserve their garments undefiled in that Sardis.'[91] Now he was to make trial of London Grace for himself and he commenced his ministry on December 19, 1779, with a sermon in St. Mary Woolnoth. 'I stand here as a pattern of the long-suffering of God', he declared, 'and, having obtained mercy myself, I have encouragement from my own case to hope that the strongest prejudices may be softened by the power of His grace.'[92] He was indeed in a new and distinct scene of action, for his church in Lombard Street was in the heart of London. It was in an opulent neighbourhood, close to the Royal Exchange and the Bank of England. The Lord Mayor would sometimes attend and it was looked upon as one of the most important of the city churches. That one who had spent his boyhood in the streets and docks of foreign cities, and his twenties off the coasts and swamps of far-away Africa, should now be called to minister in the church of the chief magistrate in the first city of the world, was a turn of providence so real to his mind that scarce a single day would pass without remark upon it in one way or another.

For twenty-eight years, from December 1779 to December 1807, he exercised that ministry in the heart of London with the most unwearied diligence, a ministry that gave him a position of great influence in the ranks of the Evangelical party. There was little variety of interest or anecdote in a life that was so stationary; sometimes the course of a single day might stand for an account of the whole year. He preached in St. Mary Woolnoth both before and after noon on Sundays, and he held a morning service there on Wednesdays. He helped other clergy as well, and preached as often as six times a week even when he was above seventy years of age. The poor were drawn by his ministry at once and their numbers soon embarrassed the wealthier members of his congregation. The troubled and tempted found an asylum and a sympathy in his home which they could scarcely find in like degree in all London besides. His friendly and hospitable home was open to visitors of all ranks and denominations every Tuesday and Saturday, and he soon won a wide reputation as a wise and sagacious counsellor in the things of God. He also held breakfast parties which were open to friends by his invitation; 'they were perhaps the most edifying' of all these occasions, so wrote one of his guests, 'for the good old man…was then fresh and communicative, always instructive, always benevolent.'[93] His droll and ready wit, his kind and cheerful eye, his ripe purity and deep piety, made him a host in a thousand; he was a conversationalist of no mean order and his social habits helped to gather round him many who were yet to stand high in Church and State. He lived to see the adult grandchildren of his early hearers in his congregation, and his name was treasured in their hearts long after he had gone to his rest. Thus his London years were crowned with success of the highest order, for he was used to lead the lost and weary into rest at the feet of Christ; and the decision of mind and the singleness of heart with which he sought them have become part and parcel of the traditional inheritance of the whole Church of Christ militant here on earth.

Newton was a man of large and generous affections; he could live no longer than he could love. He had no children of his own, but two orphan nieces of his wife's were entrusted to his care. They had more of his heart than most children have in the case of the fondest parents, and it was a great grief to him when one of the two passed away after a long illness in October 1785. He enshrined her memory in a narrative of her death and character, and a copy of this little tract fell into the hands of Mrs. Sherwood early in 1804. She never forgot the time or the circumstances in which she read that tract; she could hear the strains of the hundredth Psalm sung by her husband's regiment while she sat reading and wondering why the dying girl should feel such intense anxiety to be assured that she had a new heart. 'What could she mean, I thought, by a new heart? Is this the same as the new birth?…I then for the first time began to suppose that there must be something more in this matter than I had hitherto supposed.'[94] Newton, no doubt, never knew that his little tract had borne such fruit; he had given it to the world simply as a tribute of love to the dear child who had filled his home with holy gladness. Mary Newton, his wife, he loved with a love that excelled, a true lover's passion that knew no abatement for fifty years. Many a time he had walked out from London in the days before they were married and had climbed Shooter's Hill near Blackheath to look towards her home in Kent: 'Not that I could see the spot itself…for she lived far beyond what I could see,' so he once told Cecil; 'but it gratified me even to look towards the spot; and this I did always once and sometimes twice a week.'[95] It was the same deep love that filled his heart as he subscribed his last letter to her in August 1785: 'I shall never find words fully to tell you how much I owe you, how truly I love you, nor the one half of what my heart means when I subscribe myself, Your most affectionate and obliged husband.'[96] He never wearied of saying that this was the main hinge on which his whole rescue had turned, and her death in December 1790, after great pain in her last long illness, was a crushing blow to his whole being. She sent for him on the Sunday morning of December 12 as he was preparing for church and they took a final farewell as to this world. She faintly breathed a familiar and endearing name and gave him her hand while he prayed by her bedside. He was as unable to speak for tears as she was for weakness, and he had to leave her alone; but he soon came back and told her that if her mind were in a state of peace it would be a comfort to him if she could raise her hand. She held it up and waved it gently to and fro. Sight and speech failed that night, but she lingered three days more; then she passed quietly away. Newton arose and worshipped God in a way that surprised his friends, but the wound could only be healed by their reunion in another world.[97]

He was notorious in his London years for his homely benevolence; friends loved to throng his home, while his servants grew old in his employ. It had been his to help William Cowper with the talent which drew forth his rich stream of poetry; it had been his to fire Joseph Milner with the ideal which called forth his great work on history. His two closest friends were now Thomas Scott and Richard Cecil, who found in him a heart of gold; two more younger friends were John Venn of Clapham and Charles Simeon of Cambridge, who found in him a tower of strength. In a letter of March 1791, old Henry Venn of Yelling gives us a hint of the bond between Newton and the younger generation: 'Dear Simeon,' he wrote, '...paid us a visit and slept here last Wednesday but one; he gives a charming account of Mr Newton.'[98] It was to Newton that Wilberforce came in the great crisis of his early life for, in 1784, he wrote and asked him for an interview. 'He told me', wrote Wilberforce, 'he always had entertained hopes and confidence that God would some time bring me to Him.'[99] It was a happy choice that led him to one so wise and shrewd, and it helped him to reach his great decision to serve the Lord Christ and to fight the slave trade. 'The joy that I felt and the hopes I conceived', Newton recalled some years later, 'when you called on me in the vestry of St. Mary's, I shall never forget.'[100] It was to Newton that Buchanan came in the crisis of his wayward youth for, in 1790, he heard him preach and wrote to him in great distress of soul. He had left his Glasgow studies to tour Europe with the aid of a violin, but had fallen into grave straits on his way through London. His letter was unsigned, but Newton gave notice in church that the unknown author would be more than welcome to call on him. It was through this interview that the young troubadour found his way to Christ and chose a new path in life. Henry Thornton sent him up to Cambridge at the end of 1791, and Charles Simeon sent him out to India at the end of 1796.[101] Twice, in April and in November 1796, Daniel Wilson called on Newton in sore trouble of soul, and most faithfully did the old man deal with him in his longing for peace and forgiveness.[102] Twice, in January 1804 and in April 1805, Henry Martyn dined with Newton while he was waiting to sail for the East, and most graciously did the old man pray with him in his longing for grace and holiness.[103] Thus round him or within near reach of his letters, a new generation of clergy was rising up in those memorable years who were in debt to him for their spiritual encouragement and whose lives of noble service were to be of untold significance for their Church and country.[104]

Newton was a foundation member of the Eclectic Society which was established in 1783 'for the investigation of spiritual truth.' There were fortnightly meetings in the vestry of St. John's Chapel, Bedford Row, and it quickly grew with members in the country as well as in London. It soon became the great London centre for the noblest clergy and all the most influential laymen in the closing years of the century, and John Newton was recognized as the Nestor of the society in ripe wisdom and sage counsel for nigh on five and twenty years. It was his sheer goodness rather than his greatness that gave him such singular influence; it was the manifest abundance of the grace of God that was with him. The whole man rang with the strong and vibrant voice of evangelical truth; his old age shone with the bright and lambent flame of experimental faith. His Letters and Sermons were drawn from the wealth of his own experience, for he had plumbed the deeps both of guilt and of grace. 'With respect to my acceptance in the Beloved', he wrote, 'I know not if I have had a doubt of a quarter of an hour's continuance for many years past. But oh! the multiplied instances of stupidity, ingratitude, impatience, and rebellion, to which my conscience has been witness!'[105] 'My heart is like a highway, like a city without walls or gates,' he said; 'nothing so false, so frivolous, so absurd, so impossible, or so horrid, but it can obtain access, and that at any time or in any place.'[106] He stood as high above most men in his knowledge both of the human heart and of the Gospel life as did Sir Isaac Newton in the field of science and of philosophy, and he would have nothing to do with mere hearsay in the great concerns of the soul. 'I set no value upon any doctrinal truth,' he wrote in 1759, 'farther than it has a tendency to promote practical holiness.'[107] 'We do not deal in unfelt truths,' he wrote again in 1777, 'but we find ourselves that solid consolation in the Gospel which we encourage others to expect from it.'[108] He had a clear insight into the ways of faith and feeling, and his own deep humility is apparent in so many remarks. 'In my judgment', he wrote, 'they are the happiest who have the lowest thoughts of themselves and in whose eyes Jesus is most glorious and precious.'[109] 'O to be little in our own eyes!' he exclaimed on January 7, 1767; 'this is the groundwork of every grace!'[110] His whole heart went with the truth as he sought to bring it home to the hearts of others, and he was ever anxious to meet men in their place of need with the news of Christ and His fullness. 'The more you know Him the better you will trust Him,' so he wrote to one of his friends; 'the more you trust Him, the better you will love Him; the more you love Him the better you will serve Him.'[111] He loved to trace the hand of God in all the events of life, however trivial they might appear, for he saw that as a sinner he had no right, and as a believer he had no reason to complain.[112] He loved to bring the balm of truth to all the sorrows of life, however desperate they might appear, for he knew that as a rule it is much easier to bear the pains of suffering in our own persons rather than in the persons of those whom we dearly love.[113] We hear his own cheerful faith in vigorous exercise as he exclaims: 'May you praise Him for all that is past and trust Him for all that is to come!'[114] It would not be hard to name his favourite text if we may judge from frequency of quotation: 'But of Him are ye in Christ Jesus, who of God is made unto us wisdom and righteousness and sanctification and redemption' (1 Cor. 1: 30). Nor is it hard to see how he loved to rehearse the Names of Christ as in his most famous hymn: 'Does He not call Himself a Saviour, a Shepherd, a Friend, and a Husband?'[115] So for the space of nigh on four and forty years, he fulfilled his ministry; a minister of grace rather than a messenger of wrath, a Barnabas much more than a Boanerges, rich in genial sympathy and in generous interest, full of godly wisdom and of kindly humour, altogether 'one of the purest and most unselfish of saints'.[116]

The turn of the century in 1800 found John Newton alone of the early leaders of the Evangelical Revival still in active harness. His early friends, Whitefield and Grimshaw, had gone the way of all the earth long before. John Wesley had passed on in 1791 and Henry Venn was called home in 1797. Newton himself was now seventy-five years of age, while Scott was still only fifty-three and Cecil fifty-two. Newton and Romaine were the only two Evangelical clergy who had churches of their own when he first came to London in December 1779, and Romaine, that iron pillar of the truth, unmoved by the smiles or frowns of the world, had died in July 1795. Thus 'old Newton' was now revered as a kind of patriarch and was trusted as a sort of oracle by the men of a new generation. A sound scholar and diligent pastor, a clear thinker and dignified author, he stood for those ideals of doctrine and practice which the whole Revival had embodied for England. His life story might have formed the background for a Defoe to work upon had it not been even stranger than the strangest fiction. We can still see the old man with his spare stature and kindly face, the old sailor jacket now laid aside in the first city of the world. He used to stand in his pulpit clad in a full-sleeved preacher's gown with wig and bands; he used to sit in his study robed in a damask dressing-gown with a velvet cap.[117] It was his wont to rise early in the morning, but then he was seldom abroad in the evening. But the marks of age were upon him while old friends dropped off like autumn leaves, and a letter from Scott as early as February 1795 tells its own tale: 'Mr Newton is tolerably well, perhaps the happiest man to be met with; but he grows old, and seems in all respects to break.'[118] His calm judgment in things divine was still firm and clear, and his grasp of the truths which he had cherished so long was as strong as ever. The last entry in his journal consists of but two lines and it was on the anniversary of the day of his great deliverance nigh on sixty years before: 'March 21, 1805 (New Calendar) : Not well able to write, but I endeavour to observe the return of this day with humiliation, prayer, and praise.'[119]

His mind was much burdened with the slave trade which was still flourishing in spite of Wilberforce, who had brought its evils before the House of Commons year after year. He was in doubt whether he would live to see it suppressed, but late in 1804 he wrote to cheer the advocates of abolition who were gathering strength for the final struggle. 'The prospect', he wrote as he saw that abolition must come, 'will give me daily satisfaction so long as my declining faculties are preserved.'[120] At this great age it was observed that he was never more lively or collected than when in the pulpit and he still preached with much of his old animation, even 'when he could no longer see to read his text'.[121] But his voice and memory sometimes failed him after he had reached his eightieth year; his sight had nearly gone and he was so deaf that he could hardly join in conversation. In January 1806, Cecil tried to persuade him to retire, but he only raised his voice as he made reply: 'I cannot stop! What? Shall the old African blasphemer stop while he can speak?'[122] But from that time onward old age took rapid strides; sight, hearing, and recollection all failed exceedingly. He preached for the last time in October 1806, on behalf of a fund for the Trafalgar widows. The rough waves and wild storms of his early life were now long since past; a calm sea and a fine sky lay before him as he steered for home. He was free from pain and cheerful in spirit, but his faculties declined until it was trying to rouse them. In March 1807 an Act for the Abolition of the slave trade was passed by both Commons and Lords and, a few days later, received the Royal Assent; but the shout of triumph that went up from countless hearts came too late for him to do more than give back a faint but thankful echo. It was in that same month of March that Charles Simeon observed in his Diary:

> I dined alone and then went to Mr Newton's; he was up in his bedroom and in a very feeble state. He sat in a great chair and flannel was thrown over his feet. He was…fed as a child. He did not know me till I told him my name and, even then, scarcely seemed to notice me in consequence of his own feebleness of mind and body.[123]

But William Jay of Bath saw him very near the end and he seemed quite sensible at the last. The luminous mind and eloquent lips were almost past effort, but Jay carried home one priceless remark which ought to be treasured as long as time endures: 'My memory is nearly gone, but I remember two things,' whispered old John Newton; 'that I am a great sinner and that Christ is a great Saviour.'[124] Then he added: 'Did you not when I saw you at your house in Bath desire me to pray for you? Well, then, now you must pray for me.'[125] A day or two later, on the Monday evening of December 21, 1807, in his eighty-third year, he fell asleep, leaning as he would say on the arm of 'a love that will not be wearied, cannot be conquered, and is incapable of change.'[126]

Bibliography

Works by the Rev. John Newton

Works, Vols. I-VI, edited by the Rev. Richard Cecil (3rd ed., 1824).

Cardiphonia, with an appreciation by Dr Alexander Whyte (Morgan & Scott, 1911).

Biographies of John Newton and Other Works Quoted

Richard Cecil, *An Authentic Narrative of the Life of John Newton, written by himself; with a continuation by the Rev. Richard Cecil* (no date).

Josiah Bull, *John Newton of Olney and St. Mary Woolnoth* (2nd Ed., no date).

H. C. G. Moule, *Christ's Witness to the Life to Come*, Chapter X (1908).

F. H. Durnford, *'The Life and Works of John Newton' in* The Churchman (January, April, June 1942).

James Stephen, *Essays in Ecclesiastical Biography* (New Ed., 1875)

G. R. Balleine, *A History of the Evangelical Party* (New Ed., 1933)

M. Seeley, *The Later Evangelical Fathers* (19,3).

Robert Isaac and Samuel Wilberforce, *The Life of William Wilberforce* (Five Volume Ed., 1838).

Samuel Wilberforce, *The Life of William Wilberforce* (One Volume Ed., 1868).

Thomas Scott, *The Force of Truth, An Authentic Narrative* (R.T.S., 1929).

Gilbert Thomas, *William Cowper and the Eighteenth Century* (1935).

Michael Hennell, 'Newton's Authentic Narrative—Why You Should Read It', No. XIV, *Theology*, Oct., 1948.

3

Thomas Scott
1747–1821

Thomas Scott was born on February 16, 1747, in a small farmhouse at Braytoft, the tenth child in a family of thirteen. He was brought up some six miles from the sea in the low-lying fen country of Lincolnshire, where his father struggled for many years against storm and flood which were wont to turn his farm into a marsh scarcely fit for more than sheep or cattle grazing. He was small of stature and frail in health, but he faced narrow circumstances and stringent difficulties with patience and courage. He was a man of no common mental gifts and vigour, and he made up for the want of early education by sheer energy of intellect. It was his ambition to have at least one son in professional life and he spared no cost or sacrifice to have his eldest son trained as a surgeon. But the death of this son on a naval sloop cut his hopes short and his choice fell next on his tenth child who was as yet still in early boyhood. Thomas Scott had inherited from his father a courage and tenacity which were to hold through thick and thin, and he was blessed with more than his father's share of physical health. He had the same strong matter-of-fact intellect and he developed the same passionate love for reading. He was taught to read and spell as a child by his mother and he early began to learn Latin at a dayschool two miles away. At the age of eight he was sent to a parish school at Bennington; at the age of ten he was sent to a grammar school at Scorton in Yorkshire.

There he was to spend five long years, without one visit from his friends, without one visit to his home. Thus he was fairly launched on the sea of life in his early teens; he was left to take the helm and steer his course as best he could without a father's guiding hand.

Scorton was a hamlet in the parish of Bolton, some one hundred and forty miles from Braytoft; it was so well off the beaten highways that he never even saw or heard a stage-coach in his school days. He was taught to translate Latin with ease, but he could not compose and still less could he versify. 'God has not made me a poet', he observed in later years, 'and I am very thankful that I never attempted to make myself one.'[1] He came to feel that his conduct at school was as loose as want of money or qualms of conscience would allow it to be, but he never learned to swear or to take the name of God in vain. On his return home at long last in June 1762, he spent some weeks with relatives and then was bound by his father as an apprentice to a surgeon and apothecary at Alford. Here his master set him an example of wrong life which he could not fail to observe; here, too, his church-going habits were first disturbed by a round of duties from dawn till dark on Sundays and weekdays alike. But in two months he was dismissed and sent home in disgrace for some unnamed act of misconduct. Thus his father's favourite plan was disappointed and his blameless family name was discredited. His father refused to pay off the balance of his premium; the surgeon refused to give up the papers of his indenture. This led to a complete impasse and closed the door in other directions; he was still bound as an apprentice and was not free to make a fresh engagement. This was the last drop in the cup of mortified family pride and it set in motion a long train of events which were full of bitterness and frustration. 'I was left to encounter a degree of displeasure and mortification…which were hard enough in themselves to be endured,' he wrote, 'and to which my unhumbled heart was by no means properly disposed to submit.'[2] He was in the sixteenth year of his age, but was still an entire stranger to the comforts of faith. He knew not yet that he was a sinner in danger of wrath or in need of mercy, nor could he recollect that he had so much as offered one prayer up to this time from his heart in secret.[3]

If he could not be a surgeon then he must needs be a shepherd, and for nine years he was given for his mede all that was toilsome and dirty on his father's farm. The fen lands were often in flood and he had to meet with scenes of hardship for which his early life had little prepared him. He was as much of a drudge as any servant in his father's employ and was almost as little known beyond the circle of his neighbours. Like David, he had to follow the ewes that were great with young, and the worse the weather the more needful it was that he should tend his flock. There was no fear that he would lead a life of ease or form habits of indolence; the wet, the cold, the constant exposure were no mild trials and they often left him ill with ague and fever. He was so ill at times that his very life was held in despair and these repeated illnesses sowed the seed of obstinate maladies which clung to him through life. 'Yet a kind of indignant, proud, self-revenge kept me from complaining of hardship,' he wrote, 'though of reproach, and even of reproof, I was impatient to the greatest degree.'[4] The thought of God and of eternity would at times press itself upon his mind, but he tried to stifle his fears and to put off his repentance to a more convenient season.[5] When illness came he would pray for pardon and trust that all would be well if he died; when health returned his fears would vanish and he would live as carelessly as before. He had none but the lowest and roughest companions, who were wholly destitute of faith and who tried to fan his rebellious spirit with the flatterer's cunning. His mind was corroded with this deep but seething discontent, and his temper was soured to a degree far beyond its native harshness. He was a great trial and a source of keen provocation to his father, for he behaved with studied disrespect, not to say with downright insolence.

Yet he still had times of remorse and his day-dreams were all of the clerical profession and of literary distinction. Thus in leisure moments and on winter evenings he read all that he could lay his hands on. 'I had scarcely anything to study relative to the languages and other subjects on which my heart was set,' he observed; 'a few torn Latin books I had and a small imperfect dictionary, but not one Greek book except an Eton grammar.'[6] Meanwhile, the hope that he would one day inherit the farm on which he was working helped to buoy him up in his general misery; but the accidental discovery that the lease of the farm was left by will to an elder brother and that he was merely to be undertenant of some marsh lands which would barely support a single man, dried up his hopes, such as they were, and brought all his smouldering discontent to a climax. He would shake the dust of the farm off his feet as soon as he could and would turn to Letters or to Orders as a more congenial way of life! Thus he took up his Greek grammar and read it through and through; and he made what use he could of his Latin books while his father looked on, bewildered and astonished. He had fallen in with an old Socinian Commentary on the Bible, which had stripped sin of its ugliness and had robbed death of all that was terrible. His fears were soothed, his conscience was silenced, and he saw no need for a change of heart; he thought only that if he were ordained he would be free to aim at real literary renown. He kept all this to himself for the time being, but at length, in April 1772, at the age of twenty-five, he avowed his plans in the worst possible spirit. He came in one evening, wet and weary after a long day of constant toil and fatigue, and heard himself held up to blame by his father in what he felt was a most undeserved criticism. He flared up at once in angry passion and threw off his shepherd's cloak and swore that he would wear it no more. He marched out of his home and lodged that night with his elder brother, fully resolved to seek Orders as his future calling.

Morning found him in a better frame of mind, but not less determined to seek a new way of life. It was weaning time and he had left a large flock of ewes; this led him to return home first and do what was needful for them. Then he turned round and set out for Boston, where the clergyman was one with whom he had some slight acquaintance. This man took down a Greek New Testament and put it in his hands; he was amazed to hear him read the text freely, giving the translation both in Latin and in English. He then promised Scott an introduction to the archdeacon who was due in Boston a week later, and Scott returned home to help his father until the day arrived. A keen sense of filial duty had put his first resentful feelings to flight, for he knew how much his help was needed for tasks which his father could no longer perform with his own hands and yet would not entrust to his servants. In due time he had an interview with the archdeacon, who was impressed with his ready answers and his freedom from all disguise. The archdeacon agreed to represent his case to the Bishop of Lincoln and gave him good reason to hope for an early ordination. Thus encouraged, he spent his small savings on books and went off to live in Boston where he could pore over Greek and Latin authors to his heart's content. He was still in complete darkness as to all things spiritual; he knew nothing of personal conversion or genuine holiness. 'I lived as before,' he confessed, 'in known sin and in utter neglect of prayer.'[7] But regard for decorum made him more correct in his public deportment, and this became the ground for a curious suspicion when he went up to London for the June ordination; his new code of strictness in outward life exposed him to suspicion as a Methodist, and he was turned away on the pretext that his papers had not arrived in time! But the bishop promised to admit him to the September ordination if he could secure his father's consent and a clergyman's testimonial!

This filled him with despair, for his father seemed to be unalterably opposed. 'If his consent were necessary,' he thought, 'there could be...no hope.'[8] He made his way home on foot and walked some twenty miles to complete his journey on the last morning; then he dined and donned his shepherd's dress and sheared eleven large sheep before tea. That was no mean day's work and it showed the energy of his character! But his family were soon roused in his favour and his father was at last induced to give the written consent which had been stipulated by the bishop. Thus he became a candidate for Orders at Buckden the next Michaelmas and his letters home tell of his fellow-ordinands. One was a Methodist in outlook: 'He forms a very good contrast to some of the company,' wrote Scott, being 'so sanctified that a song, a game at cards, or a joke, is to him a most capital offence. This I could overlook, but his opinions are not mine; and I had a duel with him on my first arrival concerning justification by faith alone.'[9] The others were very different in spirit: 'The remainder are Oxonian and Cantabrigian bucks, who know more of the wine and the girls of their respective universities, and of settingdogs, racehorses, and guns in the country, than of Latin and Greek, or Divinity.'[10] Thus, on September 20, 1772, he was ordained deacon at Buckden and six months later, on March 14, 1773, he was ordained to the priesthood in London.

> Thus with a heart full of pride and wickedness; my life polluted with many unrepented, unforsaken sins; without one cry for mercy, one prayer for direction, or assistance, or a blessing upon what I was about to do; after having concealed my real sentiments under the mask of general expressions; after having subscribed articles directly contrary to what I believed; and after having blasphemously declared, in the presence of God and of the congregation, in the most solemn manner, sealing it with the Lord's Supper, that I judged myself to be inwardly moved by the Holy Ghost to take that office upon me, not knowing or believing that there was a Holy Ghost, ...I was ordained.[11]

This was the stern judgment which he pronounced on his own head in after years; he thought it 'the most atrocious wickedness of his life'.[12] But he did not regard it in that dark light at the time and much was to transpire before his conscience awoke in bitter remorse.

Scott accepted the curacies of Stoke Goldington and Weston Underwood near the river Ouse in the pleasant county of Buckinghamshire. Village life was large and populous, but the people were poor and ignorant; half of them had little knowledge at all outside the trade of lace-making to which they had been born. There were no schools for the poor and many of them never came to the church; but Scott had scant thought for their souls, for his aims when he was ordained were as low as they could well be.

> My views, as far as I can ascertain them, were these three: A desire of a less laborious and more comfortable way of procuring a livelihood than otherwise I had the prospect of; the expectation of more leisure to employ in reading, of which I was inordinately fond; and a proud conceit of my abilities, with a vainglorious imagination that I should sometime distinguish and advance myself in the literary world.[13]

He took pains in preparation for the pulpit and kept up his public duties with an eye to his own future; he was soon known by his speech and actions as a son of the soil, and his advice was much valued by the local farmers. But his studies now lay nearer his heart than social visits or public duties and he cut himself off from the common round of calls and pastimes. 'I neither shoot, nor hunt, nor course, nor fish worth a farthing,' he told his sister in September 1773; 'neither seem to have any desire to learn.'[14] 'I spared no pains,' so he recalled, as he looked back on these early studies; 'I shunned as much as I could all acquaintance and diversions, and retrenched from my usual hours of sleep.'[15] Within nine months of his ordination he had read the Greek text of Josephus in full and was up to his ears in Hebrew. 'Some twenty weeks ago I knew not a letter,' he wrote in September 1773; 'and I have now read through one hundred and nineteen of the Psalms and twenty-three chapters of Genesis.'[16]

But Greek and Hebrew had more than a monopoly of his time; they had usurped a kind of pre-eminence in his soul.

He is sketched by his own pen in *The Force of Truth* as a proud and morose churchman, negligent of all private devotion, ambitious for quick public promotion, and wrapped up in the webs of sophistry and scepticism. 'As to the rest,' he said, 'I still lived in the practice of what I knew to be sinful and in the entire neglect of all secret religion; if ever inclined to pray, conscious guilt stopped my mouth.'[17] But this and that slowly began to shake him out of his complacency, and he fell once more into apprehensive fears of eternal misery. Conscience reproached him with base hypocrisy; it grew more and more clamorous in its remonstrance. But he still lived without any personal religion, for he did not dare to pray without some reformation in his conduct as a man and minister. Yet he could neither hush nor appease that inner voice and at last he began to try out prayer as a means of self-amendment. This soon straightened up his outward conduct, but made him more proud and worldly in heart than ever. He thought his own scheme of doctrine was the exact standard of truth; and what, we may ask, was that scheme? 'I was nearly a Socinian and Pelagian,' he wrote, 'and wholly an Arminian.'[18] He was what we call a Unitarian, and he thought that his own superior abilities would prove him more than a match for any antagonists who crossed his path. But one Sunday in May 1775, his eye fell by chance on the Eighth Article, and its statement on the authority of the Athanasian Creed. He had twice subscribed to the Articles already, but he had done so merely as a matter of course; his conscience had been asleep and his signature had seemed no more than a necessary form. But the problem of subscription now leapt to the fore in his thoughts and such scruples occurred to him that he felt he could not subscribe again at any cost. But he did not reach this resolution without a stern struggle, for he knew that preferment in Church life would hinge on subscription to the Articles. But though he was still far from light in things spiritual, he would not budge on a matter like this, and he resolved to lead the life of a necessitous curate all his days rather than that he should forswear himself by a false subscription. 'Thus my views of preferment were deliberately given up,' he wrote, 'and…I was left as far as mere human prudence could discern with little other prospect than that of poverty and distress.'[19]

One of his close neighbours at this time was old John Newton, and he had heard ere this from one of his parishioners that he was a very singular character. 'He gave Mr Newton full credit for blameless and benevolent conduct and for diligence as a minister,' wrote Scott; 'but he was a Methodist and an Enthusiast to a very high degree!'[20] Scott went to hear him preach, but was convinced that his text was aimed straight at him and it was long before he would hear him again. But, in January 1774, two of his parishioners lay at death's door and he failed to visit them as he had not been called in. Then he heard that Newton had walked all the way from Olney to see them more than once and his conscience smote him with the thought of his own neglect:

> Directly it occurred to me that whatever contempt I might have for Mr Newton's doctrines, I must acknowledge his practice to be more consistent with the ministerial character than my own. He must have more zeal and love for souls than I had or he would not have walked so far to visit and supply my lack of care to those who as far as I was concerned might have been left to perish in their sins.'[21]

In May 1775, he met Newton in a room full of clergy and tried to draw him into debate. Newton would not be drawn, but sent him a little book a day or two afterwards. Scott had begun to think well of Newton, but looked on his religious sentiments as rank fanaticism. Thus he seized the chance to engage him in controversy and wrote him a long letter in which he veiled his real motives under an offer of friendship and a professed desire to know the truth. Newton observed it thus in his Diary: 'May 18, 1775: Received an unexpected letter from Mr Scott, my brother curate near me, very long and frank; it seems dictated by a spirit in search of the truth.'[22] This led to a correspondence which was carried on to the end of the year, and Newton's series of eight letters may still be read in his *Cardiphonia*. They are a model of patient wisdom and gentle candour, avoiding argument and inviting confidence. 'It is the strain of evident sincerity which runs through your letters that gives me a pleasing confidence the Lord is with you,' he wrote on June 23, '...He has directed you to the right method—searching scripture with prayer. Go on and may His blessings attend you.'[23]

This long and friendly letter took Scott by surprise, but he still tried to lure him on into debate. On July 14, Newton wrote again: 'I have such a low opinion of man in his depraved state that I believe no one has real sincerity in religious matters till God bestows it.'[24] His next letter was on August 11 : 'I feel myself much interested in your concerns and your unexpected, frank application to me, though you well know the light in which I appear to some people, I consider as a providential call which binds me to your service.'[25] The fourth letter was written on September 6: 'You seem to expect that I should remove your difficulties, but it is my part only to throw in a word occasionally as a witness of what the Lord has been pleased to teach me from the Scriptures and to wait for the rest till He who alone is able shall be pleased to communicate the same views to you.'[26] The fifth letter on October 21 gently remarks on Scott's silence; Newton felt sure that he had a desire to be useful to the souls of men, yet that he lacked the one thing needful.[27] This drew a hot reply from Scott and the sixth letter was written on October 28:

> This [the illumination of the Spirit] as you bid me be explicit, is the one thing which I think you at present lack. And I limited my expression to one thing, because it is our Lord's expression and because that one thing includes many. As I said before, I cannot give it you, but the Lord can; and from the desire He has raised in your heart I have a warm hope that He will.[28]

Newton had gleaned from Scott's letter that he was a little displeased and he assured him that he wished him as well as he could wish his own soul; but there was no reply and he wrote a new and long letter on November 17 which closed with an earnest appeal:

> What I write, I write simply and in love, beseeching Him who alone can set a seal to His own truth to guide you and bless you…I am desirous to keep up my correspondence with you because I feel an affectionate interest in you, and because it pleased God to put it into your heart to apply to me.[29]

Still there was no reply and, on December 8, he wrote his eighth and last letter:

> I still retain a cheerful hope that some things you cannot at present receive will hereafter be the joy and comfort of your heart…I should think what remains might be better settled viva voce, for which purpose I shall be glad to see you or ready to wait on you when leisure will permit and when I know it will be agreeable; but if we should never meet in this world I pray God we may meet at the right hand of Jesus in the great day when He shall come to gather up His jewels'[30]

Newton's patience had not been in vain and his hope was to have a glorious fruition. But the time was not yet and his Diary simply notes: 'December 11, 1775: Much of my leisure employed this week in finishing a long letter to Mr Scott which will probably close our correspondence, unless the Lord is pleased to work upon his heart by what I have already sent or by some other means.'[31]

Scott did reply to this letter in a few days, and the correspondence was then broken off at his own request; but he wrote in friendly strain and it did please the Lord to carry on His work by other means. Newton had told Scott all along that he would one day come over to his view of things and he had told his friends that

Scott was feeling his way towards a knowledge of saving truth; and so it was, though Scott could not bear to be told. But he could not suppress a profound and growing concern for his character and his ministry, and this concern grew so urgent that he could not halt in his search for truth. In the summer of 1775, he had exchanged the curacy of Stoke Goldington for that of Ravenstone, while he retained the curacy of Weston Underwood. 'At this place', he wrote, 'I resided about two years and it proved as it were a Bethel to me; here I read the Scriptures and prayed; here I sought and, I trust, found in a considerable measure the knowledge of the truth as it is in Jesus.'[32] It was now his resolve to accept no authority but the Word of God and to search that Word with the one object of finding out whether the Articles were in tune with Scripture. He was still far from an unreserved submission of mind and heart to the Divine Revelation, but he was now willing to ask of God light and wisdom. 'I was very far indeed from being a little child, sitting humbly and simply at the Lord's feet, to learn from Him the very first rudiments of divine knowledge,' so he confessed, '...for though I began to allow it probable that in some few matters I might have been in an error, yet I still was confident that in the main my scheme of doctrine was true.'[33] Letters written at this time bring out his growing sense of conscientious service. 'I was before too apt to judge by comparison and to think I did enough if I did rather more than others,' he wrote in July 1775; 'but now I find that...I can never do enough so long as I leave anything undone which it was in my power to do.'[34] Again, in October 1775, he wrote: 'My conscience must be my judge in this world and my Saviour in the next; and to them I appeal for the rectitude of my intentions.'[35] His strength and decision of character, his faith in God's Word and Providence, his indifference to preferment, and his high regard for the ministry, were fast developing with all the vim of a new and most impressive discovery.

It was this new line of conduct that led Newton to hope so well of him, and it is from this time that we must date his close study of the Bible and his constant habits of prayer. In the spring of

1776, Burnet's Pastoral Care led him to set up a weekday lecture in Weston and at Ravenstone for the exposition of Holy Writ. He wrote:

> My congregations were small, but very select at Ravenstone, on an average not more than forty...and at Weston often under thirty. Yet I have reason to think that these services were specially blessed to others, and they were peculiarly comfortable to my own soul; most of my few hearers I considered as my children.[36]

But his studies in the Bible were now driving him from Socinian strongholds, and he was trying to occupy a kind of Arian position which still fell short of a full and candid belief in the Trinity. In December 1776, Law's *Serious Call* made him strive to improve his devotional life: 'I became', he wrote, 'more frequent and earnest and, I trust, more spiritual than heretofore in my secret addresses to the Majesty of heaven.'[37] Bit by bit he began to preach in a new strain and he was soon amazed to find people coming to him in great distress about their souls; they asked him what they should do to be saved, and he hardly knew how to make reply. 'I knew not well what to say to them, my views being greatly clouded,' he wrote, '...but being willing to give them the best counsel I could, I exhorted them in a general way to believe in the Lord Jesus Christ.'[38] But he himself did not yet know the true nature of faith and this made him still more urgent in his prayerful readings of the Scriptures; 'and under every difficulty', he said, 'I constantly had recourse unto the Lord to preserve me from ignorance and error, and to enable me to distinguish between the doctrines of His Word and the inventions and traditions of men.'[39] Thus there was much going on in his mind and soul, and the slow dawn of a new day could not be hid. Newton met him again in May 1776, and the note in his Diary marks the progress since their correspondence had closed six months before:

> May 9: Mr Scott dined and spent the afternoon with me and stayed church. We had some free conversation and, though he does not see things clearly, I have reason to hope the Lord has begun a good work in his heart. Lord! confirm my hopes, and teach him, that he may be a blessed instrument of teaching others![40]

The year 1777, when he reached the age of thirty, saw the final settlement of his views. In January, he fell in with Hooker's *Discourse on Justification* and his balanced statements on this fundamental doctrine were a great help to him. Hooker was a recognized pillar of the Established Church, at least as far from Methodism as Scott could claim to be, and the result was that after many doubts and some months of hard thinking, Scott was won right over. 'I was convinced', he wrote, 'beyond the possibility of doubt that all men were so notoriously transgressors of every Law of God, that no man could possibly be justified in His sight by his obedience to any of the Divine Commandments.'[41] On Good Friday, he preached on the Atonement and we hear him declare:

> I explicitly avowed my belief that Christ as our Surety and Bondsman stood in our law-place, to answer all our obligations and to satisfy Divine justice and the demands of the Law for our offences; and I publicly renounced as erroneous and grievous perversions of Scripture all my former explanations and interpretations of these subjects.[42]

This was the first doctrine in which he was fully brought to own the truth in public, though for two years, with no little earnestness, he had been an inquirer. But he was much discouraged in other ways and this induced him to resume his communication with John Newton. 'His discourse so comforted and edified me', he wrote, 'that my heart, being by his means relieved from its burden, became susceptible of affection for him.'[43] He was still reluctant to own him as a friend before the world, but he began to steal away from time to time to spend an hour or two in his company. Newton's Diary suddenly lights up with brief notes which tell the story, and we can read between the lines of his successive entries.

> September 2, 1777: A visit from Mr Scott yesterday morning. O my Lord, I thank Thee for Thy goodness to him; I think he gets forward in the light of Thy truth.[44]
>
> September 15: Drank tea yesterday with Mr Scott. Was rejoiced to see how Thy goodness has confirmed the hopes I conceived two years ago. Though his views were then very dark…yet I could perceive Thou hadst given him a sincerity which I looked upon as a token of Thy further favour. And now he seems enlightened and established in the most important parts of the Gospel, and will, I trust, prove an instrument of usefulness in Thy hand.[45]
>
> November 10: Breakfasted yesterday with Mr Scott. The Lord has answered my desires and exceeded my expectation in him. How gradually, and yet how clearly, has he been taught of God the truth of the Gospel and favoured with a single eye to seek that truth above all!…What an honour and mercy should I esteem it to be any way instrumental in this good work! All the praise be to God![46]

Meanwhile, since Good Friday, his views had been cleared up on one point after another, and his scheme of thought and doctrine was not far from its full maturity. He had come to receive and to rejoice in the doctrines of the Atonement and the Trinity, and in Justification by Faith alone; but he knew well in what dislike and contempt such doctrines were held, and he felt that to own them would mean a complete sacrifice of reputation for Christ's sake. It was while he still shrank from such an avowal that he met with Venn's book on the Prophecy of Zacharias. 'I was no stranger to the character he bore in the eyes of the world', he wrote of Venn, 'and I did not begin to read this book with great alacrity or expectation.'[47] But Venn taught him what no man then living had more right to teach him, and that was an utter contempt for any motive which might prevent or delay a full and wholesome witness to the truth:

> I should as easily be convinced that there was no Holy Ghost as that He was not present with my soul when I read what Mr Venn has written upon this subject. It came to my heart with such evidence, conviction, and demonstration, that it lifted me up above the world and produced that victory which faith alone can give. I became at once ashamed of my base ingratitude and foolish fears, and was filled with such consolation and rejoicing, even in the prospect of sacrificing my character and running the risk of infamy and contempt, as made me entirely satisfied on that head. And some few seasons of unbelief excepted, I have never since been much troubled about being called an Enthusiast or a Methodist.'[48]

He was at last convinced that John Newton was right and the close of the year found him resolved once more to go and hear him preach. He was still a stranger to much of the power of these truths in his own heart and he found that Newton's preaching seemed to open up the secrets of the soul with a new reality. Thus he came to know that peace which passeth all understanding and that joy which no man taketh away: 'These the world could not give me, were I in favour with it,' he wrote; 'of these, it cannot deprive me by its frowns.'[49]

In December 1778, Newton's Diary hints at a new development: 'December 11: Breakfasted with Mr Scott. Heard him read a narrative of his conversion which he has drawn up for publication. It is striking and judicious, and will, I hope, by the Divine Blessing be very useful.'[50] This narrative of his pilgrimage through the wilderness of doubt and unbelief was published in February 1779 under the title of *The Force of Truth*. The style of the book was revised and improved by William Cowper, but its contents came fresh from his own heart. It was not a narrative of dramatic adventure like that of John Newton; it was rather a history of internal disturbance like that of John Bunyan. The first thousand copies took ten years to sell, but after that as many were sold in each fresh year; it was translated into Dutch and French, and it passed through many English editions. It is a clear and candid treatment of the spiritual phenomena which led up to his change of heart, and it compels our deep respect from first to last by its luminous picture as well as its intrinsic merit. Daniel Wilson summed up its disclosure of thought and character with perfect sympathy:

> We here behold a man of strong natural powers, entrenched in the sophistries of human pride, and a determined opponent of almost all the chief truths of the Gospel, gradually convinced and subdued. We see him engaging in a laborious study of the Scripture with opinions and prejudices firmly fixed, and reluctant to admit a humiliating scheme of theology; yet borne on, contrary to his expectations and wishes and worldly interest by the simple energy of truth. We view him arriving, to his own dismay, at one doctrine after another. We behold him making every step sure as he advances, till he at length works out by his own diligent and most anxious investigation of the sacred volume, all the parts of divine truth, which he afterwards discovered to be the common faith of the Church of Christ, to be the foundation of all the Reformed communities, and to be essentially united with every part of Divine Revelation.[51]

These words were penned long years after *The Force of Truth* first saw the light of day, but they point out the real nature of Scott's travail of soul and his triumph at last with unerring accuracy.

The Force of Truth is the record of a cool and cautious search for the truth with much, very much, prayer and meditation, carried out over a period of nigh on three long years. Scott read through the Bible in those three years many times, giving the strictest attention he could to every part, while from morning to night his thoughts had run incessantly on the great truths of the Gospel. He was driven inch by inch from all the strongholds of his own reasoning, and was forced to submit by slow degrees to the teaching of the Divine Revelation. The last doctrine to which he was brought to accede was that of Personal Election and Final

Perseverance and, as late as August 1777, he told Newton that he felt sure that he would never share his views on this subject.

> To this he answered that if I never mentioned this subject, he never should, as we were now agreed in all he judged absolutely needful; but that he had not the least doubt of my very shortly becoming a Calvinist, as I should presently discover my system of doctrine to be otherwise incomplete.[52]

It was a theme which soon pressed itself upon his mind; was it in the Bible, or not? He found that the Scriptures would teach it, in spite of every effort to twist and turn, and by Christmas of the same year he had begun in a cautious way to make use of this doctrine for the consolation of believers. The whole cycle of truth was then complete, and for nigh on fifty years he lived to preach it; and the lapse of time did but add to the stability of his convictions and the tenacity with which he clung to them as the things that are seen began to fade back from his view:

> I never gave up one tittle of my sentiments till I could defend it no longer, nor ever submitted to conviction till I could no longer resist…the strong man armed with my natural pride and obstinacy…had built himself many strongholds and kept his castle in my heart; and when one stronger than he came against him, he stood a long siege; till being by superior force driven from one to another, and all his armour in which he trusted being at length taken from him, he was constrained to recede. So that the Lord, having made me willing in the day of His power, I was forced to confess, O Lord, Thou art stronger than I, and hast prevailed!'[53]

All these facts are set out with an integrity of soul and a simplicity of style in a way which makes it certain that *The Force of Truth* will still be held in honour when Scott's other works are read no longer, and we can add our glad Amen to his own words of praise as we trace all that God hath wrought: 'For ever blessed be the God of all long-suffering and mercy, who had patience with such a rebel and blasphemer, such an irreverent trifler with His majesty, and such a presumptuous intruder into His sacred ministry!'[54]

The seven years which followed his cordial reception of the Gospel were years of great blessing to his own soul, and the change in his life soon showed itself in his parish duties. He came to look upon Ravenstone as the favourite centre of his ministry, for there he saw more in the way of fruit for his labours than in any other sphere of service. A large number of those who had been careless and ignorant as to the things of God were brought to be earnest and devoted Christians, and a serious impression lay on the whole parish beyond anything which he was afterwards to see. He had been greatly impressed by the words: 'Necessity is laid upon me; yea, woe is me if I preach not the Gospel' (1 Cor. 9: 16). These words were on his mind when he penned his sermons and when he stood in the pulpit, and by the close of the year 1777 he had begun to have frequent visits from those who were under concern for their souls. His own heart was much drawn out in this new ministry, and he spared no pains to lead them into the full comfort of the Gospel. In March 1804 he recalled his Ravenstone days with wistful interest:

> Even at Ravenstone I remember complaining in a New Year's sermon that for a whole twelve month I had seen no fruit of my preaching; yet it appeared within the course of the next twelve month, that not less than ten or twelve had been brought to consider their ways during that discouraging year, besides others, I trust, that I did not know.[55]

His friendship with Newton was now open and unconcealed: 'I continually see great cause to bless God', he wrote, 'for giving me such a friend to be so near at hand on all occasions.'[56] In January 1778, Scott heard Newton preach once more and began to attend his weekday service from time to time. Newton asked him to preach in due course and wrote of it in his Diary

> My heart rejoiced and wondered. O my Lord, what a Teacher art Thou! How soon, clearly, and solidly, is he established in the knowledge and experience of Thy Gospel, who but lately was a disputer against every point! I praise Thee for him. Often in my faint manner have I prayed to see some of my neighbours of the clergy awakened. Thou hast answered prayer. O may it please Thee yet to add to the number![57]

Regular communication thus grew up between them and, in June, Newton heard him preach again at Weston. 'It is the first time I have heard him since he began to preach extempore,' he wrote; 'his discourse was clear, copious, judicious, and animated.'[58] On December 11, he had breakfast with Scott and we can still read his remark: 'I think I can see that he has got before me already. Lord, if I have been useful to him, do Thou I beseech Thee make him now useful to me.'[59] On December 31, he heard him preach once more in the church at Weston and we read his comment: 'How should I wonder and rejoice! Surely when Thou wilt work, none can let it. What liberty, power, and judgment in so young a preacher! May Thy comforts fill his heart, and Thy blessing crown his labours.'[60] Twelve months later, in December 1779, Newton left Olney to become vicar of St. Mary Woolnoth in London, and he greatly desired Scott to succeed him at Olney. But Scott did not share his viewpoint in the matter, for he foresaw many difficulties: 'I felt great reluctance to comply with the proposal,' he wrote, 'both because it would remove me from Ravenstone…and also because…I was sure that my plain, distinguishing style of preaching, especially as connected with my comparative youth, would not be acceptable there.'[61] Scott was right, for so much opposition was stirred up that the very man whom Newton thought most improper secured the curacy. But within twelve months this man was obliged to resign, and a deputation came to Scott from Olney with an earnest plea for him to accept the vacant cure. He still felt most reluctant to give his consent, but he gave in to the persuasion of his friends. Thus, in 1780, he resigned from the curacy of Ravenstone and became joint-curate of Olney and Weston. But then, to his intense chagrin, he had to put up with Newton's bitter experience, for he found that the late curate of Olney was now appointed as his successor at Ravenstone. On August 23, 1816, long years later, he looked back on this change and wrote of it with simple wisdom: 'When Mr Newton left Olney, I seemed to have lost my counsellor; but carrying my difficulties immediately to the Lord, I believe I was eventually no loser.'[62]

Olney was not a congenial sphere of work for a man like Scott, even though it had been served by Newton for fifteen years. Newton's last year or two had been disturbed by a troublesome element in the parish and this grew a great deal worse in Scott's time. There was much religious profession, but not much practical holiness; there was Calvinistic doctrine, but with it Antinomian licence. Newton's meekness and Scott's severity were both hard put to it, and Scott's efforts to bring them to a right mind met with scant success. On February 1, 1781, he wrote: 'Olney is, I apprehend, as difficult a charge for a minister as can well be imagined, and I greatly feel my insufficiency; but if I look to Jesus I cannot be discouraged.'[63] On July 4, he wrote again in pictorial vein: 'I have taken a farm which is a good deal out of heart; I am breaking up the fallow ground, ploughing and harrowing and sowing. But what sort of a crop I shall have, harvest time will best show; only I am sure I shall reap in due season, if I faint not.'[64] But he remained unpopular with the people and could only draw small congregations in a town of two thousand five hundred inhabitants. He was often straitened and sometimes discouraged, but he persevered in every service to which they had been accustomed; thus he kept up Newton's weekday lecture though not more than fifty or sixty would attend. His chief comfort was at Weston where he had been the means of good to many. 'They love me, and are a comfort to me,' he wrote, '…and the Lord adds to their number…from time to time.'[65] There were a few even at Olney who clave to him, and some of them were converts of his own. Thus Newton observed in 1783: 'Mr Scott has some, and some of the best, who are affectionately attached to him.'[66] He was received as a good and upright man and a good preacher, but he was looked on by many as legal, unsound, and Arminian. He summed up the whole case in a few terse words of his own; he was convinced that the preaching of the age in which he lived was not sufficiently practical or experimental:

> Indeed, Adam's race seem determined that the glory of the good and the blame of the bad shall go together. The Arminian takes the blame of the bad to himself, and thinks it but reasonable that he should have the glory of the good too. The pseudo-Calvinist gives God all the glory of the good, but seems to think it reasonable that He should bear the blame of the bad also. But the true Christian says, To me, even to me alone, belong shame and confusion of face for all my rebellion, impenitence, unbelief, and sloth all my days; but to God alone belongs all the glory of the good wrought in me or done by me.[67]

It was in October 1782 that he was asked to let the first floor of the vicarage to Lady Austen, who wished to lodge close at hand to William Cowper and Mary Unwin. A door was made in the garden wall so that the two ladies and the poet soon made up, as it were, one family. They dined alternately in Mary Unwin's home and in Lady Austen's rooms, and they lived on terms of closest intimacy. It was in Scott's vicarage that Lady Austen proposed The Task and that it was undertaken; it was in Scott's vicarage that she told the story of John Gilpin and that Cowper turned it into verse. But the goodwill between the two ladies cooled off and, to Scott's no little regret, Lady Austen took her leave of his home in the summer months of 1784. Cowper's Letters charge Scott with a scolding accent in the pulpit, but Scott felt that the charge was not quite fair. 'Mr Cowper, it should be known, never heard me preach,' he wrote; 'neither did Mrs Unwin, nor their more respectable friends. Mr Cowper's information…was derived from the very persons whose doctrinal and practical Antinomianism I steadily confronted.'[68] Thus Scott was for a brief time in touch with William Cowper while at Olney, though we cannot trace his influence in the poet's life. But his name was also linked with that of William Carey while at Olney, and that in the happiest connection. He found himself asked to visit Northampton and to preach here and there in private gatherings. 'I was drawn on further and further till I was led to preach frequently,' he wrote, 'always on the weekdays…commonly to numerous congregations.…I often rode seventy or eighty miles, and preached four or five sermons between Monday evening and Thursday noon.'[69] William Carey was one of his hearers from time to time, and Scott often prayed and conversed with him, and tried to answer his pertinent inquiries at a place called Hackleton.[70] But he never knew for forty years how much Carey owed to his help and counsel. It was only a month before his last illness when he received a last warm greeting from the great Bengal missionary, who at the same time wrote of him to a mutual friend: 'If there be anything of the work of God in my soul, I owe much of it to his preaching when I first set out in the ways of the Lord.'[71] Thus if Newton helped to send a Buchanan, and Scott a William Carey to India, were they not noble forerunners of Charles Simeon and his band of men from Henry Martyn to Alexander Duff?

In September 1785, Scott was asked to submit his name to the Board of the Lock Hospital in Grosvenor Place, London, where a vacancy had occurred in somewhat trying circumstances. Martin Madan, one of Wesley's converts and a well-known preacher, had been chaplain to the Lock since the year 1758, and had held this post with no small success for above twenty years. But a literary venture with the quaint title of *Thelypthora* had now discredited his name, and he had to retire from his public ministrations, though not from the nominal chaplaincy. The Board were thus anxious to fill his place as a morning preacher in the chapel, and at the same time to choose a chaplain for the patients. But their letter to Scott came like a bolt from the blue and his reply was by no means encouraging: 'I wrote a very plain answer', he observed, 'stating my views of the Gospel and my determination to speak my mind in the plainest language.'[72] But when the election took place he was chosen by the unanimous vote of the Board. He held back his answer till the last day, and almost the last hour, for he foresaw that he would be beset with grave trials and difficulties. He soon found that the Board itself was split into parties and that the very chapel was the centre of division. The Board was governed by wealthy and titled leaders, but the preachers were paid a bare pittance by way of salary. Scott was engaged to preach at the morning service and De Coetlogon at the evening service; and the two men shared a weekly lecture on the Wednesday evenings. On Madan's death, in 1790, Scott and De Coetlogon were appointed as joint-chaplains at £100 a year and, in March 1802, Scott became the sole chaplain at £150 a year. Scott found that his preaching was in conflict with that of De Coetlogon and he arranged for a Friday lecture which would be wholly in his hands. To eke out his meagre stipend, he hoped for an appointment to one of the lectureships which were then a feature of church life in London. He held the afternoon lectureship at St. Mildred's, Bread Street, from February 1790 until March 1802, and this added £30 a year to his income; there were seldom more than a hundred in the congregation, but it was a very attentive audience. He took the morning lecture at St. Margaret's, Lothbury, in succession to Richard Cecil until November 1801, and this added £10 a year to his stipend; there was no other church in the city with a service so early as this six o'clock morning lecture, but he always had two or three hundred hearers.

Scott thus had to rise at four on Sunday mornings and would walk some fourteen miles from service to service in the course of the day. His first service was at Lothbury at six o'clock and the next at the Lock at eleven o'clock; then came the afternoon lecture at Bread Street and often a fourth service at Long Acre Chapel or elsewhere on his way home in the evening. Neither Madan nor De Coetlogon had tried to minister to the patients of the hospital and Scott was the first to visit them in the wards. Men and women were brought there from the lowest walks of life and were treated for the most repulsive and contagious forms of disease. Scott was a pioneer in his ministry among them and in this work he found his greatest comfort.

> I constantly attended twice in the week, each time preaching first in the women's wards and then in the men's. I took the plainest portions of Scripture and spoke in a strain of close address to the conscience, and altogether in a manner which I could never equal in any other place; and so as always to fix the attention and often greatly to affect the hearts of my poor profligate auditors.[73]

Scott soon saw that something more was necessary if the women were to be reclaimed for society as well as redeemed from evil; they had little alternative, as things were, on their discharge from the hospital but to return to their life on the streets. This led him to draft a plan for an asylum into which those who promised well could be received. He wrote a pamphlet and called a meeting and, at length in July 1787, after no slight difficulty, he was able to open a refuge to which some at least could go when they had left the hospital. It was only large enough for five inmates with a matron, but the scheme was opposed even by those from whom opposition was least expected. It was more than once in danger through want of funds, but it weathered such storms and won its way by slow degrees. Scott not only conceived and proposed the scheme, but founded and managed the house, ministered to the patients, and carried out the duties of a secretary without thanks and without reward. It seems to have been the first institution of its kind and it proved to be a model for similar asylums which were later founded in cities like Dublin and Bristol. It changed its name in due time from the Lock Asylum to the Lock Rescue Home, and its ministry has long been carried out in the way laid down by Scott with the finest results. His work at the Lock still offers us a noble testimony to his foresight and energy in the teeth of opposition, and to his wisdom and compassion in the cause of humanity.

But Scott's seventeen years at the Lock Chapel brought him into the firing line of a long and bitter controversy. The first glow of the great Revival had died away and had left a large class of critical adherents who were hearers, but not doers, of the Word. Scott had met men of this type at Olney, but he found himself more than ever opposed to them in London. 'The Lock', so his son wrote, '...might be considered as almost the headquarters of that loose and notional religion on which my father had commenced his attack in the country,' and which he felt himself all through life bound to combat.[74] The Lock congregation was the strenuous advocate of a view of Christian life and faith which to him was worse than a negation of the Gospel. It was ultra-Calvinistic in doctrine and Antinomian in practice, and it had become at that time surprisingly popular and prevalent in London. It was a most dangerous form of error to receive because of its close connection with the Gospel faith; it was a most difficult form of error to combat, because of its fascination for the human mind. Scott set himself against it with all the force of his rugged character and all the strength of his massive intellect, and this brought him into conflict both with the Board of Governors and with De Coetlogon. He was not a preacher who could conciliate such a congregation; he was honest and fearless, but too forthright and tactless. He had no gifts in the way of pulpit oratory and his preaching was marked by strong traits of personal character. He spent an hour in the preparation of his sermons, walking to and fro in streets and traffic; he took an hour for their delivery, timed by the old-fashioned sand-glass which has so long since passed away. He was careless in style and apt to overcharge his sermons with matter; his themes were worked out with that kind of close and well-knit argument which suits the bar so much better than the pulpit. His voice was asthmatic and dissonant, and his accent was that of a provincial who had come to London as a stranger from the country. There was always a little group who sat reverently at his feet, a group which included men of the first calibre in the life of the day. They were drawn by the originality of his matter or by the reasoning qualities of his method; they were held by his intimate knowledge of the Sacred Book, or by his intensive study of the human heart. But they were few and his foes were legion.

On Christmas Day, 1790, Wilberforce inserted a brief remark in his Diary which sums up his impression of Scott's chief opponent: 'At the Lock this evening; much disliked De Coetlogon.'[75] After Romaine's death in 1796, Newton did not hesitate to express an opinion on the state of affairs in the London pulpits: 'Mr Scott is perhaps the most ready and fluent extempore preacher amongst us.'[76] But the morning congregation at the Lock took alarm at the strong practical strain of his demands for true personal holiness, and their numbers dwindled. 'Everything conduced to render me more and more unpopular,' he acknowledged, 'not only at the Lock, but in every part of London, and numbers who never heard me preach were fully possessed with the idea that there was something very wrong, both in my preaching and in my spirit.'[77] The Board tried to dictate to him what he should preach and a crisis arose. But he met it with quiet courage and his reply lies on record as an immortal memento of true faithfulness: 'Gentlemen,' he said, 'you possess authority sufficient to change me FOR another preacher whenever you please, but you have no power to change me INTO another preacher. If you do not convince my understanding that I am in error, you can never induce me to alter my method of preaching.'[78] But though these years of strife at the Lock meant little else for him but gall and wormwood, they were years of supreme value to the cause of Evangelical truth. Scott was the first to make a strong and effective stand against the corrupt and meagre presentation of the Gospel which had become fashionable in the metropolis, and his fearless exposition of Christian virtue as well as of Christian blessing was one of the major factors in saving the Evangelical cause from possible disaster. He was almost alone in his efforts to stop the drift towards the arid wastes of Antinomianism and he went far to set the Evangelical Movement on the highway of true service and dignity. His sterling honesty of purpose and his fearless devotion to duty would have made him a strong asset to any cause; the Lock congregation might not appreciate him at his true value, but he was recognized by the inner circle of Evangelical stalwarts as one of their foremost leaders. 'He was a noble specimen of a Christian,' Abbey and Overton declare, 'and deserved a much wider recognition than he ever received in this world.'[79]

At the close of 1787, he was asked to write a series of notes on the Books of the Bible which would be published with the sacred text in weekly numbers. This was the origin of his great *Commentary on the Bible*, the chief love and the *magnum opus* of his life. The first number was written on January 2, 1788, and the last was finished on June 2, 1792, and in those three and a half years the whole script was written out twice by his own hand in full. It was compiled in distressing haste with an eye on the weekly press, and he was often called up from bed to write out further copy. 'You seem to have forgotten how I wrote,' he once observed; 'sick or well, in spirits or out, lively or dull, the tale of bricks must be delivered.'[80] There was little time to consult, and much less to transcribe from other authors; he was largely forced back, upon his own original ideas, and he had to let the results of his thinking stand their own ground. He was saddled with great difficulties in other ways, for he was no business man and he was deceived by his publishers from first to last. When fifteen copies had appeared, he was told that their funds and their credit were both exhausted. He found himself involved in endless debt and difficulty as he strove to support their sinking funds, and it was a relief to him when the first edition of three thousand copies was sold off without loss, if without gain. But he had found the sphere in which his heart was most at home and the residue of his life was spent in unwearied efforts to bring his great work to perfection. He toiled at this Commentary for three and thirty years all told, and it earned him a place in the front rank of the theologians of that generation. A second edition of two thousand copies with marginal references was published in 1809, and a third edition of three thousand copies came out in

1814. He was at work on a fourth edition right up to the time of his death and at least eight editions were brought out during his lifetime in America. Thirty-seven thousand complete sets were sold in his own lifetime and they brought the various publishers something like two hundred thousand pounds by way of profit.

Not the hundredth part of that sum ever reached the author, but he had the satisfaction of a task nobly done. Swindlers, scoundrels, critics, and suits in Chancery all had to be faced, but they could not deter him; illness, censure, sorrow, and years of penury were part of the price, but they could not defeat him. The task was never taken up but to be pushed to a finish, and was never finished but to be taken up afresh. It required skill as a textuary and force as a commentator, humble submission to each part of Holy Writ and constant attention to the whole plan of sacred truth, untiring diligence in toil and devoted holiness of heart. Thus he produced something which had been thought out by himself and not something which was merely borrowed from other men's labours. Sir James Stephen says that this exclusive reliance on his own resources brought with it an unfortunate sameness in its staple of thought; its chief defect as a result is a certain monotony, and it is most revered by those who can read it in the same grave, devout, and practical spirit in which it was written.[81] But such a man was Daniel Wilson, and he frankly bore his testimony: 'It is an original production in which you have the deliberate judgment of a masculine and independent mind on all parts of Holy Scripture.'[82] The style never varied, but was always plain and lucid. It refrained from all metaphysical niceties of exegesis; it rejoiced in an unhesitating reliance on the inspired records. It was candid and modest in its statement of doctrine; it was forceful and earnest in its statement of duty. It was true to Scripture in perspective and proportion, in symmetry and harmony, and this 'saturation of the comment by the spirit of the text' was its grand excellence.[83] No man since the days of Matthew Henry had produced a commentary which was so well fitted to mould the religious life and thought of the times; it was read aloud at family prayers in almost every

Evangelical home and it stamped its sane and sober views on a whole generation in the era at hand.[84] Daniel Wilson was a typical member of that generation and, to the end of his life, it was THE book of his choice. He never seemed sensible of its defects and never grew casual in its study. New authors arose and new comments appeared; but it had won his heart and he was not to be shaken. To him the old was better; it was wholly suited to his taste and temper. He wrote on February 1, 1838:

> After all my new authors, I turn back to my old commentator Scott with a fresh zest. I am now in Ezekiel in my annual course, and I sit with astonishment at many of his grave and deep remarks....That book is not yet sufficiently valued. I have now been reading him for forty years, and my judgment is that he surpasses all other commentators by far, with the single exception of the incomparable John Calvin.[85]

Though Scott did not attract people in large numbers he was greatly blessed to a select few. His friendship with Newton was renewed in London and was maintained in its pristine beauty until at length death came. Richard Cecil was a very close friend in his London years and an unfailing source of strength and comfort in his trials at the Lock. Henry Venn had come to know him while at Olney and one of his letters in July 1784 observes: 'No sooner was I come to Orlingbury than Mr and Mrs Scott from Olney...came in, and very glad we were to meet. He is a man of right spirit, always about his Master's business, and has a tongue given him which is a well of life, always ministering grace to the hearers.'[86] In 1797, shortly before Venn's death, Scott paid him a farewell visit: 'All his ancient fire rekindled,' wrote Scott, 'and he talked for some time in the most animated and heavenly strain.'[87] Charles Simeon had come to know him through Henry Venn, and made him welcome in later years to his Cambridge pulpit and his student hearers. It was due to Simeon's generous and vigorous exertions that the financial deficit on Scott's Bible was at length cleared up in 1813, and Scott declared that 'to him, under God, he owed the comfort of his declining years.'[88] His books were used of God to some who never heard his voice, but who in turn have left their mark on history's page. Henry Kirk White was reclaimed from the errors of Deism by reading *The Force of Truth*, and John Henry Newman said that, humanly speaking, it was to Scott's works that he owed his soul.[89] Henry Martyn, too, made mention of this in his journal out in India: 'April 26, 1807: Began Scott's Essays, and was surprised indeed at the originality and vigour of the sentiments and language.'[90] He had in his congregation at the Lock as regular attendants both Lord Dartmouth and Lord Gambier; he won the cordial affection of John Thornton and was the means of leading his son, Henry Thornton, to the point of decision in his spiritual life.[91] Then, in the year 1796, old John Newton sent young Daniel Wilson to Scott as one whose ministry would build him up in faith and truth. 'I myself was, five or six and twenty years ago,' Wilson recalled in his Funeral Sermon for Scott, 'one of his very small congregation at his lecture in the city; and I derived, as I trust, from the sound and practical instruction which I then received, the greatest and most permanent benefit.'[92] Scott and Pratt were linked with Cecil and Newton as the great formative influence on the early days of his Christian life and ministry; and there was no one whom he felt that he could more gladly honour than Scott, no one whose works he could so gladly make his habitual study. 'Thomas Scott was a wonderful man,' he used to observe; 'as wonderful in his way as Milton or Burke.'[93]

But there is one more name with which the name of Scott is linked in a way that ought never to be forgotten. Late in 1785, Newton told his young friend William Wilberforce that a minister of very superior understanding and eminent piety was about to settle in London. 'I soon found that he fully equalled the strongest expectations that I had formed of him,' wrote Wilberforce, 'and from that time, for many years, I attended him regularly, for the most part accompanied by...Henry Thornton. We used to hear him at the Lock in the morning,...often gladly following him for the afternoon service into the city where he had the lectureship of Bread Street Church.'[94] The brief entries which Wilberforce made in his Diary are enough to disclose what he felt at the time: 'January 1, 1789: I went…to the Lock; received the Sacrament'; 'January 1, 1790: Lock-Scott-with Henry Thornton.…Most deeply impressed with serious things'; 'February 13, 1791: Scott—an excellent sermon—very serious thoughts.'[95] Wilberforce never forgot the moral force and mental power of Scott's sermons; he still spoke of them with admiration in long after life as among the best he had ever heard in church or chapel. 'The strong sense, the extensive acquaintance with Scripture, the accurate knowledge of the human heart, and the vehement and powerful appeals to the conscience,' he said of these sermons, '…abounded in a greater degree than those of any other minister I ever attended.'[96] In April 1797, Wilberforce published his *Practical View of Christianity*, and Scott wrote of it in terms of the highest praise:

> It is a most noble and manly stand for the Gospel, full of good sense and most useful observations on subjects quite out of our line, and in all respects, fitted for usefulness; and coming from such a man, it will probably be read by many thousands who can by no means be brought to attend either to our preaching or to our writings.[97]

Again, in March 1807, Wilberforce carried his measure for the Abolition of the Slave Trade, and Scott wrote of him in terms of the truest joy: 'I feel a sort of self-congratulation…that above twenty years ago, I withstood with all my energy Mr—'s counsel, who advised Mr Wilberforce to retire from public life. Had that counsel been followed, the slave trade might have been continued to future generations.'[98] The lapse of years only served to increase the sense of high regard which each cherished for the other. In 1798, Wilberforce wrote of Scott with high praise: 'Mr Scott is a man of whose strength of understanding, correctness of religious views, integrity, disinterestedness, diligence, and perseverance, I think very highly.'[99] Again, in 1822, Wilberforce wrote of him just after his death:

> What a truly great man old Scott was, acting for so many years on the highest principles, not only above money, but above vainglory, or any other of the idols of men: I always valued him, but now that his character is viewed more distinctly, he really appears to have been a Christian hero![100]

Scott's long struggle with difficulty and unpopularity was not in vain, for few can leave so strong a mark on men like William Wilberforce. 'The grand point for imitation, and may we both attend to it,' so he wrote to Scott's son, 'is his integrity; he was an Israelite indeed, in whom there was no guile.'[101]

Scott's life and labours were cast in a sphere which kept him out of the way of the world at large, but he had a flair for rapid insight and solid judgment on current affairs or passing events. He was one of the most active of men in his aid for benevolent institutions, and his name is inseparably linked with two great societies which first saw the light in his day. He was wrapped up with the Bible Society in its earliest history, for he it was who, in 1787, had first really raised the question of Bibles for Wales. He had called on a friend who had told him that he could give him a few Welsh Bibles if they would be of use, and Scott had written at once to ask another friend in Wales to explore the possibilities. It was in March 1787 that he received the reply:

> You ask me whether a parcel of Welsh Bibles would be acceptable; you could think of nothing more acceptable, more wanted and useful, to the country at large. I have been often in my journeys through different parts of the country questioned whether I knew where a Welsh Bible could be bought for a small price, and it has hurt my mind much to be obliged to answer in the negative. There are none to be bought for money, unless some poor person, pinched by poverty, is obliged to sell his Bible to support himself and family....If you can procure a parcel of them for our poor people, I am sure you will much rejoice the hearts of many,...and I think I could dispose to very good purpose, and make profitable use, of any quantity you could procure for me.[102]

This was enough to fire Scott's zeal and he wrote back on May 15:

> In consequence of what you write concerning the scarcity of Welsh Bibles, I have received twenty-five from the society for distributing Bibles among the soldiers and sailors…Besides this I am collecting money to send you a hundred. I have had assistance from Mr Thornton in this, and probably shall have more.[103]

He had sent off this batch of one hundred and twenty-five Bibles by June, but was meeting trouble in his search for further copies. On January 12, 1788, he wrote: 'I have got upon a new scent, but know not how I shall succeed.…As far as I can with propriety procure either the sale or gift of Welsh Bibles, I shall count it my privilege to send them.'[104]

He was ere long hoping that, with Thornton's help, he would be able to get no less than a thousand copies. 'But alas!' he wrote on April 30, 'I have only waited for a disappointment.'[105] He did send a few more copies in the course of the year and, in February 1789, he was able to write:

> If no unexpected hindrance arises, you will receive as soon as they can be got ready and sent, another cargo of Bibles; one hundred to give away at Mr Thornton's expense, and the other two or three hundred to sell.…I believe that the whole impression of Welsh Bibles is now nearly exhausted, and I would be thankful that the Lord has made me almost without my having any thought of it an instrument of bringing a considerable number out of the warehouses to be disseminated where they were wanted.[106]

He did secure one more supply in 1792, but then there were simply none to be had. The S.P.C.K. had not issued a single copy of the Welsh Bible for thirty years, though Wales was a principality with more than half a million people. But Scott's later letters tell how the S.P.C.K. at length did agree to bring out a reprint of the Welsh Bible and, in 1799, a limited edition of ten thousand Bibles and two thousand Testaments was produced. Scott procured nearly a thousand copies, but his correspondence came to an end in May 1800 on a sad note: 'The demand has already so far exceeded the impression, that each person is put off with fewer than he applied for.'[107] The S.P.C.K. felt that they could do no more, and this led Charles of Bala to lay the whole problem before the Religious Tract Society in London. He told the now famous story of Mary Jones, who trudged with bare feet thirty miles over the mountains, only to learn that the last Bible had been sold long months before. But if they were to print Bibles for Wales, why not for the kingdom? And if for the kingdom, why not for the whole world? Thus, in 1804, the British and Foreign Bible Society was born and Scott, who was by then out of London, rejoiced to hear of its progress. In 1816, he spoke for the Bible Society at a county meeting, and his address depicts the aims of his whole life in the clearest colours:

> Time was since I can remember when, if I had possessed the means in other respects, I should hardly have known how to reach out the blessing beyond my own contracted circle. But this Society, and others of a similar nature, so to speak, lengthen my arms and by concurring heartily in the designs of those who conduct them, we may stretch out our hands to the inhabitants of the east and of the west, of Africa, of Asia, of America, as well as of Europe, and give to them the light of life.[108]

Scott's interest in the Bible Society was second only to his interest in the Church Missionary Society, and his ardent desire for world evangelism was nearly as old as his own Christian life. He told the L.M.S. in 1804:

> An early acquaintance with the writings of President Edwards, Brainerd, and the New England Divines, gave my mind a peculiar turn to this subject, the nations unacquainted with Christ have ever since been near my heart, and I never thought a prayer complete in which they were wholly forgotten. This was the case several years before Societies for Missions…were established, but I could do no more than offer my feeble prayers.'[109]

Thus, in due course, he was one of the first and most urgent in pressing upon his brethren the need to form a Church society, and he became one of the most active in putting that design into operation. It was on February 8, 1796, that Simeon first proposed his question to the Eclectic as to what steps they could take to promote a mission to the heathen world from the Established Church. Seventeen members were present, but his only support came from Thomas Scott and Basil Woodd; but it was this discussion that set things stirring and the progress of time proved it to be the origin of the Church Missionary Society. The question came before the Eclectic again three years later on February 18, 1799, and it was resolved to call a special meeting to give it full consideration on March 18. It then fell to John Venn to introduce the points at issue in a speech on the great question: 'What methods can we use more effectually to promote the knowledge of the Gospel among the heathen?' Simeon, Scott and Woodd, Grant and Pratt, were all in favour of action; Scott urged that it was their bounden duty to do more than had yet been done, and that they ought to form a society within the Church. As a result the Society for Missions to Africa and the East was born at a meeting on April 12, and Scott was one of the twenty-four foundation members of the first committee. Three days later he was chosen as the first honorary secretary, and he held this office until his removal from London three and a half years later. 'We mean to begin on a small scale, and afterwards to enlarge it if we can,' he wrote on September 28, 1799; 'and we have no fear of not getting money, if the Lord will but form us missionaries.'[110] The new Society soon lay off 'the Bishop and his Clerks', where, if not wrecked, it might rot for all that Scott could see; but he held it to the course of duty in the belief that their difficulties would be removed as need arose. A family memorandum written at the time of this crisis in August 1800 affords us a noble glimpse of the faith that buoyed him up when most were ready to despair: 'What will be the final issue—what the success of these missions? We know not now; I shall know hereafter. It is glorious and shall prevail; God hath said it, and cannot lie.'[111]

Scott and Venn were the two whose names are pre-eminently identified with the early struggles of the Society and Scott's indomitable labours were of no less value than Venn's inimitable wisdom. 'His courage and faith again and again carried the day when more timid counsels nearly prevailed,' and the force and energy of his character were a distinctive element in the development of the society.[112] He was not always sanguine as to its success, and he was apt to share in secret the common fear that it would come to little; but this put him on his mettle, and he resolved to work and not to faint. 'I wish to do what I can, or at least to attempt it,' he wrote on October 29, 1800; '…I cannot become a missionary; but I can labour, and I have a little influence.'[113] Old John Newton was asked to preach the first annual sermon before the society, but it was Scott who took his place when he fell ill. That Whit Tuesday, in the year 1801, was a wet day and a bare four hundred were all who came to hear him in St. Anne's, Blackfriars. 'We did expect a crowded church on this most important occasion,' Mrs. Scott wrote to her son at Hull; 'but alas! our hopes were damped.'[114] But Scott dealt in masterly argument with the accusation that it was an uncharitable thing to fear lest the heathen should be lost, and his sermon helped to nail the colours of the struggling Society to the mast in a way that his heirs ought never to forget. He plied the labouring oar as secretary to the close of 1802, and his resignation then was only due to the fact that he had to move his home away from London. Active operations had scarce begun when he retired, but the preliminaries were complete; and he did not cease from his labours even when he could no longer keep his hand on the helm. In 1806, much time and thought were spent on the problem of how to train missionary students, and the upshot was that both German and English candidates were sent to study under Scott. The first party of six students came in 1807, and he carried on this labour of love until failing health compelled him to give it up in 1814. He shrank from no difficulty and his trainees did well. In June 1808, he wrote in semi-humorous vein to his son: 'Mr Pratt begs that your father will begin to teach the missionaries Susoo and Arabic, of neither of which languages has he any knowledge! He felt very uncomfortable about this for a day or two; however, he has now begun to study these new languages with them.'[115] There was great energy and resolution of spirit in the man who could thus calmly meet and master the difficulties of a barbarous dialect like Susoo or the intricacies of a major language like Arabic; he was in his fifty-third year and his health was broken, but teach them he would that he might also teach them Divinity.[116] In 1811, he gave a singularly wise and comprehensive valedictory address and, in 1812, he was made one of the first honorary life governors of the society. In 1813, he went down to Bristol to form an auxiliary branch of the society and, in 1814, he bade farewell to his last missionary trainees. Well might the C.M.S. Minute after his death pay its tribute in terms that summed up his labours with a noble kind of fullness:

> With that comprehensive knowledge of the heart and of Scripture which stamped on his sentiments an early maturity that for almost half a century grew more mellow, but without withering or decay—he laid down for us those principles of action, stimulated us by those motives, encouraged us by those promises, and suggested those practical measures, the truth and wisdom of which are receiving fresh evidence every returning year.[117]

In July 1802, Scott was instituted to the living of Aston Sandford, near Bledlow at Buckden, where he had been ordained thirty years before. There was no parsonage in this tiny parish, and he had to build a house for his family out of his small revenue. He then resigned from the Lock and they moved to Aston in the spring of 1803. He had spent the years from 1772 to 1785 in the country and from 1785 to 1802 in the city; he was now to spend the nineteen years from 1802 until 1821 at Aston in great quietness and privacy. The whole village was one of the smallest in the kingdom, for it only contained two farmhouses and a few labourers' cottages. The roads were so bad that a wet season made them impassable and the local population did not number more than seventy people. But he found a surprising sphere of usefulness in this retired corner and his small church was soon packed full. He would expound in his kitchen on the Sunday evenings of the summer months and the weekday evenings of the winter months to all who would come.[118] Daniel Wilson tells us that his communicants came from all parts and grew so in number that he could count on a hundred who would meet round the Lord's Table.[119] Aston was more encouraging to him than any other scene of his labours since his days at Ravenstone. 'The poor people expressed great delight', his son records, 'at finding his preaching beyond their expectation so intelligible to them.'[120] They looked up at his plain countrified figure and saw in him a son of the soil like themselves; his strong accent and his choking asthma did not put them off, for they were not so nice in their tastes as the fashionable crowds in London. Constant good was done for many who were worldly and careless, and not a few who had been profligate and dissolute, were brought to the feet of Christ. He was at his best by the bedside of the sick or with the problems of the soul, and he built up an earnest body of well-instructed Christians in Aston Sandford.

Nor was this all. His own earnest piety found vent in a life of active benevolence and he evoked a warm response on behalf of various interests. Schools were built and societies were formed for the relief of the sick and needy. He found leisure for the pursuit of his reading and studies in a way that he had never known in London, and ten or twelve hours of the day were often spent in poring over his books with pen in hand and print in view. He toiled at his Commentary, seeking to revise and improve each new edition with unflagging industry; he thought out and wrote a number of books which were characterized by close argument and a determined tone of Scriptural truth. His style was always grave and unadorned, but always clear and vigorous, and no one could mistake his manner of doctrine. After *The Force of Truth* his first work had been a *Discourse on Repentance*, which was written at Olney in 1785. 'I wrote and enlarged it for the press,' he once recalled, 'commonly with a child on my knee or rocking the cradle, and my wife working by me; for a study and a separate fire were more than my purse would allow.'[121] His means were still spare and his life frugal when he made his home at Aston, but things had altered a great deal; he was freed from the cares which had harassed his early years, and he could work and write in ease and comfort of mind and body. Daniel Wilson tells us that 'he was always at work, always busy, always redeeming the time, yet never in a hurry.'[122] He worked away with his students at Hebrew or Susoo and he spared no toil to give them a sound and comprehensive view of truth. Visitors as well as candidates found their way to Aston from time to time, for few men were so well qualified to give counsel to young Christians or young Ministers. It was well known that no selfish plea of credit or interest could make him swerve by a hair's breadth from the line of truth and duty; it was no less well known that he had made himself, by his own unwearied perseverance a truly learned man, a wise and deep theologian. His Aston years thus found him recognized as a most loyal and useful servant of the Gospel in the front rank of the whole Evangelical movement.

'A certain roughness of exterior impressed many persons with the idea that he was harsh and severe,' his son remarked; 'it was reserved to those who knew him more intimately to be fully aware how kind and feeling a heart he carried within.'[123] Christian convictions not only fortified the strength and firmness which were his by nature, but also brought out all that was tender and gracious in a way that seemed to grow more beautiful with the passage of time. He kept up a close and affectionate correspondence with his sisters from the time when he first left home, and his letters breathe the spirit of love for all his family without the least disguise. In the end he outlived all twelve brothers and sisters, and for years he was acknowledged by them as their truest friend and benefactor. After his own spiritual experience, he could not rest until he had brought each of them to find in Christ their All in all. This was far from easy when he essayed his first approach, but he persevered in the spirit which a few words from one of his letters indicates: 'O my dear sister,' he wrote on July 27, 1779, 'I wish you as happy as I am myself, and I need wish you no happier in this world.'[124] In December 1774, he proposed by letter and married a widow while still in his first curacy, and his choice fell on one whose prudent, friendly, kind, and cheerful spirit went far to win all who conversed with her.[125] The thought occurred to them that they should pray with each other, although he had only once been present in a home when family prayers were held. They grew side by side in grace and truth, and their habits of household worship were maintained all their lives long, without interruption except through illness or absence from home. He took advantage of these occasions to expound the Scriptures to the household circle, and his remarks often rose far above any written comment in their point and fullness. 'I have never seen his soul', so his son recalled, 'more thrown into his countenance than on these occasions. [126]

Two children were born at Ravenstone, of whom Anne died at the age of four and a half, a rare flower of infant grace and beauty. The other was dedicated to the ministry, though not without conditions; it was only 'if it please God to spare his life and mine, and to give him a head and a heart meet for so sacred and important a function'.[127] Scott would rather his son were anything or nothing, if he were defective in either direction. Three more sons were born while he was in the country, and a son and a daughter after he had moved to the city; but two of these sons like little Anne were caught away from earthly love in their early childhood. Then, in 1790, his cup of sorrow was filled full, for his wife passed gently away. 'The Lord gave and the Lord hath taken away; blessed be the Name of the Lord,' he wrote; 'I would say so from my heart, though it aches when I attempt it.'[128] He was left with three sons and a daughter, himself involved in toils and difficulties enough to crush his health and spirits alike. It was less than twelve months later when he married again and his second wife was one whom his son described as 'an unspeakable blessing to him and his for more than thirty years.'[129] Very strict, but very loving was the home life his children knew; rebuke and punishment, even direct admonition, were barely known to them. Scott's temper and habit of life bore out the truth and sincerity of his prayers and teaching with irresistible force, and they all trod in his footsteps as time went by. His three sons were ordained and his daughter married a clergyman. 'O home,' he once wrote in 1808, 'how I love thee! because I love those at home!'[130] Grandchildren in due course came to take chief place in his heart and prayers; deaf though he was, he seemed to have a strong attraction even for very small children, and they would spend as much time with him as could be allowed. When two of his grandchildren came to bid him farewell less than twelve months before his death, he read them his daily portion from the Bible. It chanced to speak of the blessing which the old patriarch bestowed on his grandsons (Hebrews 11: 21), and he was so moved that he could hardly proceed. 'All my children are, I trust, serving God, and my anxiety as far as that is concerned is about my grandchildren,' so he wrote in February 1821; '…I pray in hope that they will be gathered one by one,…and in this hope, I use such means as I can.'[131] Happy man that he was, for they were an honour to his name and a blessing to the Church.

Sir George Gilbert Scott, the famous architect, was one of his grandsons, and his Recollections sketch him in his old age as a venerable figure.

> My grandfather was, as I remember him, a thin, tottering old man, very grave and dignified. Being perfectly bald, he wore a black velvet cap with silver buckles, and black silk stockings, and a regular shovel hat. His amusement was gardening, but he was almost constantly at work in his study. At meals when I chiefly saw him, he was rather silent owing to his deafness.…One day as we sat at dinner a very

> old apple tree, loaded with fruit, suddenly gave way and fell to the ground to the surprise of our party; and I remember my grandfather remarking that he wished that might be his own end, to break down in his old age under the weight of good fruit.[132]

Sir James Stephen says that his face was harsh and his eye unlit, his voice was rough and his gait uncouth, his manner was absent and inattentive, his temper was hasty and overbearing.[133] William Wilberforce was not blind to this side of Scott, and had expressed himself on the subject as early as 1798: 'Mr Scott is a rough diamond, and almost incapable of polish from his time of life and natural temper.'[134] Daniel Wilson in his Funeral Sermon placed his finger on the same faults: 'His failings…lay on the side of roughness and severity of temper, pride of intellect, and confidence in his own powers.'[135] But his asperity in personal points and his deficiency in popular gifts were no more than the rough exterior of the real man; behind that harsh, unfaced surface, there was the glowing diamond light of a noble character. He used himself to say that it was no excuse for a man to argue that he had no turn for a virtue of this kind or that kind, for all virtues ought to be the turn of every earnest Christian.[136] The difficulties and discouragements of all his early years are the proper foil to the virtues of his latter days, and we must not forget that he had to face a long climb and a long fight before he could stand up on the sunlit summits of peace. He was honest and candid almost to a fault, severe in his self-judgment and conscientious to the last degree; and the result was that seldom or never did he have to repent of what he had done when he had prayed it over, and then acted up to the light he had received.[137]

He was a man of sound and original qualities as well as of strong and energetic character; diligence and industry were like second nature to him, and they carried him through toils and labours from which most men would shrink in a palsy of sheer alarm. A clear judgment and close reason went hand in hand with a determination of mind and a perseverance of soul which formed the rock basis of his manhood and gave solidity to all his ways. He was tenacious of purpose and determined in conduct to the very verge of obstinacy, but purpose and conduct alike were nerved and steeled by his aim to serve God and God alone. He had learned to live in severe frugality and brave independence, and he was a noble illustration of one who proved himself superior to earthly ambition and worldly attraction. 'I trust I speak as a Christian minister when I say that toleration and protection are all that God's servants can reasonably expect in the devil's world,' so he had written in December 1792; 'and in fact, this is all they should desire!'[138] He was not by nature a man of strong social habits, but a kind and feeling heart made him ever think with sympathy and act with charity when he found others in need or trouble greater than his own. The grand secret of his triumph in the struggles of a long and hard life lay in his twin habit of meditation and intercession. He tried in his lifetime to pore over the words of eternal life with the earnest meditation of one who was wholly given to things divine; he thought on his death-bed that he had failed less in the great task of intercession than in any other.[139] These facts would be remarkable in any life and they help us to understand the simple dignity of his ideal: 'I trust I only desire to live that I may serve the Lord and recommend His Gospel,' he had declared in February 1795; 'and perfect holiness and obedience are the heaven I hope and long for.'[140] Scott could lift up his head and stand erect in the midst of all his trials and anxieties, for he sat loose to the things of time and held fast to that which is eternal. Sir James Stephen was right in saying that the seeds of every Christian grace were constantly germinating in his soul, and that their energy grew more and more prolific as the time drew near when they were to burst into perfect bloom in the heavenly paradise.[141]

Scott had a strong constitution, but his normal health was by no means good; he never recovered from the privation and exposure of his shepherd life at Braytoft, and he was a lifelong victim of ague and asthma, of cold and fever, and of various disorders which were internal and recurrent. On his itinerant tours from Olney he would often sit up through half the night in some strange bed, choked with asthma and longing for daybreak.[142] In 1783, he was stricken with a nervous fever while in Shropshire, which laid him so low that he thought the end had come. In 1801, he suffered a violent asthmatic attack in London and he feared that he would die of suffocation. 'I did not feel much of what the Apostle mentions of DESIRING to be with Christ, and I was convinced for that very reason that my Christianity was of a small growth,' he told his son; 'yet I trusted that it was genuine.'[143] After 1814, he was all but a prisoner in the neighbourhood of his own home and, on January 2, 1821, we hear him observe: 'I have not been out of my parish, or at the further end of it for several years; one service on the Lord's Day seems to overdo me.'[144] His time was shared between the study and his garden, and for his last ten years his wife was his only companion as his sons and daughter had all set up homes of their own. He was grave, but cheerful in his bearing, and he met his daily lot of pain and weariness with a calm and patient spirit. It was observed that his feelings of a kind and gentle nature seemed to blossom more and more, while those of a harsh or hasty spirit seemed to wither and die. His mind was still alert and as full of vigour as in his prime, and he applied himself to his studies much as he had ever done right on to the end. But when failing health began to confine him to his home and its precincts after 1814, his thoughts turned more and more to the great world of the unseen beyond. 'I desire, and I trust shall not in vain desire', he wrote in May 1816, 'the help of your prayers…that I may close well.'[145] He felt that the end of the race would soon hove into view, and it was his greatest longing that he should be found running at his best when the last lap lay before him.

In June 1819, Daniel Wilson came to see him and sat with him till near midnight. 'This morning', he wrote of the next day, 'he gave us a most beautiful exposition of Romans 10: 12.' He 'expounds twice a day, has above a hundred communicants, is popular and beloved in his neighbourhood, and has fuller churches than ever.'[146] But old age and extreme deafness, and a frame worn out by long toil, could not but take their toll, and his eyes were towards the world above. 'Oh, how my heart leaps and exults within me', he exclaimed with unusual fervour, 'at the thought of so very soon joining the glorious company before the Throne of God!'[147] On March 4, 1821, he was in church for the last time; then catarrh and fever broke out and his final illness set in. He was in pitiable distress, thin and emaciated; but his spirit was full of heavenly consolation. He could not claim much joy: but there was a deep and solid trust and his mind was content and in peace. All his tempers seemed to bespeak a soul ripe for heaven, and the very virtue which he most feared would fail, that of patience, was most exemplary. A last message came from Daniel Wilson which made mention of the good he had done, but he disclaimed it with holy vigour: 'This is doing me harm,' he cried; 'God be merciful to me a sinner is the only ground on which I can rest.'[148] But no one could tell him what death was like, and the iron strength of his constitution made him tremble at the prospect of the final struggle. He exclaimed on March 27:

> Oh, it is hard work to die, death is a new acquaintance, a terrible one, except as Christ giveth us the victory and the assurance of it. My flesh and my heart seem as if they wanted to fail and could not; who can tell what that tie is which binds body and soul together? How easily it is loosened in some; what a wrench and tear is it in others! Lord, loosen it, if it be Thy will![149]

But there was no struggle when the end came, and he suffered much less in the act of dying than he had done for many hours before. At six-thirty on the Monday evening of April 6, 1821, he made a sign for his head to be raised, and a young friend held him up in his arms. Scott leant his head on his shoulder and looked upward as if towards heaven; the look that stole over his face was a look of ineffable joy and composure, a look as of glory begun. He was sinking just as calmly as an infant falling asleep and in a few moments, without sigh or struggle, it was over. 'Father Scott', as he was so affectionately called by Henry Venn the Younger, had ceased to breathe, and that was all; he had fallen asleep in his seventy-fifth year with placid and perfect peace, in the arms of the Lord Jesus.

Bibliography

Works by The Rev. Thomas Scott

The Force of Truth, An Authentic Narrative (R.T.S., 1911).

Essays on the Most Important Subjects in Religion (no date).

Commentary on the Holy Scriptures (no date).

Biographies Of Thomas Scott And Other Works Quoted

John Scott, *The Life of the Rev. Thomas Scott* (1822).

A. C. Downer, *Thomas Scott, the Commentator* (1909).

Josiah Bull, *John Newton of Olney and St. Mary Woolnoth* (2nd Ed.).

Robert Isaac and Samuel Wilberforce, *The Life of William Wilberforce* (1838).

Josiah Bateman, *The Life of Daniel Wilson (1860).*

William Knight, *Memoir of Henry Venn* (1882).

G. R. Balleine, *A History of the Evangelical Party* (New Ed., 1933)

M. Seeley, *The Later Evangelical Fathers* (1913).

James Stephen, *Essays in Ecclesiastical Biography* (New Ed., 1875)

J. H. Overton and F. Relton, *A History of the English Church in the 18th Century* (1909).

Eugene Stock, *The History of the Church Missionary Society*, Vols. I-III (1899).

4

Richard Cecil
1748–1810

Richard Cecil was born in Chiswell Street, London, on November 8, 1748, the child of old age and many sorrows. His mother was over fifty years old when he was born, and more than ten years had elapsed since the birth of her last child. Her heart sank with sorrow in her time of travail, and she little thought that this child was to be the comfort and honour of her latter days. She came from a pious family, who for generations had served God as Nonconformists outside the pale of the national Church. Her grandfather used to save up money for the aid of the Dissenters in prison cells, and her mother used to carry it with her own hands to these sufferers for conscience' sake. She shared in the spirit of her forebears and was a woman of great worth, given to faith and good works, one who plied her needle to enlarge her private purse for charity. She was the daughter of a London merchant and she had become the wife of a London merchant, for her husband was a scion of the Burleigh family and the head of a long-established firm who were scarlet dyers for the

East India Company. He had inherited a large tract of ground in Chiswell Street, on which his home, his dyehouse, and his garden were well situated, and he was in affluent circumstances in those days when untold wealth was drawn from the magic Orient. He had been brought up with a classical education and was a man of wide reading and sound literary judgment. He was a strict Churchman and took his son with him to church from childhood days; but it is not so clear that he shared the rich vein of faith and piety which distinguished his wife.

Their child grew up at home, with garden and dyehouse for his playground, and his boyhood seemed to offer promise of future distinction. 'I used to imagine', Daniel Wilson declared long years afterwards, 'that I saw revived in him all the fine talents of his great ancestor, Cecil, Lord Burleigh, that distinguished ornament of the reign of Elizabeth.'[1] He wrote so well that some of his boyish pieces found a place in the periodicals to which he sent them on hazard; his own father once refused to believe that he was the author of a certain poem which he had read in one of these publications. He was intended for a mercantile life in the old family tradition and was placed in two large city houses to learn the ways of business. But he evinced the most determined aversion to trade and at the same time developed a passion for art and literature. His father would find him at picture sales when he ought to have been in the warehouse, or else trying his own hand at art when he ought to have been in the office. At length, unknown to his parents, he set out on a tour of France to see the great paintings of the greatest masters, and he only turned home when his means failed. He was wonderfully versatile in interest and genius; his aesthetic and literary tastes taught him to love all the Arts. But his passion ran to painting beyond all else, and at length his father allowed him to leave his uncongenial life in the warehouse. It was proposed that he should be trained by a friend of the Cecils in Rome, but some unforeseen circumstance put this plan out of court at the last moment. Soured with disappointment, he lived on at home with his books and music, writing poetry and playing the violin; above all, improving his skill as an artist. But it was a dilettante mode of existence, for he was not being trained to paint with character. It was, in fact, an unhealthy kind of life for a young man who could live in the lap of luxury with no better motive than his own tastes and whims. Nature had given him a strong bent to a life of idolence and sin; now his father and his circumstances seemed to encourage it. Only the grace of God could recover him for a life of honour and usefulness.

Richard Cecil was truly a child of providence, yet in early life he had no value at all for religion. He had many remarkable escapes from sudden death or violent accident, but they never turned his heart in a Godward direction. Once he fell through broken ice into a garden tank and was rescued when almost frozen to death; once he was caught by his coat in a mill-wheel and was rescued when within an inch of being crushed to death. Deep and constant was his mother's anxiety to see him walk in the ways of godly manhood, but her desires long seemed to be of no avail. She bought him Watts' *Hymns for Children and Janeway's Token for Children*, and they impressed him for a time; but his goodness, like the morning cloud, passed away at noon, and her early hopes were rudely blighted with what looked like tragic disappointment. As the boy grew, he grew in wickedness; he made such progress in sin that he learned to glory in his shame. But there were some restraints and his conscience was never seared. His own father had one pious servant whose faith gave him a dignity which the lad knew not how to value, but which made him feel that the servant was, in fact, his superior. This man induced him on one occasion to go and hear Whitefield; he was seventeen or eighteen years old at the time, and it must have been near the close of the great preacher's English ministry. 'It had no sort of religious effect on me, nor had the preaching of any man in my unconverted state,' he recalled; 'my religion began by contemplation. Yet I conceived a high reverence for Mr Whitefield; I saw a commanding and irresistible effect, and he made me feel my own insignificance.'[2] But he soon fell in with certain infidel books and he began to call darkness light, and light darkness. He became a kind of apostle for unbelief and he strove to instil his views into others. Such was his grim success that in after years, when he tried to undo his work and reclaim their souls, his efforts were in vain. We are not surprised that when young Daniel Wilson came to him for advice long years later, and told him of the time and mode of his conversion, he had somewhat to say: 'When I mentioned the dreadful lengths of iniquity into which I had sunk', Wilson wrote, 'he stopped me when I called myself the chief of sinners to put in his claim to that character; and this was the point in which he said he exceeded everyone; that he kept a kind of school of infidelity, and used to have a number of young men, and teach them to ridicule the Bible.'[3] Thus he devoured the works of the sceptics in that age of reason when doubt and unbelief were at a premium; he stuffed his head with intellectual difficulties which seemed to lead God to the edge of the world and then bow Him out of the Universe. Was not this the sorry case of Newton in his early years of profanity and unbelief? It was, in part at least, the fashion of the age in which they lived. But while Cecil seemed to harden his heart and to resist the call of God on the plea of infidel arguments, we may well doubt whether his unbelief had more than a surface hold on his mind. He could not bear to read books which dealt with the Christian way of life in a wise and searching manner; conscience would gather strength and fears awoke in his soul as he thought thereon. He was at least preserved from the wicked by-ways of life into which John Newton had strayed, and his profession of unbelief was never required to stand a first-class trial. Moreover, like Newton, Cecil had a mother who yearned over him with ceaseless yearning, and the child of so many prayers and tears could never perish.

Cecil could not deceive himself on the subject of his mother's warnings; they hung on the wheels of evil, and he only drove with difficulty in the path of youthful folly. He was wretched when by himself, because it was just then that her words could least be stifled. 'I was a professed infidel,' he said; 'but then,

I liked to be an infidel in company rather than when alone.'[4] Her words stuck in his mind like barbed arrows, and tears often fell from his eyes as soon as she was out of sight. 'My mother', he said, 'would talk to me, and weep as she talked; I flung out of the house with an oath, but wept too when I got into the street.'[5] Her tenderness was more than he could bear, and he could not shake his mind free from her entreaties. Then came one eventful night when he lay in bed and his thoughts turned to his mother. He began to reflect on the many trials and sorrows which beset her, and then on the patient and cheerful spirit with which she faced them. This led him to think that it was through her private life of prayer and Bible reading that she had won such strength and poise. 'She has a secret spring of comfort of which I know nothing,' he thought, 'while I who…seek pleasure by every means, seldom or never find it.'[6] But if there were any comfort in religion, why should he not enjoy it as well as his mother? He would seek it at once from God, and he rose up without ado to pray. But then he remembered that his mother's comfort in prayer was linked with faith in Christ, and how was he to pray in that Name in which he would not believe? He threw himself down on his bed again in utter confusion, murmuring: 'This Christ …stands much in my way, and can form no part of my prayers!'[7]

But the next day he had recourse to compromise, and he began to pray to God as the Supreme Being. Had he been told at this juncture that he was not seeking God in the right way, he might have been discouraged from seeking Him at all; but he was more than ever indebted to his mother for her truly wise and patient conduct as she looked on.[8] He now gave ear to her words of loving wisdom and talked out his problems with her without reserve. 'The Christian will look back throughout eternity with interest and delight on the steps and means of his conversion,' he used to say. 'My father told me this! My mother told me that! Such an event was sanctified to me! In such a place God visited my soul! These recollections will never grow dull and wearisome.'[9] He now began to read books and to hear sermons and, one by one, he found that his difficulties were cleared away. He found it hard to break off his old and favourite connections, but light went on streaming into his soul and this led to gradual amendment of life. At length he made a full and clear discovery of the truth that, so far from standing in his way, Christ was The Way for all who come unto God by Him. Cecil used to say in later life that a whole volume might be written on the varied means by which God leads men to think of Him and take their first steps towards Him; further, that the story of a man's own life makes all other lives seem dry and vapid when set beside his own.[10] No one else can read or feel the story of his life as he can himself, and he for one never ceased to recall with a thrill of sacred wonder all the way which the Lord God had led him. 'I have tried to find rest elsewhere; I have fled to shelters which held out great promise of repose,' he wrote; 'but I have now long since learned to turn unto Thee. Tell me, O Thou Whom my soul loveth, where Thou feedest, where Thou makest Thy flocks to rest at noon?'[11]

His father was perplexed by this change of outlook, and not without alarm for his future. He had made two experiments on his behalf, and each had failed; he would not go into business, nor would he take up an artist's career. Now his father told him that if he joined the Sectaries, or Nonconformists, he would do no more to help him, alive or dead; but if he would enter the Church, he would gladly bear the expense of a university training. Cecil embraced this new offer at once, and in May 1773 he took his place in Queen's College at Oxford. Thus, as in the case of Newton, it was just a little extra weight in one scale that tipped the balance in favour of the Church of England : 'Mr Cecil said that, when he was first convinced of sin', wrote Daniel Wilson, 'he had no idea of being a minister; but his father was a high Churchman and…forced him to go to College.'[12] There are but few details of his Oxford career, but a man like Cecil in his early twenties would make the most of its opportunities. Once God had made the light to shine out of darkness into his heart it would illuminate all his mental gifts and early training with new strength and lustre. He seized the chance to fill out his knowledge of the Classics in a way that laid the basis of his later reputation as a man with the instinct and training of a scholar. He was wedded to the study of Greek and strove to make himself a real master of the niceties of that noble language. Pratt tells us that his incessant application to this subject, mainly by candle-light, brought on an almost total loss of sight for six months or more.[13] Yet he refused to give either Arts or Science an undue place in his scheme of things, for he felt that such were the very idols of the heathen world: 'And what are they who now follow them with an idolatrous eagerness', he asked, 'but like children, who are charmed with the sparkling of a rocket, and yet see nothing in the sun?'[14]

Oxford was in low water in all things spiritual and he could get little help from man for his soul. It was barely five years since six students at St. Edmund Hall had been expelled from the University on account of their Evangelical convictions, and the storm had left an angry swell in Oxford circles which had not yet had time to die away. Lady Huntingdon's plan to educate converted men for the ministry had been rudely terminated as far as Oxford was concerned, and she had felt compelled to open a college of her own at Trevecca in Wales. Thus few men of spiritual standing were to be found at Oxford in the 'seventies, and Cecil had to learn what it means to walk alone. He was still young in faith and in experience, and he had to contend with many sore conflicts in mind and soul. The heirs of the Holy Club were all now dispersed, and he had to put up with the insults which the profligate love to aim at piety. The rags of infidel thought still wrapped themselves round him in that casual atmosphere and this, indeed, was a trial which overtook him from time to time as long as he lived. 'I know not', he confessed, 'that I have any other which is so particular in its attacks upon me.'[15] Once, while walking in the physics gardens, he saw a fine pomegranate tree cut almost right through the stem, down near the root, and he asked the gardener why this had been done. 'Sir,' he was told, 'this tree used to shoot so strong that it bore nothing but leaves. I was therefore obliged to cut it in this manner; and when it was almost cut through, then it began to bear plenty of fruit.'[16] This came home to his mind as a vivid illustration of his own case and he went back to his rooms comforted and instructed. Thus, in spite of coldness and of opposition, he kept up his witness and became known for his piety. His later life was not to lie in a sphere where much variety of incident would form a large feature, but it was to be one of far-reaching importance for the Church at large; and he gained much that was to fit him for his work in the way of knowledge of the human mind and quick insight into character from his experience in the bleak and frigid air of Oxford.

In September 1776 he was made a deacon, and in February 1777 he was ordained to the priesthood by the Bishop of Lincoln. Thus he received Orders at the hands of the same prelate who had ordained Newton in 1764 and Scott in 1772; little, perhaps, did the bishop think that he had ordained three men who were destined to head the van in the second generation of Evangelical clergy! It is pleasant to trace this link between Cecil and the two men with whom he was to form so close a bond in after years; but it is a striking contrast to turn from rough diamonds, like Scott and Newton, to the highly cultured man who was to stand by their side. It would seem that Newton first met him in 1776, not long after he had been ordained, and he wrote to his wife from London: 'I heard him at St. Antholin's; he is a good speaker, and a good preacher for a young man.'[17] He took his Arts degree with great credit in Lent 1777, at the age of eight and twenty, while his title as curate at Rauceby placed him with the very man in whose house, some eighteen years later, the first hint was made of the possibility of a Mission to the Heathen by the Church of England. But his stay at Rauceby was short enough, for his value was soon discovered. At his vicar's request, he left Lincolnshire to serve three small churches at Thornton, Bagworth and Markfield, in Leicestershire. This was a provisional arrangement until the son of the deceased vicar should be of age to take up the livings. He found very little in the way of true religion in these centres, but he gathered round him a flourishing congregation and left behind him a goodly band of true Christians. Above all, the vicar-to-be was led to embrace the truth and in due time became a faithful shepherd of the flock entrusted to his care. These were fruits the value of which all could observe, and they cheered his heart with a joy which no one could remove.

Cecil then returned to Rauceby, but was at once offered two small livings at Lewes in Sussex. He was gladly released to take this fresh charge, and his sense of responsibility seemed to grow with each new sphere of service:

> A minister is to be in season and out of season, and therefore everywhere a minister, he will not employ himself in writing secular histories; he will not busy himself in prosecuting mathematical inquiries. He will labour directly in his high calling, and indirectly in a vast variety of ways, as he may be enabled; and God may bless that word in private, which may have been long heard in public in vain.[18]

But the house in which he lived at Lewes was so damp that his health soon became seriously impaired; he was afflicted with some rheumatic disorder in the head and, in the end, was disabled from all duty for several months. He was obliged to appoint a curate to serve the two churches, and this swallowed up the meagre income of his living. The death of his parents at this juncture left him without private means and he had to make shift with somewhat straitened circumstances. But he held on to both livings for the express purpose of keeping up a true ministry at Lewes, and he persevered in this for a number of years until he was sure that he could resign the charge into the hands of a trusted successor. But ill health had compelled him to leave Lewes himself, and he found a house at Islington where he hoped to recuperate. This was a change which led him to accept invitations to preach in various London churches and chapels, and it was soon clear that he would be no less welcome in the city than had been the case in the country.

Evangelical clergy would have been almost without a voice in London for a whole generation had it not been for the proprietary chapels and occasional lectureships which were then a feature of the Church and city. The proprietary chapels came into being as Chapels of Ease, in semi-private hands, and were allowed by the bishops as the simplest way of coping with the demands of a growing population. The Law did not encourage division of old parochial districts, and so would not expedite erection of new parish churches in the crowded suburbs. Chapels of Ease thus came into being with lay proprietors who claimed the right to choose their own preachers, and it was their choice of Evangelical clergy that linked the chapels with those who were shut out of Church and pulpit elsewhere. It now fell to Richard Cecil to have a call to what was by far the largest chapel of its kind in London; this was the Chapel of St. John's, Bedford Row, which stood in the parish of St. Andrew's, Holborn. It had been built in the reign of Queen Anne as a means of relief from the noisy High Church rector who then held the living. This was Sacheverell, who had left the Whigs for the Tories in hope of promotion, and had thrown the whole country into a state of ferment with the old cry that the Church was in danger. He was impeached by the House of Commons, and was sentenced to have his books burnt and to keep silence for the space of three years. But the Queen gave him the living of St. Andrew's, Holborn, and this led the dissatisfied parishioners to build St. John's, Bedford Row, as a Chapel of Ease in 1713. It had served a useful cause for almost seventy years, but then it fell on evil days, and Sir Eardley Wilmot, the chief proprietor of the Rugby estate on which it stood, advertised in vain for a clergyman who would take it.

At length he was given the name of Richard Cecil by the Archbishop of Canterbury and he sent him a warm invitation to come and take St. John's. Cecil found that the buildings were out of repair and would require a large outlay to put them in order; he found that the income came from pew-rents and that the pews were all underlet. He had no private means of support and he would not run the hazard of a large debt which he could not see how to pay off. Thus he would have declined had not two earnest friends of the chapel now come forward with a timely offer of help. One was Mrs Wilberforce, the sister of John Thornton and correspondent of John Newton, and she offered her bond to secure Cecil from loss if his undertaking should not succeed. The other was William Cardale, and he promised to lend the full sum that might be required to put the chapel in a proper state of repair. Thus, one by one, all his scruples were met and his mind was made up. It was in March 1780 that he entered on the ministry at St. John's, which was only to terminate with his death thirty years later, and he soon became known as a valuable acquisition for the Evangelical cause in the heart of London. St. John's, Bedford Row, was only a proprietary chapel, not a parish church, but his long ministry gave it an importance which was perhaps second to none in the Church life of the city. It was redeemed from the backwaters of debt and ruin in which he found it, and it soon became a centre of Evangelical thought and activity which could almost rival John Venn's church at Clapham. Indeed, the great laymen who made up the Clapham sect came to look on St. John's as their other home when they were in London, and Cecil was drawn into the full stream of philanthropic endeavour and missionary enterprise which characterized their lives. Thus, he was called of God to live and labour in a sphere where he could help to guide and mould the life and thought of the whole movement in its second generation.

Cecil found that he had a difficult and arduous path to tread in his first years at St. John's. Mrs. Wilberforce and her friends naturally expected that he would preach in the same strain of doctrine and appeal as he had done elsewhere, but he soon saw that the majority of his congregation were quite opposed to the spirit of the Gospel. He had to make up his mind as to what was the right course to pursue with an eye to the future, and he was faced with two alternatives. He might at once boldly show his colours and preach as he had done in his country livings or his London lectures; this would soon drive away the old hearers, but would attract a new and select congregation with a large and assured income. Or he might start with more caution, and try to lead the old hearers into a real love for spiritual truth by gentle degrees; this would work out for the good of benighted souls, but would disappoint his chief patrons and expose him to misunderstanding. But he bravely chose the second alternative and for seven years at least he had to pass through deep waters of trial. His friends could not perceive his aim or share in his motives; they felt that one who did not shun to preach a full Gospel elsewhere was now trimming his sails in Bedford Row. This was hard to endure, but he was not the man to shrink from the path of duty:

> Some seem to think that in the choice of a wise way, there lurks always a trimming disposition, there are men doubtless who will sacrifice to self even Christ Jesus the Lord; but they of all men are farthest from the thing. There is a secret in doing it which none but an honest man can discover.[19]

At first the chapel was but thinly attended and the repairs consumed the small annual revenue from the pew-rents. He was so anxious to spare his hearers from any fresh burden that, for three years, he went without emolument at all and was content to live on the trifling income which he received from his lectures at Orange Street Chapel. For eighteen years he paid the entire, interest on the money lent for the repairs, and it was not until 1798 that his friends rallied once more to his support and paid off the last debts on the chapel buildings. He sought not theirs, but them, and he would not force the pace; the work of winter had to be done as well as the work of summer, and he held on his way with faith and patience.[20] His very soul abhorred the thought that any man should be discouraged from hearing the free offer of salvation through having to pay his way into a seat, and he would not raise the pew-rents lest dying men should turn away from the word of the living God. He set his face against all the irregularities which so often prevailed in the city churches on the part of vergers, and he strove to model the whole conduct of the service in the spirit of holy and ordered harmony. He soon made St. John's known for the vitality of its worship; all parts of the service were carried out in unhurried but unbroken succession from the first sentence to the last Amen. The prayers were read without chanting, and a psalm was sung after the second lesson as well as before the communion service and sermon. The organ in St. John's was a beautiful instrument, and it was played by Cecil's daughter with an unfailing sympathy for the sentiment of the hour.[21] The whole service was grave and devotional in tone and was designed to help men to worship God in spirit and in truth. There was no parochial charge in the strict sense of that term attached to the chapel, but the minister of St. John's was free to attend to the needs of his own people. Cecil had to labour chiefly in the pulpit or with his pen, but he was an earnest pastor of those on whom he could look as his flock. Thus, the passage of time saw the congregation increase until St. John's became famous; the old hearers, as well as his patrons, were reconciled, and new hearers came in from all quarters to attend his ministry.

But great as was the value of the chapels, the influence of the lectureships was greater still. It had been a custom in Elizabethan and Stuart times for pious benefactors to create endowments so that regular sermons in parish churches could be supplemented by additional lectures which would not be a charge on parish funds.[22] The parishioners were free to choose any ordained man whom the bishop was willing to license, and he was free to lecture once a week at some hour when the church was not in use for an ordinary service. This old system opened a new door for the Evangelical clergy in Hanoverian days and they made their message heard by means of lectures while the normal sermons were still denied to them. William Romaine held a lectureship of this kind at St. Dunstan's, Fleet Street, for almost fifty years, and Henry Venn gave three London lectures each week while he was curate at Clapham. Thus, it is no surprise when we learn that Richard Cecil was not only in charge of a Chapel of Ease, but was also engaged for certain lectures in London churches. He first took up work of this kind when he retired from Lewes to live in Islington and for some years he was called to preach a Sunday lecture at six o'clock in the morning at Lothbury. He found the walk at that early hour not without peril in the winter, for most of the street lamps were out and few people were yet astir save those who prowl about for prey. He often encountered rogues of the night, their dark lanterns in hand and designs still darker at heart. But God preserved him in all his ways and he was never molested. He was at length forced to engage a hackney coach for the journey to and from the church, but this was rendered necessary, not through danger to life or limb, but through fatigue to a nervous constitution.

He took special delight in this early lecture on a summer morning, for then he found that his hearers were often made up of men and women who were out for an early walk; they would saunter without a thought into the church and some of them at least heard and embraced the truth. At length ill health and the anxiety of his friends led him to give up this Lothbury lectureship; he lost nothing but a labour of love, for the trifling income was barely equal to the weekly expense. But he had been appointed to the lectureship at Orange Street Chapel, and this supplied his sole slender means of income for the first three years of his ministry at St. John's. These were evening lectures which were held twice a week, and he kept them up for many years, on Sundays and Wednesdays. These Orange Street lectures came to an end when the chapel was dismantled for structural repairs, but the congregation was moved to Long Acre Chapel where a new arrangement was made. Richard Cecil and Henry Foster were to take the Sunday evening lecture alternately at Long Acre Chapel and at Christ Church, Spitalfields; each was to be in charge for three years, first at one centre and then at the other. Cecil entered on his work at Spitalfields in September 1787, and again in 1793 and in 1799; but for the last three years it was almost wholly discharged by his curate, owing to extreme ill health, and he could not renew the engagement. On the first night that he was to take this lecture, he had to leave a child at death's door in his wife's care; but he went on his way, saying that 'the walls were to be built in troublous times'.[23] He went with a heavy heart to do his duty, but it pleased God to heal the child, and his ministry at Spitalfields was greatly blessed. He drew a vast congregation from the poorest classes to that great church, and they used to hear him in the breathless silence of a most impressive interest. Thus, for many years he carried on these lectures at the same time as his ministry at St. John's, and his voice was lifted up for Evangelical truth to new congregations in the heart of London.

Richard Cecil came to London at a time when Evangelicals were still a small and despised body whose preachers were ostracized by most parish clergy. As late as June 1798 Wilberforce summed up the state of affairs in dark enough terms: 'It is my fixed opinion, formed on much reading, consideration and experience, that there has been for many years among the majority of our clergy a fatal and melancholy departure from the true principles of Christianity and of the Church of England.'[24] Whitefield had built the Moorfields Tabernacle and the Tottenham Court Road Chapel, and Wesley had built the Foundry and many other chapels in the heart of London; but for many long years William Romaine was the only beneficed clergyman of Evangelical character in the city north of the Thames. In 1749 he was chosen for an afternoon lectureship at St. Dunstan's, Fleet Street, and in 1764 he became Rector of St. Anne's, Blackfriars. Henry Venn and Thomas Jones were the only two among the London clergy who looked up to him in his early years; but Venn moved to Yorkshire in 1759 and Jones died at Southwark in 1762. Thus Romaine stood alone. It is not a little striking to think of this solitary preacher who rose up like John the Baptist in the moral wilderness of London, and told out the vital call to repent and believe for thirty long years almost alone.[25] Then, in December 1779, Newton came from Olney to be Rector of St. Mary, Woolnoth, and in March 1780 Cecil was placed in charge of St. John's, Bedford Row. Romaine was much older in years and in Orders than either Newton or Cecil; he was grave and scholarly in habit, quiet and retiring in spirit, and as inflexible as a pillar of iron in the Temple of Truth. Friendship with him was not easy to cultivate, but he gladly welcomed two new recruits to the ranks of the London ministry. What they thought of him is clearly seen in Newton's remark after his death in 1795: 'He was the most popular man of the Evangelical party since Mr Whitefield, and few remaining will be more missed.'[26] Romaine's mantle was to light on Cecil rather than on any other London minister, for he had his cultured mind without his studied reserve; Newton's friendship was to fall to Cecil rather than to any other city clergyman, for he had his kindly charm without his rugged candour.

Newton was in his fifty-fifth year when he came to London, and Cecil in his thirty-second; their first meeting, four years before, had forged the initial link in an intimacy which was to ripen more and more for thirty years. It is pleasant to think of this friendship between the polished young scholar and the rugged old sailor; the one looked up to the other with a sense of profound veneration and seemed to find in him his beau-ideal of a truly converted minister. He spent many an hour with him as his companion in those years of momentous influence, and watched over him with the most tender care and solicitude when life and health began to fail. Then he prepared the narrative of his life for the press and brought out a complete edition of his works; it was his last tribute to one who had helped to bring heaven down to earth for him. But those years in London put him in touch with the great and the good from all quarters, and he came to know most of the early fathers and honoured heroes of the Evangelical revival. Thus, throughout the eighties, good old Henry Venn of Yelling was wont to spend a month or two each summer in London, when he would preach for Rowland Hill in Surrey Chapel. He and Cecil had met at least as early as 1783, and a cordial affection had sprung up between them at once. Thus, when Venn had spent May and June in the city in 1786, he wrote of his visit with playful humour: 'Mr Cecil says

I do very wrong to come for so short a time; he would persuade me to undertake for half the year.'[27] Then, in 1785, the London ministry was again enriched by the appointment of Thomas Scott to the Lock Chapel; he owed even more to Newton than did Cecil, and it was but natural that the two should be drawn together in bonds of more than ordinary strength. Then there was Henry Foster, for long the friend and curate of Romaine, no less the friend and colleague of Cecil, a man of true piety and devotion;[28] and there was John Thornton, the friend and patron of every good man and every right cause, a generous benefactor to Cecil's wife at a time of gravest anxiety, and one whose praise was sung by Cecil with peculiar feeling.[29] Above all, there was William Wilberforce, with whom he had so much in common both by nature and by training. He was staying with Wilberforce at Battersea Rise in August 1793, when 'the first timbers' of *The Practical View of Christianity* were being laid; the whole book was discussed between them in detail, and was strongly recommended by Cecil.[30] What Wilberforce thought of Cecil can be made clear by two entries in his journal: 'Mr Cecil came to dinner, and *tete-a-tete* with him...Much pleased with Cecil; he is living like a Christian. Oh that I were like him!'[31] Again, in 1794: 'Dined with Cecil; he is a true Christian. The nearer he is approached, the better he appears.'[32]

Richard Cecil was an original member and one of the founders of a society long since famous in Evangelical history. In 1783, three London clergy and one layman met in the Castle and Falcon Inn in Aldersgate Street. The three clergy were the veteran, John Newton, and his younger friends, Richard Cecil and Henry Foster.

These three, with their lay friends, Eli Bates brought into being the Eclectic Society as a club where they could meet for Christian fellowship and pastoral discussion. Thenceforth they met once each fortnight in the vestry of St. John's, Bedford Row, and their numbers soon grew to twelve or more London clergy, with as many country members, who were always welcome when they happened to be in the city. The new society thus became a centre where almost all the Evangelical clergy were wont to meet, and not a few of the leading laymen in the city were also chosen as members. It soon proved its value as a means of keeping the scattered and solitary units in touch with each other, and it rendered a unique and priceless service to the Evangelical cause as the years passed by. Those who came drank tea in Cecil's vestry and then settled down to discuss some fresh problem which had been chosen in advance for the meeting. Numerous topics came up for discussion over the years and difficult questions were threshed out among themselves in the light of Scriptural teaching. What is the best preparation for the pulpit? What is the best method of comforting afflicted consciences? How can we distinguish between true and counterfeit Christianity? What is the best mode for the visitation of the sick? Such were problems which each member tried to handle, and Pratt's records of the Society show that no one played a more important role than Cecil himself.

His name is linked far more intimately with the history of the Eclectic than the bare fact that it was held in his vestry; he was at his best in such a meeting, where his keen psychiatric mind and his fine literary style gave a peculiar interest to his contributions. Thus, the Eclectic came to be a fellowship of the London clergy which was recognized as a counterpart to the Clapham Sect as a fellowship for the London laymen, and some of the greatest movements in the later story of the whole Church rose out of the debates of this little Society. It was, for example, at a meeting convened by the Eclectic on April 12, 1799, that the Church Missionary Society was born. John Venn was in the chair, with fifteen clergy and nine laymen over whom to preside, and these twenty-five men took the momentous decision to found a Church Society for missionary work. Richard Cecil and Charles Simeon had both taken a keen interest in the earlier discussions, but could not be present on this historic occasion; Cecil was laid aside with a severe illness, and Simeon was then engaged in his Cambridge duties. But the meeting chose them both as members of the first committee, and the third annual sermon was preached by Cecil on the words of Isaiah: 'Prepare ye the way of the Lord' (Isa. 40: 3). He dealt with the moral state of the heathen, the right means for their recovery, and the motives which should induce men to take up the task. It was full of incisive thought and bold epigram, and there were some very striking features in its appeal. He said that the sons of earth, the slave-traders, had brought reproach to the very name of Christianity, and that the sons of hell, the French revolutionaries, had gone far to root it out altogether. 'May we', he cried, 'as the sons of God in the midst of a crooked and perverse generation, shine as lights in the world!'[33] Many other plans of benevolent design and of philanthropic intent were discussed and matured in the vestry of St. John's, Bedford Row; and they never found a warmer friend or advocate than Cecil, though his health would not allow him to take so active a part in their prosecution as he must have desired.

Cecil had thus won the regard of the fathers of the Evangelical movement, such as Henry Venn and Romaine; he had also become the close friend of its chief captains among his own contemporaries, such as Thomas Scott and Newton. He was now to exert a deep and decisive influence on those who were to rank as its leaders in the coming generation, and this was made abundantly clear in the case of Josiah Pratt and Daniel Wilson. Cecil knew Pratt's father, who was an old member of Riland's church at Birmingham; Cecil, indeed, used to say that he had never seen a fairer copy of the character of our Redeemer. Pratt was born in 1768, so that he was twenty years the junior of his future friend and helper. In 1789 he took his place in St. Edmund Hall at Oxford, and in 1792 he was ordained as a deacon on a title to the church at Bewdley. Five years later he was anxious to exchange his place in the country for one in the city and he gladly rose to Cecil's invitation to come and help him in St. John's Chapel. Thus, in 1797, he took a house near Bedford Row, and married the woman of his choice. Cecil's keen insight and shrewd judgment of men's motives and men's feelings, his wide knowledge and clear vision in Church problems and Church parties, marked him out as just the man to act as friend and guide to one who in turn would be a wise father to many sons. How much Pratt owed to those seven formative years with Richard Cecil we can never assess; but they saw him develop a rare strain of faithfulness in the service of souls. When he first took up his duties at Bedford Row he was somewhat shy and downcast. It was then that Cecil gave him advice which he never forgot: 'Never mind, Pratt; make yourself useful, and the time will come when you will be wanted!'[34]

Pratt left Cecil in 1804 to become curate to John Newton at St. Mary Woolnoth, and there he stayed until Newton's death in 1807. Meanwhile he had played an active part in the formation of the Church Missionary Society and had followed Thomas Scott as secretary. He held this office from 1802 to 1824, and was the main pilot of the Society in its first twenty-five years. He proved himself a born statesman, one whose very instinct it was to think on an imperial scale for the Kingdom of God. He was singularly unobtrusive by nature and habit, but he had great business talents, backed up by a practical, sagacious and comprehensive mind. He had a quick and unerring eye for the heart of a problem, and he worked with ceaseless care and wisdom for the right solution. He was blessed with a rare combination of absolute loyalty to the faith and practice of his own Society, and of generous sympathy to the aims and motives of other men and missions. His name must stand second only to that of the greatest of all secretaries, the second Henry Venn, in the annals of a hundred years, and we are not surprised to know that Vexin always referred to him in an affectionate way as King Pratt! In 1813 he had begun to produce a monthly paper which he called the *Missionary Register*, and in 1824 he resigned from the Church Missionary Society in order to give his whole time to its demands. It was not confined to his own Society, but was meant to give a systematic account of all missionary effort. Materials were gathered with endless patience, and details were arranged with consummate skill. It was a work which showed astonishing powers of toil and industry in its technical character, and astonishing breadth of love and sympathy in its general management. There has never been a paper at all like it in complete and thorough information, and the Church owes more than it has ever recognized to his untiring energy. When he passed away, in the year 1844, Daniel Wilson bore a simple testimony to the great worth of Cecil's early curate: 'To no one was I more attached than to him who was spared to me and to the Church the longest, the Rev. Josiah Pratt, my honoured brother![35]

Daniel Wilson was first put in touch with Cecil by his father at a crucial stage in his life, and no man was better fitted to give him wise advice on the points at issue. Wilson's father had placed him in a large London warehouse with a view to a good merchant career, and he had grown out of boyhood as a professed sceptic, in spite of a godly mother. Then came that great change in which good old John Newton played no small part, and he was filled with enthusiastic desire to give his life to the ministry. But his father demurred until at length it was arranged that the whole case should be referred to the judgment of Richard Cecil. Thus, on March 26, 1798, after much importunate prayer, but not without fear and trembling, he made his way to St. John's. He sat down opposite the sofa on which Cecil was then forced to recline, and was put at his ease by an assurance that he would be heard without prejudice. 'I related the abiding desire of my soul towards this work', he wrote, 'and the different steps which had brought me before him as a judge.'[36] Cecil could not have heard Wilson's story without surprise at the curious resemblance which linked it with his own early experience; things could not have been more fitly ordained than for Wilson to have come to the very man who had trod the self-same path before him. We can hardly wonder that he expressed himself thoroughly satisfied with his call to the work of God's vineyard and urged him by all means to press on his way. 'I seize the first moment to acquaint you with the blessed event of my interview with Mr Cecil,' he told a friend; 'I have not time to enter into particulars. To sum up all in one word—he is fully persuaded that I am called of God to the work of the ministry, and advises me by all means to go on with it.'[37] Wilson's father was satisfied with Cecil's judgment and gave consent for his son to leave the warehouse. Thus, in May 1798, he placed himself under Pratt who was then Cecil's curate for guidance in study and reading; and in November 1798 he took his place in St. Edmund Hall at Oxford where Pratt had been ten years before.

On August 1, 1801, Wilson left Oxford and went down to Chobham for the benefit of Cecil's advice and instruction: 'God grant', he would pray, 'that I may turn what I have learned to my own profit, and the promotion of His glory!'[38] On September 20 he was ordained as Curate of Chobham, and he laboured there for two years until his appointment to the staff of St. Edmund Hall. Cecil often came for a brief visit, always full of instructive and original conversation. No time was lost in idle talk; he would begin at once with some topic of the ministry, or some volume on theology. Sometimes he would discuss some theme from his own life, and would open up a rich and copious stream of spiritual wisdom and experience. Then, perhaps, an attack of pain would overtake him and he would lie down on the floor, often turning on his face for a time to hide his feelings. Then it would pass and he would resume his attitude and continue the discussion. Wilson could not forget such scenes as these and he loved to gather up the crumbs which thus fell from the rich man's table. His journal notes preserve many a short saying which had stuck in his mind. 'Mr Cecil used to say', he recalled, 'that it is not by men of great powers God does His work, but by men of holy love.'[39] He felt that there was real danger lest in trying to learn at Cecil's feet he should at length copy him too closely; but he strove to correct mistakes and to supply defects in his own style in the light of Cecil's teaching, and to adapt himself in turn of mind and in spiritual frame to Cecil's disposition.[40] In the passage of time, Wilson was brought down from Oxford to take Cecil's place at St. John's, and he carried on the tradition of his ministry at Bedford Row for a decade after his death. It fell to Pratt to prepare Cecil's *Life and Remains* for the press; it was

Wilson's lot to preach two noble funeral orations from his pulpit in St. John's on his death. 'Tenderly do I recall all the scenes of my youth when I first came to you as pupil in 1798,' so he wrote to Pratt in 1834; 'and earnestly do I remember the example and advice of Mr Cecil and yourself. I ever trace to that connection under God's blessing the right direction of my mind and studies when I entered College.'[41]

Cecil had none of the robust health and vigour of a man like Newton; his whole life was full of physical suffering and personal affliction. It made him see that though men wish and wish that things were other than they are, the one thing they should do is to lie quietly in the hands of God.[42] He felt that he could name twenty cases wherein he wished that God had done otherwise than He had; but he came to see that had he had his wish, it could only have led to sorrow and mischief.[43] He had rheumatic tendencies of a serious character in his own frail constitution, and for many years he suffered from some form of sciatica. But he carried on his duties without intermission until one Friday evening, in December 1798, when he was seized with an acute attack of pain. His condition was thought dangerous and he was forbidden to preach while the symptoms prevailed. But he determined to keep a Sunday morning engagement for which he had been advertised, and he gave out as his text the last verse but one in the last book of the Bible. Not more than five minutes had passed before all could see that he was in extreme pain, but he struggled on for twenty minutes all told. Then he dismissed his flock with that Benediction which brings the Bible to a close. Many who heard him that morning thought that they would never listen to his voice again. He was confined to bed throughout the long winter months which ensued, but his heart was comforted in the school of affliction. 'I have learnt more within these curtains', he said, 'than from all the books I ever read.'[44] His friends were careful to note and treasure up the gracious sayings which he let fall in the course of this long illness, and they disclose far more of his inner life than outward records could be made to depict. Newton came to see him on the Monday and heard him say: 'It is consistent neither with reason nor religion to oppose sufferings to the love of God, for whom the Lord loveth, He chasteneth, and scourgeth every son whom He receiveth.'[45] John Venn called to see him the same evening and him he told: 'I am not afraid to die, but I am afraid to be worn out by pain; nature shrinks at this prospect.'[46] He felt that he had been too much occupied in preparing to live, and too little in living; that he had read too much for mental pleasure, and too little for his work's sake. He was thankful that he had learnt in some degree to take pleasure in his infirmities, though he could not speak so when his pain was extreme; then he was glad if he could just bear it, and not murmur, and he could say that no murmur had as yet risen in his heart. He knew that the spirit of prayer did not come of its own accord in time of affliction, but he could not do without it: 'If this be not poured out upon man', he said, 'he will like a wounded beast skulk to his den and growl there.'[47] But so far from growling was he that his prayer went up night and day: 'O Lord! let me have anything but Thy frown, and anything with Thy smile!'[48] That smile shone down indeed, and he could tell his friends: 'I have great peace—not a ruffled breeze night nor day—and this is all grounded on the doctrine of Jesus Christ. Give up that, and I should have no sleep tonight.'[49] Very slowly his health in some measure returned and God was pleased to add twelve more years to his life. He took up his duties once more in St. John's, but he was henceforth obliged to sit down in order to preach with ease. Sleepless nights left him weak and far from well, and none of his hearers ever knew the pain which each new morning forced him to bear. 'I am thankful for five minutes' freedom from suffering,' he once remarked; 'how forgetful have I been of fifty years of tolerable ease!'[50] Pain was like a dagger thrust deep into his side, or a worm at the root of his constitution, but no word of complaint ever seemed to fall from his lips.[51] He was wonderfully upheld in the pulpit, and men were made to feel that his sufferings were not in vain. He acquired a keener insight for the vanity of all earthly affairs, so that he could strip off the mask of the world that is to let others see its poverty and emptiness; he attained a higher foresight for the dignity of all divine events, so that he could draw back the veil of the world to come to let others see its plenitude and majesty. It gave him a criterion of new value informing his judgment of men; he watched them in the school of affliction. 'I consider how a man comes out of the furnace,' he said; 'gold will lie for a month in the furnace without losing a grain.'[52] It gave him a criterion of new wonder in forming his judgment of God: 'God is omniscient as well as omnipotent,' he said; 'and omniscience may see reason to withhold what omnipotence could bestow.'[53]

This stern illness made it clear that he would have to give up his lecture at Spitalfields when the current term of three years expired; but he believed that 'God denies a Christian nothing, but with a design to give him something better.'[54] Thus, in 1800, Samuel Thornton made him the offer of two small livings at Chobham and Bisley, with a view to giving him some respite from his heavy duties at Bedford Row. He met this proposal at first with a decided and repeated refusal, but at length he gave in to the earnest persuasion of his friends. Chobham was a pleasant agricultural village in Surrey, and Bisley was a retired hamlet three miles away. It was only two years since the illness which had threatened his life, and his health was still much broken; but he went down at once on a visit to his two new centres and bent all the powers of his mind towards the care of a new flock. He found all in disorder and the people sunk in ignorance and immorality. They were rude and irreverent, and religion was neither valued nor understood. There were but few hearers in church, and the Sabbath was a day of sport and recreation. On his first visit to Chobham he was sitting in the vestry prior to the service and was so pained by the noise and uproar from the gallery that he burst into tears. His heart was full of the prophet's grief as he cried: 'Can these bones live?' (Ezek. 37: 3). But the bones did but wait the breath of life and all was soon transformed. He engaged a curate all the year round, but he arranged to take the three summer months himself. There was no house where he could live in a private manner and he was forced to rent a room in the village. He set up two extra lectures on each Sunday and one week-day evening, and soon won over the farmers of the parish by his disinterested arrangements in the matter of tithes. He made his style conform to the capacity of his hearers and soon gathered two large and attentive congregations. It was not long before it could be said, as of Zion in olden times: 'This and that man was born in her' (Ps. 87: 5).

His first curate was Hugh Pearson, whom he engaged in 1800 and who was destined to become Dean of Salisbury; his next curate was Daniel Wilson, whom he engaged in 1801 and who was destined to become Bishop of Calcutta. Cecil used to pay an occasional visit to them apart from the summer months, and he seemed to find welcome relief in these short trips to his Surrey livings. But he often rode home racked with pain, pale, speechless, and emaciated; he would throw himself down on the sofa, with his face buried in his hands. Then the paroxysm of pain would pass and he would rise in an instant to engage in conversation with his customary cheerfulness and dignity.[55] In his very first year he received rare encouragement, for it was in 1800 that the well-known Arthur Young chanced to spend the night at Chobham Inn one Saturday evening. His *Travels in France* had been published on the eve of the Revolution, and he was now Secretary to the Board of Agriculture. He heard Cecil preach next morning from the Book of Jeremiah, and he was so impressed by his telling appeals and his tender pathos that he walked the three miles to hear him at Bisley the same afternoon. He then heard him preach from the Parable of the Ten Virgins and, like the whole body of those rustic hearers, he listened with breathless awe from the first moment when he announced his text: 'The door was shut' (Matt. 25: 10). It led Arthur Young to seek an interview with the preacher, and the evening was spent by the two in animated conversation. The best results ensued, and the Name of Christ from that time forward shed a calm and steady light on his path to the end of the way. Cecil had won his man because he had learnt to speak the truth in love, and it reminds us of his own pointed remark:

> The love of some men is all milk and mildness; there is so much delicacy, and so much fastidiousness. They touch with such tenderness; and if the patient shrinks, they will touch no more. The Gospel is sometimes preached in this way till all the people agree with the preacher; he gives no offence, and he does no good.[56]

Cecil's hand was tender, but he did not fear to use the lance and scalpel to probe the soul and bring the sinner to the feet of Christ. Wilson recalled those Chobham days long years after, during his brief visit to England in July 1846: 'I have once more been permitted to preach in Mr Cecil's pulpit at Chobham after forty-five years from my first coming here as Curate. Blessed be God for what He has done in this parish by Mr Cecil and the two Jerrams!'[57]

Cecil had all the gifts of intellect and all the powers of utterance that a city preacher could most wish to possess, and his talents were linked with the highest regard for the credit of his office. 'The ministry is a grand and holy affair', he said, 'and it should find in us a simple habit of spirit, and a holy but humble indifference to all consequences.'[58] He was a painstaking minister and an accomplished orator, and he adorned the pulpit with gems of sane thinking in words of great beauty. There was an unusual strain in his make-up which made all that he thought or did altogether his own; he could hardly preach a single sermon without a touch of novelty as well as dignity. His cast of mind, his style of speech, his appearance and utterance in the pulpit, were all so out of the ordinary, yet at the same time so appropriate that they lent a charm and fascination to his preaching which no one else could hope to imitate. Few men of his age were more distinguished for a large fund of original thought combined with a firm grasp of apostolic truth. His skill in arresting attention and convincing the intellect, his power in arousing conscience and commanding the feelings, were unrivalled in his own day. He would appear in the pulpit with animated features and, sitting or standing, would deliver his soul with great variety of expression. He was graceful in manner, forceful in action, and almost dogmatic in his tone of moral authority; but this tone of authority was softened by a note of urbanity, by the unction and the tender feeling which rose from the springs of personal affliction. He was a close student of all human nature, and this was a large part of his secret; he was careful not to weary, and he was a master in the art of apt and telling illustration. He knew how to adapt himself to the tastes and feelings of his congregation and would choose a fresh text four and five times a day rather than preach the same sermon to new hearers for whom it had not been prepared.

He had an uncommon flair for arresting attention and then retaining interest. 'What is the end of exciting attention', he would ask, 'if there is nothing deserving attention?'[59] Sometimes one brief sentence, even a word, sufficed to rivet every eye and every ear; sometimes the most startling methods were called into service to force those to hear who were not wont to listen. 'If a man cannot so feel and think as to bend all subjects naturally and gracefully to Christ', he said, 'he must seek his remedy in selecting such as are more Evangelical.'[60] He took endless pains with his art, and he also tried to help his younger brethren in the kindest manner. Thus he tried to correct Wilson's loud voice, and the faults of vehement action which threatened to become habitual;[61] and he tried to improve Martyn's soft speech, and the want of expressive manner which threatened to make him unimpressive.[62] Pratt's son summed up his gifts as a preacher in striking terms in his edition of the *Notes of the Eclectic*:

> There is no doubt that amongst a group of these good men, Mr Cecil stood pre-eminent as a preacher capable of commanding the attention of a congregation, and producing upon them a corresponding effect....All his effort in the pulpit was directed first to engage attention, and then repay it. His most striking sermons were generally those which he

> preached from very short texts, such as: My soul hangeth on Thee, All my fresh springs are in thee.…In these sermons the whole sermon had probably struck him at once, and what comes in this way is generally found to be more natural and forcible than what the mind is obliged to excogitate by its own laborious efforts.[63]

Daniel Wilson summed up his qualities as an orator with glowing praise in his two magnificent funeral sermons:

> When his subjects were of the grander order and his powers were on the full stretch, there was a comprehension of mind, a native dignity, a sublimity of conception, a richness and fertility of imagery which captivated and astonished his audience. No one can form an adequate notion of his powers as a public speaker from his printed sermons. Like every true orator, the soul of his discourses lay in a large degree in that pathos, that touch of nature, that surprising originality, that sublimity and grandeur of expression, which must considerably evaporate with the affections which produced them. I have on the whole no fear of affirming …that he was not merely one of the most eminent preachers of his day, but one of a totally different order from others—a completely original preacher.[64]

Cecil published but few of his sermons, though his notes were prepared for the press by the hands of friends after his death; they were deemed a kind of model for pulpit work, but they lack the fire and lustre of a personal utterance. In 1785 he published a collection of psalms, which were chosen in line with his own taste and that of his congregation. It was very conservative in tone and not till the seventh edition were hymns allowed a place beside the psalms. But the psalms were culled from the best versions available, and there were selections from men like John Milton and Addison. It was a beautiful collection and it deserved the vogue it long enjoyed. His *House of Mourning* was much valued as a manual of devotion for the bereaved, and his *Life of Newton* is still valuable as a completion of Newton's own Narrative. But he published nothing that would win him literary fame, though he had a well-deserved reputation as an intellectual light. The fact was that he had many imperfect manuscripts which might have been sent to the press, but feeble health and public toils meant that they were never polished and never finished. During his last illness they were all consigned to the flames, and the only one to escape was a small manuscript of his sayings which his wife had preserved. Almost all that we know of him we owe to the notes and recollections of friends, and it was Pratt who made it his special task to gather up his *Remains*. Pratt was so struck with the original flavour of his remarks, in the course of many conversations, that he began to note them down and at length gave them to the world. Cecil can still best be studied in the pages compiled by Pratt's labour of love. Here are all the hall-marks of a scholarly mind and a liberal heart; here are all the keynotes of a developed faith and a practical life. They are suffused with the warmth of human kindness; they are enriched with a wealth of honest wisdom. Brief as they are, they are nevertheless a real contribution to Evangelical literature.

It is clear that Cecil was a conversationalist of the highest order and his sayings clung like proverbs once they came to be known. The lives of men like Scott and Wilson show how often he was quoted among his friends. Would we see his felicity in the use of picture language? We may hear him describe the growth of a soul in humility: 'The blade shoots up boldly, and the young ear keeps erect with confidence; but the full corn in the ear inclines itself towards the earth, not because it is feebler, but because it is matured.'[65] Would we try his accuracy in the art of human judgment? We may watch him dissect the thoughts of the heart from experience: 'Man seems formed to be a hero in suffering, not a hero in action. The hero of the world is the man that makes a bustle...But what is the real labour of this man, compared with that of a silent sufferer?'[66] How well he understood the yearnings of unsatisfied desire! He could sum it up with penetrating simplicity: 'We often want to know too much, and too soon; we want the light of tomorrow, but it will not come till tomorrow. And then a slight turn perhaps will throw such light on our path that we shall be astonished we saw not our way before.'[67] How well he understood the feelings of disappointed conflict! He could state it all with remarkable analysis: 'All of us live to make discoveries of the evils of the heart, not of its virtues; all our new knowledge of human nature is occupied with its evil.'[68] He could speak plainly enough on the way of evil: 'The approaches of sin are like the conduct of Jael; it brings butter in a lordly dish! But when it has fascinated and lulled the victim, the nail and the hammer are behind!'[69] He could speak sharply enough on the end of evil: 'He who like Samson…lays his head in the lap of temptation will rarely rise again as he lay down. He may say, I will go out as at other times and shake myself; but he wists not that the Lord has departed from him.'[70] All this helps to explain the terms in which Wilson wrote to Cecil's daughter from his far-off See in May 1852:

> I received a few days since my eight copies of your venerable Father's *Thoughts*, and I shall be glad of twelve more copies being sent for me. The work is invaluable. The intertwining of the mysteries of Christ with the feelings and practice of daily life is unequalled. I know nothing like it in the compass of Theology.[71]

St. John's, Bedford Row, and the Eclectic Society were the natural rendezvous for friends of the Evangelical cause whose work lay in the country, but who came, from time to time, to London. This brought Cecil into close touch with some of his greatest contemporaries, and it is of no slight interest to trace such connections. Thus, the first six months of the year 1805 brought Henry Martyn to London on no less than three occasions, preparatory to his departure for India. On his first visit he tells us briefly in his journal: 'January 11th 1805; we called on Mr Cecil, with whose conversation I was much struck and edified.'[72] His next visit was in the month of March, and there is another brief record: 'March 10th: Walked to St. John's Chapel, Bedford Row; Mr Cecil preached very well on Jonah.'[73] Then, in

April, he left Cambridge and came up to London to wait for the sailing of his convoy. Nearly three months were spent in the city before he did of length embark, and he found a constant source of delight in Cecil's preaching and conversation. On April 23 he called on Cecil and received some advice on how to write to good effect; on April 28 he had tea with Cecil and was charmed with the conversation which seemed to be his common table talk. His brief remark is itself a comment on the kind of renown Cecil had won among his friends: 'He was very striking, as usual, in his observations.'[74] That night he read prayers for Cecil who preached on the godly sorrow which leads to repentance: 'It was a most able sermon, powerfully engaged the attention,' Martyn observed; and then he adds: 'And yet I cannot say my feelings are devoutly affected by this sort of preaching.'[75]

Martyn, in the Cambridge tradition of sermon-making, could not at once give his heart to Cecil in the Oxford tradition of pulpit preaching. On May 15 he read prayers for Cecil again and heard him preach in a most striking manner on Rev. 3: 21: 'I was encouraged to determine to fight,' he wrote; 'but oh! what pride, and hardness of heart, and forgetfulness of God, have I to recollect this day!'[76] On May 19 he heard Cecil again, on 1 Thess. 3: 18, and found himself moved to tears as he saw the bond that knit the pastor to his flock, feeling that God had not caused any such connection to exist between him and his people.[77] Two days later Cecil came to see him and spoke with his wonted vigour on the work of the ministry, leaving him astonished and confounded at not being swallowed up in his sacred calling.[78] On June 3 he went to the Eclectic, where they discussed the state of the nation. There were nine clergy present as well as himself, but he comments only on one: 'Mr Cecil spoke admirably!'[79] He dined three times with him in the next two weeks and received wise advice both on his pulpit address and on his private affairs. On June 17 he was again at the Eclectic, when they discussed the measure and means of happiness. Again he passed over all the speakers in silence except one: 'Mr Cecil spoke very sensibly!'[80] On June 23 he heard Cecil preach on the Shepherd Psalm, and on June 24 he tells us that Cecil took great pains to correct his own inanimate style of delivery. 'Sir,' said Cecil, 'it is cupola painting, not miniature, that must be the aim of a man that harangues a multitude!'[81] On July 7 he was allowed to preach a farewell sermon from St. John's pulpit to a large and attentive congregation. He drank tea with Cecil for the last time when the service came to an end, and on July 8 he left London in the early morning on his way to Portsmouth by coach. Cecil had watched over him for three short months in London as Charles Simeon had done in Cambridge, and he followed him with a sense of deep fatherly affection in the few years which still remained.

But perhaps the greatest of all Cecil's contemporaries in the Evangelical world was Charles Simeon, his junior by only eleven years. Simeon must have heard of Cecil early in his Cambridge life from good old Henry Venn, who in April 1784 had written of 'the apostolical spirit, and abilities, and great grace, of Mr Cecil'.[82] Simeon was a country member of the Eclectic from the 'eighties onwards, and took an active part in the meetings when he was in London. But his visits to the city were few in number and brief in duration, and it was not until 1807 that he spent any length of time with his friends in London. Then an illness obliged him to leave his work in Cambridge for a long rest and he spent some weeks in London two years after Henry Martyn's brief sojourn there. He had known Cecil for at least twenty years, but had seldom heard him preach before this visit. He was now of necessity silent himself and he became one of Cecil's constant hearers in St. John's, Bedford Row. Thus, his journal notes have preserved some valuable observations which help to throw a broad beam of light on both men. On March 8 he notes: 'In the evening, Mr Cecil preached on Matthew xiii, four last verses. He showed that however excellent the truth was, and however confirmed by miracles, pride, prejudice, and unbelief would counteract it. He observed that there was a Privy Council at which Pride presided, and Prejudice and Unbelief were members; Truth was arraigned at their bar, and condemned.'[83] The next day he dined with Cecil and then went to the Eclectic, where they discussed the proper boundaries of typical interpretation. Cecil and Simeon were at one in their firm belief that all typology should be treated with great caution, lest fancy should run away with reason.

The next Sunday, March 15, he was in St. John's twice, and he tells us:

> Mr Cecil preached with considerable animation on Zaccheus, Luke 19: 4–5. In the evening, I heard Mr Cecil again, on Psalm 4: 3. On the whole, the effect of Mr Cecil's sermons seems to be to strike the imagination, and to please. There is much point, but no flow. He wounds with an arrow; but does not close and wrestle with men, or draw them by persuasive arguments. I think some other preachers on the whole more likely to convert souls, but few more likely to instruct and please. I was remarkably alive and attentive at both times, so as almost to have lost my wonted stupidity.[84]

Simeon's hopes were thus raised as it were in advance as the next Sabbath drew near, and he wrote on the morning of March 22: 'I am now going to Mr Cecil's church…and I hope I shall meet my God there.'[85] Few men were more thoroughly qualified to judge of the value of his preaching, for Simeon had made the whole subject his grand study for years. Thus, on April 5, he records his thoughts again, and concludes with italics: 'At Mr Cecil's church, I was not so devout in the prayers as I sometimes am, nor was I much impressed with the sermon; but I find that the more I hear Mr Cecil, the more I like him!'[86] Simeon found in Cecil a man who shared his own views of the great controversy of the age to a remarkable degree. Cecil loved to insist that the right way to interpret Scripture is to take it as we find it and not to try to force it into any particular system. He would not have a man clip or curtail any passage, whether it spoke the language of the Calvinist or of the Arminian; if God has been pleased thus to state the truth, we ought to go all the way with it in its full and free meaning.[87] He held, like Simeon, that all extremes are open to error: 'The reverse of error is not truth, but error,' he said; 'truth lies between these extremes.'[88] Cecil laboured to do in London what Simeon laboured to do in Cambridge, and these few weeks in which they met at close quarters were weeks of great value for both; but Cecil's life had only three years to run, while Simeon was to live and work for thirty years.

Richard Cecil does not stand out on the stage of history in the same bold relief as some of his great contemporaries, and it is less easy to paint a true portrait of the man and minister. He was like James Hervey in the delicate health which held him back from taking so active a part as his friends in the great movements of the day; but while Hervey gave time and talent to literary toil, Cecil burnt all his manuscripts. He was like John Fletcher in the scholarly tastes which gave tone to all his thought and preaching; but while Fletcher was tucked away in the rural cure of Madeley, Cecil stood in the heart of London. He threw the weight of his support behind all good causes and did all that he could to aid his friends in their philanthropic activities; but his own distinctive part in the great spiritual movement of the age was in a wider channel, and his contribution was made in a way which others could not imitate. Samuel Wilberforce, who had often heard him at Bedford Row, described him as 'the one clerical genius of his party'.[89] This is without doubt an overstatement which fails to give proper credit to some of his fellow Evangelicals, but it serves to remind us of certain aspects which were salient in his character. Cecil was the most cultured and refined of all the Evangelical leaders in London at the turn of the century; social birth and breeding were linked with mental gifts and training which qualified him to represent the Evangelical cause with great success in the Metropolis of all England. On many points, indeed, he held wider and far more liberal views than were at all common either in his own party or in the Church at large. His friends must have heard with no mild surprise what he had to say on some themes, such as the width of God's mercy towards the heathen,[90] or the value of the *via media* in doctrine.[91] But his views of truth were clarified with the passage of time, and grew still more vivid in the last days of his final illness.[92]

He was always a strict Churchman and would not break through the order and discipline of the Church to gain his own ends; but he had no doubt that an Evangelical ministry was the surest road to success in winning souls.[93] 'Many people labour to make the narrow way wider,' he used to say; 'they may dig a path into the broad way, but the way to life must remain a narrow way to the end.'[94] He toiled hard to make St. John's a worthy centre of light and influence, for no man on earth in his judgment could be so pernicious a drone as an idle clergyman; [95] and the secret spring of all his labours lay in a life of prayer which for him was a matter of habit rather than of rapture.[96] 'I have a favourite walk of twenty steps in my study and chamber,' he once declared; 'that walk is my oratory.'[97] Two old portraits hung on the walls of his study, one of the martyr Bradford, one of the Scottish Leighton; and they never failed to speak to his heart of what true faith and holiness are.[98] He had learnt that to school the heart is the grand means of personal religion,[99] and he knew that his strength lay in a thoroughly humbled and dependent spirit.[100] His friends were proud of his piety and character, as they were proud of his dignity and scholarship; grace and gifts were combined in his life to adorn the Gospel of the great God and our Saviour, Jesus Christ. Gentle and cultured in tone and temper, modest and brilliant in thought and action, earnest and striking in pulpit delivery, pungent and sparkling in private conversation, a man who won the secret of faith and patience from a life full of pain and distress, he served his age in a way which no one else could have done and left his mark on some who were to stand in the first rank of the Evangelical succession.

In 1807 Cecil suffered a slight paralytic stroke, but was not disabled from his work in the ministry; but on March 2, 1808, less than three months after Newton's death, he had a second seizure which deprived him altogether of the use of one side of his body and brought all his public activities to a final standstill.

He spent some months at Bath, and then, in September 1808, he went on to stay at Clifton in the home of a friend whom God brought to his aid. Towards the close of the year he wrote to Wilson, who thus retailed it to his friend Pearson: 'Mr Cecil sent for me to Clifton, and urged me much to take St. John's as his Curate. I then agreed that in the course of two or three years, if God should please, I would yield to his wishes.'[101] He left Clifton with this in mind, but thought little further of the affair. But in March 1809 Cecil's health began to decline still more seriously and he journeyed slowly back to London. His shattered nerves could not stand the summer heat, and in May he moved to the home of a friend in Tunbridge Wells. But this long-continued illness had a sorry effect on his chapel; the congregation was growing restless and the income was much reduced. This led him to write once more to Wilson, who thus tells the story:

> A letter from him reached me...to state that his health was very rapidly declining, that things were falling to pieces at the chapel, and to urge me to take it wholly as minister whilst his life remained to him, and the power to consign it legally. I was seized with the utmost consternation, and...hurried to town to weigh the summons. I found Mr Cecil too far gone to be capable of giving advice, but his mind was fixed on me as his successor...And I left London on Saturday virtually minister of St. John's.[102]

Thus, in October 1809, an arrangement was made to secure two hundred guineas a year to Cecil and his family, and Wilson became minister-in-charge in succession to his friend and father in the faith.

In the same month Cecil returned to London, and in April 1810 he took a house at Hampstead. In 1798, though racked with pain, his mind retained its full vigour; but from 1808 his mind was no less sick than his body.

> The energy, and decision, and grandeur of his natural powers gradually gave way, and a morbid feebleness succeeded; yet even in this afflicting state, with his body on one side almost

> lifeless, his organs of speech impaired, and his judgment weakened, the spiritual dispositions of his heart displayed themselves in a very remarkable manner. He appeared great in the ruins of nature, and...the habit of grace which had been forming in his mind for thirty or forty years shone through the cloud'[103]

He spent his whole time in reading Scripture and one or two trusted divines like Leighton and Gurnall; and he said that he had never seen so clearly the truth of the doctrines he had striven to preach. His wife found texts in his Bible after his death which he had marked with a trembling left hand: 'R.C. Amen!'[104] As death drew near, his one topic was Christ, and his long and gracious habits of prayer remained like the light at evening. His mental faculties were in a state of slow decay, but Wilson found in him such 'a resignation, a tranquillity, a ripeness of grace, a calm and holy repose on the bosom of the Saviour...that there appeared nothing left for grace to do.'[105] Shortly before the end he told Wilson with unforgettable solemnity: 'I know myself to be a wretched, worthless sinner, having nothing in myself but poverty and sin; I know Jesus Christ to be a glorious and almighty Saviour...and I cast myself entirely on Him.'[106] Later on he asked one of his family to write down his dying statement: 'None but Christ! None but Christ! said Lambert, dying at a stake: the same, in dying circumstances, with his whole heart, saith Richard Cecil.'[107] The name was signed with his left hand in a manner hardly legible through infirmity. But despite the inroads of disease on mind and intellect, which eclipsed his comforts and depressed his feelings, his wife and friends saw that he seemed to grow riper for glory as he travelled nearer the grave; riper in his child-like simplicity, in his utter humility, in his self-abasement, in his exaltation of Christ as All in all. At length, on August 15, 1810, at the age of sixty-one, his life so full of physical pain, so rich in heavenly thought, so well redeemed by loving labour and noble friendship, fell like a shock of corn in its season, and was gathered up in the arms of the Eternal for His garners on high.

Bibliography

Works by The Rev. Richard Cecil

Sermons, edited by the Rev. Josiah Pratt (1839).

Original Thoughts on Various Passages of Scripture, edited by Miss Catherine Cecil (1848).

Biographies Of Richard Cecil And Other Works Quoted

Josiah Pratt, *The Life and Remains of the Rev. Richard Cecil* (1854)

M. Seeley, *The Later Evangelical Fathers* (1913).

J. H. Overton and F. Reiton, *A History of the English Church in the 18th Century* (1806).

Robert Isaac and Samuel Wilberforce, *The Life of William Wilberforce* (1838).

Josiah Bull, *John Newton of Olney and St. Mary Woolnoth* (2nd Ed.).

William Carus, *Memoirs of the Life of the Rev. Charles Simeon* (1847).

Samuel Wilberforce, *Journals and Letters of the Rev. Henry Martyn* (1837).

Josiah Bateman, *The Life of Daniel Wilson* (1860).

Eugene Stock, *The History of the Church Missionary Society*, Vols. I-III (1899).

5

Daniel Wilson
1778–1858

Daniel Wilson was born in Church Street, Spitalfields, on July 2, 1778, the eldest son of a well-to-do silk merchant and manufacturer. He was delicate as a child and was brought up under a nurse in the country. But this early weakness passed right away after some years and he grew in health and vigour with buoyant spirits and handsome features. At the age of seven he was sent to a small school at Eltham in Kent; then, at the age of ten, he was placed under the Rev. John Eyre at Hackney. But his schooling came to an end in June 1792, when he was no more than thirteen years old and, six months later, he joined his uncle's warehouse for a seven years' apprenticeship. His hours of work were from six in the morning to eight in the evening, for the social reforms of Lord Shaftesbury's day were still in the womb of the future. But he always snatched an hour or two before he fell asleep at night for the study of French and Latin, or for English composition. His scrapbooks were written in the clearest hand as if they had been prepared for the press, and they all disclose a love of literature and a skill in composition which are most uncommon in such circumstances. It was said in after years that he used to read in boyhood for recreation, in manhood for information, and in old age for relaxation; but it was the habit of close study after a long day's work when he was only in his teens which made him a student of new authors and large volumes to the end of his life. His desk in the warehouse did not seem to offer much of a field for the cultivation of literary tastes; but the ore would crop out.

Thus the world seemed to lie before his eyes, a world of wealth and interest; he had but to tread in the track which his father had marked out for him, and stores of wealth lay at his feet. He was young and vigorous, strong and resolute, with great energy and great decision of intellect and character, and he was sure to take the lead either for good or ill. He came from a godly home where the light of Revival had shone for more than one generation, for his mother's father had been one of Whitefield's friends and trustees. His own parents shared their Sundays between church and chapel, but his uncle was a strict and faithful churchman, who went to hear men like William Romaine and Richard Cecil, Thomas Scott and Basil Woodd. His own early tutor and lifelong friend, the Rev. John Eyre, had been Cecil's curate at Lewes in 1780, and was a devoted adherent of the Evangelical Movement. But as a boy Wilson was far from God and deep in sin. 'I was constantly acting against a better knowledge,' he wrote in 1796; 'but I loved my sins, and could not bear to part with them.'[1] He was guilty of marked irreverence in church and posed as a sceptic before his friends; he lived altogether without prayer and seldom read his Bible. He took refuge in a false view of the Gospel and liked to think that it was out of his own power to help himself. Thus he hushed his conscience with the thought that he had done all that he could do, and he remained quiet and at ease as the willing slave of sin and Satan. He was impetuous in temper, imperious in passion, and his friends were more or less like-minded. Such was the natural character of one who stood on the threshold of life with all the lure of wealth and fortune before him. But then the Grace of God began to work upon this character, and a conflict ensued which was to end in an unqualified self-surrender to the Lord Christ.

On the evening of March 9, 1796, he was warmly engaged in denying man's moral responsibility in view of God's absolute sovereignty, and in asserting the folly of all human exertion if grace be irresistible. A friend ventured on the reply that God had not only chosen the end, but had also fixed the means. Wilson then said that he had none of those feelings towards God which He required and approved. 'Well, then,' his friend replied, 'pray for the feelings.'[2] He carried it off with a joke, but the verbal shaft had struck home. Thinking that he would still say that he had done all he could, he knelt down that night to pray for the right kind of feelings. All the feelings for which he prayed at once awoke to life and action; he was thrown into consternation, and he grew restless and uneasy about his soul. He was in great confusion, but he did not try to hide his anxiety. There was none of that concealment or postponement which is so common and so hurtful to the early growth of a soul. He lost all interest in the world of business and became quite another man in his search for the one pearl of great price. Three days later, on March 11, he wrote to Eyre with a sorrowful confession of his inward darkness: 'When I rise from my knees and open the sacred Word of God, I endeavour to ejaculate a petition that God would open my eyes to understand His truth; ...but alas! I find it a dead letter.'[3] On April 20 he had an interview with John Newton at St. Mary Woolnoth, and heard him inculcate the salutary lesson of waiting patiently upon the Lord. 'The words of Mr Newton, that unbelief is a great sin and should be prayed against as such, continually recur to my mind,' he told his mother a few days later; 'alas! my heart is unbelieving and hard, but I hope I endeavour to pray to the great Redeemer to give me a believing heart.'[4]

His conscience grew very sensitive to each new change in the realm of his soul, but long months were to wear away before he passed out of darkness into light. No man could have been less like a hypocrite in his dealings with God from the first day of his spiritual awakening, but the work of grace was to be slow and thorough. Day after day he left the warehouse and went down into the cellar to pour out his heart in a prayer of anguish that if God would not deliver him from the guilt and condemnation of sin hereafter, He would at least deliver him from its power in the present so that it should not make him wretched in this world as well as in the world to come. [5] Night after night he sat up long after his cousin had fallen asleep, not in common studies as of old, but to pore over God's Word or to kneel in long-continued prayer. The year came to a close and the new year grew old while the shadows still hung over his soul; but rest of heart came at length like morning light spread out upon the mountain-tops in his use of God's appointed ordinance. There is no clear account of the final steps which led to this change, but on October 1, 1797, he knelt for the first time before the Lord's Table to share in the memorial feast of redeeming love. 'I have nothing but mercy to tell you of,' he wrote next day to his mother; 'Oh! that my heart was but melted with love and gratitude to my dear Redeemer for such rich grace as He is continually showering upon my soul!'[6] And on October 4, he told John Eyre: 'To you I confess it, though it ought perhaps to be a cause for shame, that I have felt great desires to do anything to spread the Name of Jesus; and that I have even wished, if it were the Lord's will, to go as a missionary to heathen lands.'[7] Thus the first flush of peace and joy found vent in a desire which was to be fulfilled thirty-five years later when, in October 1832, he stood on the banks of the Hooghly as the Bishop of Calcutta.

There was perhaps something unusual in the spiritual experience of Daniel Wilson; something quite out of the common in the depth of his penitential sorrow and his self-abasement, as well as in the long lapse of eighteen months before he found pardon and peace. But there was a purpose in it all, for his was a life marked out for God. We can still trace the inner history of his soul in his private journal and his many letters. The first entry in his journal was made on December 26, 1797, and it was kept up in minute shorthand until June 13, 1801. It was kept in Latin, but was less continuous from August 1801 to September 1807, but then there was a long blank for twenty-three years until 1830. It was resumed in French from January 12, 1830, until his departure for India in June 1832; and then it was carried on in English to the close of his life. The most remarkable fact about his letters was the careful way in which his friends preserved them. They were numbered by the hundred and these were not merely single letters, but whole series, each of which ran to tens or scores. These letters were treasured up by his friends long before his name grew famous, and that surely goes to prove that there was always a tone of greatness in the man. Many extracts from his journal and these letters have been preserved in the biography which was prepared at the hands of his son-in-law, and they provide us with the most valuable material for a study of the interior life of his soul. They take up the story right from the time when he first found peace with God, and they prove that he was a man with gifts of wisdom and with breadth of vision from the very outset of his career.

His first desire for the work of the ministry found voice in the month of his conversion. He strove to repress the thought at first as a new form of the pride which he had come to loathe, but he could not until he had made it known. 'On Sunday night, October 15,' he told John Eyre, 'my soul was exceedingly drawn out in earnest prayer for direction.'[8] But his father would not hear of the idea; it crossed all the plans which he had formed. Delay thus became a duty, and he agreed to let the whole matter wait for twelve months; but he felt that God had made his call as clear as though it had been traced on his soul with a sunbeam. 'I feel all the desires of my soul continually and increasingly drawn out towards this work,' he wrote; 'and my soul yearns over the vast numbers of my poor fellow-sinners who never heard of Jesus nor of the life which is in Him.'[9] The year came to a close with the lesson that his strength was to sit still; then God began to work on his behalf and at once all wills were changed and all difficulties removed. In March 1798, his father arranged for him to interview Richard Cecil of St. John's, Bedford Row, and the result was that Cecil felt quite convinced that his call was of God. Then his father gave the desired consent for him to give up his business career and to prepare himself for St. Edmund Hall at Oxford. Thus he left the warehouse on May 1 and went to reside with Pratt as a private pupil until the university term began. No wiser or better guide could have been found, and he never ceased to cherish him as friend and teacher. 'To no one was I more attached', he declared in his charge of 1845 after Pratt's death, 'than to him who was spared to me and to the church the longest—the Rev. Josiah Pratt—my honoured brother.'[10] Six brief months with Pratt passed quickly away and, in November 1798, he took up his residence as an undergraduate in Pratt's Alma Mater, St. Edmund Hall.

Oxford was in low water at the close of the eighteenth century; academic life and spiritual truth were at the worst ebb. Students who read hard were few and far between, while those who lived for Christ were marked men. St. Edmund Hall was the recognized centre of such Evangelical life as there was, but no Charles Simeon had yet appeared to hold the flag aloft in one of the city churches. Evangelical truth was looked upon as 'the rather mysterious religion of Teddy Hall', [11] while Simeon's name had already begun to attract most of the keen men to Cambridge. Matters were not helped by the fact that St. Edmund was the weakest hall in Oxford; it had never fully recovered from the expulsion of six of its students on religious grounds in March 1768. It had yet to regain its full prestige in Oxford life, for it was still better known for piety rather than for learning. Nevertheless, men like Josiah Pratt and William Marsh had proved that even in the nineties Oxford could still produce here and there the finest type of Evangelical life and character. This was in broad outline how things stood at Oxford when Daniel Wilson came up at the age of twenty in 1798. He was handsome in his bearing, reserved in his habits, at a great handicap with regard to classical interests, but no common figure in that Oxonian environment. He found a small group of men from various colleges who met regularly in each other's rooms for Scriptural discussion. He grew apace in his knowledge of the will of God and the ways of man. 'Oh for grace to be humble, watchful, dependent, and simply devoted to the glory of my Divine Lord,' he cried; 'pray for me to be kept at the feet of Jesus, learning His Word and seeking the honour which cometh of Him only.'[12]

He gave himself to his studies with the most determined diligence and quite a tradition grew up round his name for hard work. He was said to have translated the whole of Cicero's Epistles into English and then back into Latin in order to perfect his own style! He took his degree with the highest credit in March 1802, and won the English Prose Essay Prize in 1803; he took his M.A. in 1804, and received his D.D. by Royal Mandate in 1832. He was ordained on September 20, 1801, by the Bishop of Winchester, and went straight from the palace at Farnham to the parish of Chobham. This was a small agricultural village in Surrey, of which Samuel Thornton was the patron and Richard Cecil the rector. Cecil's plan was to spend the three summer months there while his curate worked the parish all the year round. Wilson thus found that he had to preach twice a week, and he began with a sermon on Christ's welcome to all who will but come (John 6: 37). He worked through the parish from end to end, paid a visit to each little mud hut where his people dwelt, and enrolled the name of every parishioner with brief traits of character and short notes of success or failure. He learned how to unite Evangelical truth with Church order in the way which was to make him a link between the past age which had been so apt to divorce them and the new age which tried so hard to combine them. It was a true training ground for the work of the ministry, and it was high praise when Cecil himself dubbed him 'the Apostle Wilson'.[13] On March 9, 1803, he wrote:

> Seven years have passed since the Grace of God came with power to me, who was buried in total darkness. I acknowledge myself to be the vilest of the vile, and I grieve over it. Still the

> Grace of God is exceedingly abundant towards me; I wish to be nothing, and would cleave to Christ only'[14]

It was thus that the Grace of God prepared him for a call to join the staff of St. Edmund Hall and, in January 1804, he went back to Oxford to teach where he himself had once been taught.

In January 1804, he took up his duties as a tutor at Oxford and, in January 1807, he became Vice-Principal of St. Edmund Hall. He took up this post in Oxford as one who stood in the full stream of the Evangelical Revival. Whitefield and Romaine had been household names and lifelong friends in his family circle; Newton and Cecil had been trusted guides and honoured friends in his Christian service. He used to say in his latter years that Scott and Pratt were the two who had done more than all others to mould his intellect and build his character on the sacred pattern of Holy Writ. These were great names in the story of the Evangelical Revival; they include the greatest name of all to have been engraved on the Evangelical escutcheon. No one could doubt that the name of Wilson was in true line with this notable succession, and his call to Oxford seemed to open up a door of useful service comparable to that of Charles Simeon in the sister seat of learning. But Wilson was neither fitted by nature nor suited by office to do for Oxford the work which Simeon had done for Cambridge; he was not the rector of an Oxford church, nor yet the Fellow of an Oxford college. 'I fear Oxford,' he wrote in a Latin letter to a friend just before he left Chobham; 'I tremble to think of its Dons and its duties, and the general tone and colouring of its maxims and opinions.'[15] But he felt that to shrink from the call would prove him faithless, and his sense of duty led him to take up the challenge. He did all that he could in his own sphere at St. Edmund Hall, and his energy never flagged. He was always a hard student and he read everything which had any bearing on the ministry which he had received of the Lord Jesus. His mind was well furnished in private and was bound to overflow in public; and he laid down the great doctrines of the Bible with a forcefulness and clarity which no one could mistake. The Hall increased in numbers and rose in reputation, while it still held fast its distinctive character for piety.

Wilson was revered and admired by his students, and his influence was felt to a certain extent by the whole university. No academic tradition or conventional privilege could silence him when principles were at stake, and he was fearless in his avowal of what was right and true. In January 1810, he was asked to preach before the university, and his printed sermon quickly ran through several editions. The plain doctrine and clear logic, with a ringing appeal to each hearer's conscience, left the crowded congregation in St. Mary's Church in breathless silence. But it was in his own soul that the price was paid and his early fears were at length borne out in sober reality. He wrote in August 1806:

> It would require not merely letters but volumes to tell you all my inward conflicts and anxieties, my soul is sick. I am perplexed and overborne with college and university business. I have wandered from God. You would not believe how weak my mind is, how perturbed not to say hardened, so that I feel no love for sacred things, nor derive any profit from them.[16]

The next year his journal was laid aside, a sad presage of his interrupted development in peace and holiness. He felt that his labours as a tutor were by no means congenial to his own mind, and the passing years left him no doubt that he ought to give himself wholly to the work of a pastoral ministry. 'The gradual decay of vital piety in my own heart', he wrote in 1809, 'is too obvious and too alarming a symptom not to force itself upon my conscience. May God yet spare me for His honour!' [17] At length, after nine years, at the close of 1812, he left St. Edmund Hall, and his Oxford days were over. Eighteen years passed away and then he summed up his feelings in retrospect:

> My time at Oxford was utterly without profit as to my soul. Pride grew more and more, and carnal appetites enchained

> me…These nine years were passed I trust in the path of duty, though amidst struggles, temptations, and frequent estrangements of soul and spirit.'[18]

The one bright spot in these years at Oxford were the Sunday duties which he undertook as curate at Worton. Upper and Lower Worton lay between Banbury and Woodstock, and their united population did not exceed two hundred small farmers. There were two small churches which had fallen into a state of sad neglect, and the congregations had slumped to a bare ten or twelve. Daniel Wilson found his work at Worton a light and pleasant task in each vacation, but it involved a good deal of effort when the Hall was in term. He used to leave Oxford for the sixteen-mile drive to Worton by post-chaise at eight in the morning and he would spend the day between the two churches until the time came to return in the evening. He seemed to throw off all the cares of St. Edmund Hall in the fresh country air, and he found his way with perfect ease to the hearts of his country flock. He preached in an extempore fashion and his sermons were couched in the language familiar to all village listeners. Texts were chosen which would set out the great primary truths of the Gospel, and it was found that they lingered in mind and memory even after a lapse of fifty years. His simple language and stirring appeals, his quiet delivery and deep solemnity, were never forgotten, and they often produced a kind of trembling awe in the conscience of his hearers. There was a progressive harvest from this ministry which we can still trace through his Letters. In July 1804, he observed that his work was not without success; in May 1806, he remarked that there had been fifty-eight at the Lord's Table. 'I hope the Lord is doing something for us,' he wrote, 'and that several are seeking a better country, even a heavenly.'[19]

In 1807, he commenced a mid-week meeting as well as the Sunday worship, and each church was crowded at the time of service. A great and lasting impression was made throughout that part of the county, and crowds began to flock to the Worton churches from more than twenty surrounding villages. The church would be filled long before the bell had rung, and then the schoolroom which opened into the churchyard; they would crowd the windows, and he would speak loudly enough for all to hear. There were no less than one hundred and sixty people on one occasion who knelt together in the Communion service. Such work taught him where his real strength lay and helped him to know whither God was leading him in his ministry. Thus, in 1808, Cecil asked him to come to St. John's, Bedford Row, as his curate, and he agreed to do so as soon as his place in St. Edmund Hall could be filled. Then a letter came which urged him to throw in his lot with St. John's at once and to succeed Cecil while he still had legal power to consign his charge to another. He found Cecil far too ill to offer advice, but with his mind firmly made up. The one difficulty was that his successor-designate for St. Edmund Hall was still an undergraduate; but a solution for this problem was found when he gave a pledge that he would continue to guide and superintend the Hall until this young man could take his Master's degree. Thus, in October 1809, the whole thing was settled and he became the minister of St. John's Chapel on the understanding that he would keep the terms at his old Hall until he was replaced. But the strain of double duties at London and Oxford was great; each of them really required his whole time and thought, and it was with thankful relief that he finally left Oxford to make a new home in London at the close of the year 1812.

St. John's, Bedford Row, had been built as a Chapel of Ease in the reign of Queen Anne as a protest against the institution of Sacheverell to the parish of St. Andrew's, Holborn, and it had been served by men of strong Evangelical views. Wilson was an ideal successor to the long and fruitful ministry of Richard Cecil and all his powers were called into play by the great congregation of nigh on two thousand lawyers and merchants in the heart of London. They came from all parts of the metropolis, and few who had the welfare of true religion at heart failed to worship there at times. Thirty or forty carriages would stand in triple rows round the church doors when the London season was at its height, and every vacant sitting was filled from the moment when the doors were opened. Men like Charles Grant and Henry Thornton, Wilberforce and Macaulay, were among the regular attendants when they were in London, and the very names of these great laymen of the Clapham Sect are still suggestive of singular goodness and beneficence.[20] It was a sphere for which Wilson had rare talents, and his years at St. John's were years of great blessing. Few facts of a religious character were more deeply written on the history of that period than the crowded congregations who came under the spell of his commanding oratory. Before he went to St. John's he had only preached six hundred and forty sermons; but in the fifteen years at Bedford Row he delivered no less than one thousand one hundred and eighty-seven sermons. His regular voice, his natural style, his varied action, his graceful gestures, were the hallmarks of a splendid preacher, and Charles Simeon, who was no mean judge, used to say that he had the congregation at his feet.

No labour, no study was deemed too great in the preparation of his message; he would gather honey for his own hive from all quarters. Only a few notes were taken up into the pulpit, but his mind was clear and his heart was full. He stood as God's servant to do God's work and his power was soon felt by all. He was in earnest at a time when earnest men were still comparatively hard to find; he preached a full Gospel in an age when preachers of the Gospel were few and far between. He was steadfast where many were given to change, and moderate when others ran to extremes. His grave and dignified bearing was a solemn rebuke to the spirit of levity or unbelief, and his impassioned address to conscience was varied with an impressive pathos of appeal.[21] Such was the real secret of his great and ever-growing influence at St. John's; he soon became the most prominent Evangelical in the whole of London. The number of communicants was, as a rule, between three and four hundred, but it increased at times to as many as five hundred. The press was so great that although the words of administration were voiced to the whole rail and not to each private person, only a few minutes elapsed between the end of the morning service and the hour for afternoon worship. When the lease of St. John's was renewed in 1821, two new rows of pews were built all round the front of the galleries. St. John's vestry had been the meeting place of the Eclectic on each alternate Monday ever since its inception in 1783, and he spared no pains to enlarge and enrich its role. St. John's vestry soon became the centre of the London Clerical Education Society which he established in 1816 on the same lines as those at Elland and Bristol, to help young men of promise and piety to prepare for Orders. He brought into being the first real District Visiting Society to aim at the relief of the poor by means of laymen, and this was a novel experiment in the church life of his own day. Here he delivered his great funeral orations on the death of Cecil and then of Scott; here he put forth a constant stream of sermons and pamphlets to defend or promote the Evangelical cause. St. John's Chapel reached the zenith of its long and useful story in the days of Daniel Wilson.

Thus the fifteen years at St. John's were years of ceaseless activity. The last link with Oxford was severed in 1812, and then even the summer months were devoted year after year to the service of the Bible Society or the Church Missionary Society. Not one year passed from 1813 to 1822 in which he did not undertake extensive tours throughout the British Isles to preach or speak on behalf of these Societies at a time when they were struggling to win recognition. His frequent companion on these tours was William Marsh, who declared that the last thing which met his eyes at night and the first thing in the morning was always the sight of Daniel Wilson on his knees.[22] In 1817, he preached the annual sermon for the Church Missionary Society on the first occasion when the service was held in St. Bride's, and it was a remarkably able survey of the world and of missions at work on the field. He worked with Simeon in the campaign to plant the missionary cause for heathen souls in the universities; he worked with Wilberforce in the crusade to drive the mercenary trade in human lives from the British colonies. He was active in controversy when truth was at stake; he was ceaseless in correspondence when friends were in need. But private anxieties and public controversies, literary labours, voluminous letters, preaching duties, constant journeys, and his varied plans of useful service proved at length too great a burden even for his strong and energetic constitution. Moreover, he found that in London no less than at Oxford, the iron would eat into his soul, and a journal entry made in retrospective vein years later serves to disclose his own mature judgment on the vital points at issue: 'My course in London was strangely intermingled with great mercies from God and great miseries from my own evil heart. I can neither record nor realize all the temptations, the back-slidings, the corruptions of heart which have defiled me; it is terrible to think of.'[23]

Towards the close of 1822 his health began to fail and by November he was completely *hors de combat*. He paid a long visit to the Continent in search of health in the early months of 1823 and his return at the end of October was hailed by the congregation at St. John's with great joy. He preached twice in November, but then he was silent once more for many months. All the symptoms of his illness returned in aggravated form and his way back lay near the gates of death. We wish for his Journal to throw some light on all this, but it had long been discontinued; it had long ceased to tell of stern self-examination, of interrupted prayer or consequential pride, of wandering affection or intricate temptation in the realm of his soul. Its very silence seems to be suggestive, and the trial of prolonged illness was the chosen rod that restored the repentance and confession of a contrite spirit. On January 2, 1824, he told his sister that for some time he had drifted from God at heart and that now his earnest desire was to return in humble faith. David's Psalm of profound sorrow for sin was the very language of his own soul, for he had discovered how true and salutary were the effects of trial. He lay awake at night and found the Word of God sweet to his taste. He summed up his feelings at last with peculiar solemnity in the words of the Psalm: 'My soul cleaveth unto the dust; quicken Thou me according to Thy word' (Ps. 119: 25). Thus his spirit was chastened and softened until it was like that of a little child, full of watchful longing to catch hold of each new lesson that would impart some ray of light to his eager soul. There were many alternations between strength and weakness in the months at hand, and progress in the recovery of health was slow indeed. 'I am very poorly,' he wrote after a long interval; 'but my mind is calm, reposing on the blessed will and mercy of God my Saviour.'[24] But his voice had been heard for the last time as the minister of St. John's, for in May 1824, while he was still in search of health, he was called to the cure of souls at Islington.

The parish of Islington contained one church and one Chapel of Ease which had to serve for some thirty thousand people, a very different proposition from the select and attached congregation at Bedford Row. On May 18, he received the appointment and on July 2, he preached his first sermon; but his steps were still feeble and he was forced to retire once more until the month of November. This gave him time to pause and contemplate the whole prospect; then he went forward, strong in the Lord and in the power of His might. He had to face the fact that the Islington seat-holders were all strongly opposed to the advent of an Evangelical; they had learnt to regard the Church as their private chapel and the vicar as their private chaplain, and they felt that their rights had been infringed by the appointment of a man like Daniel Wilson. It required no little tact to introduce a new regime and yet not to lose all the old congregation; but that was his first task and he carried it through. The whole parish was mapped out in districts and house-to-house visitors were enrolled. He established an early morning service of Holy Communion and a second evening service of Common Prayer at a time when such innovations were hardly known outside the Evangelical circle. He introduced the use of the Litany on Wednesdays and Fridays, and established a church service on each Saint's Day. Seven hundred and eighty candidates were prepared and brought before the bishop at his first Confirmation; fifteen local Sunday schools were set on foot and visited in rotation in the poorest parts of the parish. They met in temporary rooms, were taught by voluntary helpers, and were run with special funds and libraries on the lines laid down by Thomas Chalmers. There had been no such stir among the dry bones of Islington since the day when Whitefield had preached his first sermon in the open air in London in that parish graveyard. Vast crowds were now once more assembled in the church, and all standing room was occupied to hear Whitefield's spiritual grandson; and though all seats were free at the second evening service, the church could not contain those who converged from all quarters for the sake of Wilson's preaching.

On January 7, 1827, Wilson observed that there were two hundred and thirty-eight communicants at the morning service; on March 18, 1827, the church was so crowded that four hundred people were turned away. More church accommodation was an urgent necessity and thus he launched his plan to build three new churches. This scheme called forth immense labour and most anxious planning; but prayer was made without ceasing, and his vision and enthusiasm swept all obstacles aside. These three churches rose up one by one at a cost of some thirty-five thousand pounds, with more than five thousand sittings, and were consecrated by the Bishop of London between July 1828 and March 1829. Good men were put in charge and they were all soon filled with large congregations. The one further need which was felt in a parish like Islington was that of a good school for the children of the upper classes, and this need was also met when such a school was opened in 1830. Meanwhile, he kept up a steady output of literary work and his style developed in strong and trenchant English. Simeon did not hesitate to describe his Preface to a new edition of The Practical View of Christianity in 1826 as 'of very singular value', and 'one of the finest compositions in our language'.[25] In 1827, he built a new and imposing library, and the ten thousand volumes which lined its walls in double rows were his great delight. Here, in 1828, he met twelve friends to discuss the subject of prayer and thus commenced what has become so well known as the Islington Clerical Conference. Its annual sessions grew in numbers and influence, until the jubilee and centenary meetings saw many hundreds in the place of the original twelve. He had also founded the great Islington Missionary Association which in those days gave all London the lead in generous offerings. On January 12, 1830, he resumed his journal and the first entry appeared in these words: 'Twenty-three years have passed since I wrote in this journal; I can scarcely say why. I believe that I ceased to write because pride gradually increased, and I could not even describe the state of my soul without some inflation which spoiled all.'[26] Thus eight years passed away while a great and permanent change was wrought. Clergy and laymen of many views were looking on while the energy of one man strove to rouse thirty thousand. Islington was a parish which soon became proverbial for strength and efficiency, for the days of Daniel Wilson were the days of its visitation from on high.

Meanwhile, in those years at Oxford and in London, God had built him a house and fixed its centre in heaven. On November 23, 1803, he had married his cousin Ann, whose father owned large estates at Worton; and he found in her a woman of great lowliness of mind and true charity of heart. Two sons and one daughter were born while they lived in Oxford; one son and two daughters were born after they had moved to London. For fourteen years, apart from the death of their first infant daughter in 1809, the sound of joy and laughter rang all through their home. 'We are', he wrote in 1816, 'the most merry and happy household in London.'[27] But, in 1818, his daughter Ann, a child of great promise whose piety and affection had endeared her to all, died with distressing suddenness at the age of seven. In the morning she was said to be in no danger; in the evening she was called away while on her father's knee. 'How can I tell the distressing event? We have lost our sweet daughter Ann'; so he broke the news to a friend. 'She died last night in my arms and has taken our hearts with her; or rather, may she have drawn them more closely to that Saviour into whose bosom she has fled!'[28] This wound was still unhealed when the last born, William, was seized with a severe illness and his mind was partly clouded. He grew up to the age of five and then, in June 1821, he passed gently away. 'Thus have three children been removed and one half of our little flock transmitted to the heavenly pastures,' he wrote; 'may we so nourish the remainder as to fit them by their Shepherd's grace for the same divine glory!'[29] His two sons, Daniel and John, were at Oxford in his early years at Islington and were left motherless by the death of his wife after a long and painful illness in the May of 1827. Her last thoughts clung to the children with the tenderest affection; among the few fragments of broken speech that fell from her lips as the end drew near, she was heard to murmur: 'Dear John! Dear Dan!'[30] Daniel was the elder of the two and he was ordained as curate of Worton in December 1828; but John!

No one had shown such great promise as this much loved child had done in the morning of his life; but the very gifts which had made him a favourite in his home and with the godly seemed to lay him open in a special manner to the temptations of the wicked. He took rash counsel and formed loose habits; he found himself with the evil-minded and soon drifted from bad to worse. The fears of all who loved and watched him with eyes of tender anxiety were too surely confirmed and, at length, he retired to live on the Continent with his father's unhappy consent. This blow was more bitter than death to his father; he found it hard for faith even to bear the trial:

> I do not know when I have suffered more…Satan has come in like a flood and in ways I could least expect.. I know that my own sins as a man, a parent, and a minister, deserve far more than I have suffered; I know that this dispensation is designed to humble, teach, and purify.[31]

John was followed with ceaseless prayer and anxious love; but the father and son saw each other no more. He was attacked by a fatal illness while on the Pyrenees in August 1833, and his brother at once hastened over to be at his bedside. 'Oh my dear, dear brother,' was his first exclamation; 'that you should have come this long way!'[32] He soon confessed that he felt himself to be the greatest of all sinners, but he pinned his hope as he lay at death's door to the words of Christ: 'Him that cometh to Me, I will in no wise cast out' (John 6: 37). This had been the text of the first sermon which his father had preached; perhaps this was a link in the long chain of answered prayer! He had learnt to cry for mercy, and grace began to work. 'I feel myself now the vilest of sinners, but I believe I have found mercy in the blood of Christ…' he said, 'the great burden on my conscience is my horribly, horribly vile conduct towards my father.'[33] On August 27, 1833, he passed away in peace, and the report of his dying mercies was the one most longed-for comfort of his anxious father in a far-away land. Daniel Wilson was thus a lonely and widowed man after eight years at Islington, and the ties were loosened which might have held him in England. He was now free to hear God's call, while two children were left; a son to succeed him in Islington and a daughter to go with him to Calcutta.

Daniel Wilson had long been on terms of closest friendship with Charles Simeon who, for more than forty years, had made India one of the chief concerns of his ministry. Wilson's missionary zeal could not fail to be drawn to the land where Henry Martyn, and Thomas Thomason, and a score of others had gone at Simeon's behest. His interest was strengthened by the appointment of Heber to the See of Calcutta in 1822, and he had written at the time: 'I cannot close without one word respecting Reginald Heber's nomination to the bishopric of the East. Never was anything, so far as I can judge, more happy.'[34] Wilson had been followed by Heber on the rostrum at Oxford in 1803, when the Prose Essay had been capped by the Prize Poem for the year. No one could have thought that Heber would be followed by Wilson in the bishopric of Calcutta in 1832, when he would cast the spell of energy and action over the scene where the other had cast the charm of poetry and romance. In

1829, Turner, the fourth bishop of the See, paid a short visit to Islington, and Daniel Wilson pledged his parish to give or do anything they could for the benefit of India. Bishop Turner took up his words and said that he would undoubtedly call for the redemption of that pledge; but the summons for Islington to make good the promise came with the death of Turner himself in 1831. The See of Calcutta was thus left vacant by death for the fourth time within nine years and a sense of utmost consternation was felt throughout England. Three men in turn refused the appointment and Wilson felt gravely concerned lest it should fall into inferior hands. His views were placed before Charles Grant as the Colonial Secretary, and he was asked to submit a list of names for consideration. This list was drawn up and sent off with earnest prayer; then the thought came to his mind that he ought to volunteer to go himself!

Therefore he wrote again to state that if a real emergency occurred, and no one else could be found to accept the post, he was ready to let his name stand for nomination. It must be remembered that the See of Calcutta was not then a prize to be coveted, but a great sacrifice which most men avoided. The first four bishops had sunk and died within the last nine years, and the man who was to follow them would go like one who had been baptized for the dead. India was a land of exile compared with the life and glow of Islington, and his offer was wholly disinterested. 'I was compelled', he wrote, 'by conscience and by an indescribable desire to sacrifice myself, if God should accept the offering, and the emergency arise.'[35] On New Year's Day, 1832, he traced the call again: 'The thought first entered my mind on December 11; I cannot tell how or why. I felt in my heart a great desire to dedicate myself to this missionary bishopric, if the Lord would accept me.'[36] Some weeks of delay served to chasten his mind and to subdue his will; then, at the end of March, his appointment was announced. Old friends rejoiced with trembling, for they felt how uncertain was his tenure of life and health; but all who wished well to India and the cause of missions were delighted. 'The appointment of

Daniel Wilson to Calcutta!' exclaimed good old Simeon. 'What a blessing to India! His loss will be sincerely felt in Britain; but God has yet the residue of the Spirit.'[37] His consecration was fixed for April 29, and it was with solemn feeling that he applied to himself that morning the words of St. Paul to the Elders of Ephesus: 'I also go to India under somewhat similar circumstances with the Apostle, in that I know not the things that shall befall me there; but his God will be my God and his Father my Father, and therefore none of these things move me.'[38] It was on June 19 that he embarked on the admiral's yacht at Portsmouth and he found Charles Simeon already on board to join him in valedictory prayer. Then at length he put out to sea, and the desire of his heart in the first glad flush of conversion to spend his life in the missionary service of the Gospel was now after thirty-five years to be satisfied.

The long voyage by the Cape came to an end at last on November 5, 1832, when they dropped anchor in the Hooghly and he landed to a salute from the fort guns. He drove at once to Government House and was then installed in the cathedral by his old friend, Archdeacon Corrie. He gave a short address to some twenty clergy and missionaries whom he met at dinner and told them that he had been before the Church to some extent for thirty years; he would still adhere to the principles which he had always professed, but would endeavour to fulfil the new duties to which he was called with the strictest impartiality.[39] The jurisdiction which his see involved in 1832 was immense, for it stretched from India to Australia and it embraced both Burma and Malay. He brought great talents for organization to his task and his forceful vigour was soon to electrify the sleepy East. He was by no means perfect in character, but his faults were the faults of a strong man. He was fifty-four years of age and he had a wealth of experience behind him; he was now to be spared to rule the Church in his Indian Episcopate for a quarter of a century. Those twenty-five years proved him to be a great man and a first-class bishop, and he did a noble work for India. He saw that the proper method of administration in that vast and scattered See would be by means of Episcopal Visitation, but he wisely spent the first two years in Calcutta in order to accustom himself to the climate and to get a firm hold on the reins of office. The arrears of business were small, but the confusion of the first months was appalling. Diocesan records had all disappeared and he was thrown back on common sense and traditional knowledge. But he had joined the committee of the Church Missionary Society in the year 1810 when Indian problems were first being agitated, and he had been active in all the plans which had been put forward in the twenty years or more since that time. Thus his mind was richly furnished with most necessary knowledge and it quickly ripened in his measures for the evangelization of his vast diocese.[40]

He looked all round the field at home, and then wrote long letters to Madras and Bombay, to Ceylon and Sydney, and even to China. A month passed by, and then we hear his first reflections in a letter which was written in December 1832: 'My view of the prospect before me widens every day, if only God vouchsafes me grace and strength to occupy the station as it stretches out before me on every hand, and to sustain me under the accompanying trials which must arise.'[41] He had to use great caution and seek constant advice; he had to act on first principles and meet events as they arose. He was tireless in acquiring information; no pains were spared, no views despised, and no advice neglected. Men like Alexander Duff and William Carey were laid under contribution, and the details were all written down and preserved for future use. His work engrossed him in his morning ride and in his evening drive, when others were weary with a sleepless night or jaded by a breathless day. His mind was cleared and made up not so much by thought as by conversation, and it was thus that his ideas matured and his plans were resolved. His first two years were full of anxious problems which were a heritage from the past, but they were packed as well with plans and decisions which were full of moment for the future. He took measures to set right the anomalous independence of the chaplains who were prone to resent Episcopal authority; he took steps to secure a large increase in the number of clergy and missionaries at work on the field. He saw the work of the S.P.G. and C.M.S. in Bengal; he launched a Church Building Fund for India as a whole. Quarrels were healed and lectures were established; ordinations were held and confirmations took place. His health stood firm in spite of the varied demands and the trying climate and at length, in 1834, he was ready to initiate his Primary Visitation.

This Primary Visitation was set in full motion on August 13, 1834, by the delivery of his charge in the cathedral; then, on August 24, he embarked with the usual salute and dropped down the river. He sailed across the Bay of Bengal to Penang and Singapore, where he launched a fund for the erection of a new church. Then he returned by Malacca and Moulmein, which had just passed into British hands. 'We have been proclaiming the Gospel in the Burman Empire,' he wrote, 'with China on one side and India on the other!'"[42] Then he headed back across the Bay of Bengal for Ceylon and landed at Colombo on November 7 to deal with many urgent problems. He reached Madras on December 9 and travelled inland to visit the C.M.S. stations at Tanjore and Trichinopoly. On his return he left Madras on February 23 and reached Calcutta on March 2, 1835, thus ending a journey of six thousand five hundred miles in six months and a few days. The most painful problems with which he had to deal were the problems which had to do with native caste and with the Church Missionary Society. He found himself faced with a most awkward question in the case of his old Society, though it had to do with missionaries rather than with natives; it was the vexed question as to the degree of episcopal control which was involved in the issue of an episcopal licence. He had found the problem in a tangled state, but he strove to get it settled on a proper basis. He found that the C.M.S. committee at Madras had chosen to ignore all Episcopal authority, yet theirs were the missions which had fallen into the worst confusion on the issues of caste disorder. Then he learned that certain of their Lutheran missionaries were in direct conflict with the doctrines of the Church of England and that he was refused the right to interfere. This made for a system so ruinous to the peace and holiness of new converts that he felt it threatened the subversion of Christianity itself.[43] Much as he loved C.M.S., he refused to compromise the rights inherent in his office, and a serious controversy on the question of Church Order ensued. It was only composed after three years when C.M.S. gave way, and the settlement was then embodied in four rules drawn up by Wilson and approved by the Society. 'I return now to the full tide of affectionate intercourse with the Church Missionary Society in all its ramifications,' he wrote in June 1836, 'which I only felt compelled for a time to suspend because my superintendence was rejected.'[44] The sound of strife at Madras was hushed and peace was restored with London.

The caste problem had slept for a number of years, but it had wrought untold harm in the Church; one Tanjore Christian had even bluntly said that he would give up his faith rather than part with his caste. The whole problem was now the more awkward to take up and resolve owing to the fact that caste had been tolerated in a modified form by Schwartz, and connived at as a civil rather than a religious institution by Heber. But the whole caste system was heathen and corrupt from first to last; it lay at the very root of Hindu worship and it led to endless abuse in the social life of converts to the Gospel. Wilson had been informed that the missions in the south were in a low state, but he was by no means prepared for what he found. He was startled by the statement of an official secretary that no less than one hundred and sixty-eight converts had lapsed within twelve months, and he saw that the sole cause of this landslide was the recognition of caste in the life of the Church. This made it as easy to return to heathenism as it made it simple to embrace Christianity; the bridge between the two had been allowed to stand and the only verdict he could form was that it ought to be broken down. He looked at the question simply as a matter of right or wrong, and formed his own judgment in the light of New Testament demands. He based his decision on the grand principle that there is neither Greek nor Jew in the Christian Church, but that Christ is all and in all; and on July 5, 1833, he issued a pastoral which declared that caste must be renounced, immediately and irrevocably. When this firm and faithful letter was read to the leading congregations, it met with frank revolt on the part of the Sudra Christians. The few missionaries on the field were scarcely equal to the crisis, and their hands were weakened by European interference. On March 27, 1834, he wrote to the missionaries again and laid it down that no Church office or Church money could be conferred on those who still adhered to caste. The whole system was to be torn out root and branch from the native churches, or the members of those churches were to be disowned until they had abjured the evil thing. This stern decree swept through the church like the blast of a hurricane through an ancient forest, and all that was rotten with age or putrid with sin fell before it. But the presence of Wilson in person was an urgent need and, on his arrival at the close of 1834, he dealt long and anxiously with the disaffected congregations. 'I repeat', he said at last, 'that the impassable barrier of caste must be removed.'[45] To purify the Church absolutely from such customs entrenched since the days of Schwartz was more than one man could do; but the net result was more hopeful than he at least had once dared to conceive, and the whole cause of truth and righteousness was the better for his action.

On October 13, 1835, he embarked on the second stage of his Primary Visitation. His first object was to visit the Syrian churches on the coast of Malabar and in the province of Travancore. The Church Missionary Society had sent agents to work with the heathen population, but their attitude to the Syrian Christians was a very delicate matter. They could not but see how abuse had crept into the Church and they longed to correct what they knew to be wrong; but this required a gentle hand and a master mind.[46] Wilson strove hard to hold out the right hand of fellowship and to encourage a thirst for revival. This hope was high when he resumed his journey, but later years were to prove that all his efforts were abortive. On December 12 he reached Bombay and, on December 23, he delivered a new Charge to the local clergy. 'Your Charges are the result of much, very much thought,' wrote his old friend, Charles Simeon, in August 1835; 'they quite surprise as well as delight me. There is everything suited to meet the feelings of those at home as well as those abroad.'[47] His next step was to make plans for the long overland journey which would take him through the upper provinces of India, for he knew that it was of the first importance to reach the shelter of the Himalayan Mountains before the hot season set in. This meant a succession of one hundred marches over fifteen hundred miles of unsafe and unsettled country. On January 4, 1836, he set out with a large cortege and, on February 6, he reached the border which lay between the two great presidencies of Bombay and Bengal. Here he was urged by many to retrace his steps, but he had made up his mind to go on. If there were unsettled country in front there was an unhealthy jungle behind; the whole cortege, apart from the bishop, had already suffered from repeated attacks of fever and the risks seemed at least equal. He was anxious to call at each military station in the heart of India and his visit to these distant outposts was a powerful influence for good. He used to hold morning and evening prayers; he tried to cheer the chaplain and to leave a blessing. His own sermons and conversation were never more impressive or more delightful than when he found a bare handful of two or three; he set apart someone who feared God to conduct worship on each station where no chaplain had been installed.

On June 13, 1836, he reached Simla and there, for four months, he remained. On October 10, he resumed his journey once more and pursued the same plan as before. He was soon floating down the great River Sutlej in a large native boat, with the vast domains of British India stretching out on one hand and the scarcely known territories of the Punjab reaching back on the other. He rose up on the deck and, looking towards the great unknown, he exclaimed aloud: 'I take possession of this land in the Name of my Lord and Master, Jesus Christ.'[48] The Punjab was then under independent rule and there was little prospect that it would pass into British control. But it is a simple matter of history that the Punjab very soon became not only a British possession, but a very bright centre of missionary enterprise; and it was the Punjab which stood loyal to England when all India rose in mutiny twenty years later. The whole story shows us how a man of faith has power with God and can prevail. He travelled home by the great stations at Delhi and Agra and Cawnpore, until at last on March 13, 1837, his boat dropped anchor at the mouth of the Hooghly. His Primary Visitation had taken two and a half years; he had travelled thirteen thousand five hundred miles by land and sea, and had touched the confines of Burma and China, of Tibet and Cabul. 'I cannot enter upon any one duty this first morning after my arrival in Calcutta', he wrote on March 14, 'without humbly offering my praises to the great Giver of all good for the preservation vouchsafed to His unworthy servant.'[49] Thus, by the end of 1837, the rough work of the diocese had been done, for he knew the general character of the clergy and the needs of each station. The caste problem was at least quiescent and no urgent duty was weighing upon him. The Church Missionary Society controversy had been resolved and there were seventeen missionaries at work in the south where he had found but two. He was ready to press on and to move forward.

Wilson had long fought hard to get approval for the division of his enormous See, and not in vain. Corrie was made Bishop of Madras in 1835 and Carr of Bombay in 1837; Australia was cut off from Calcutta in 1836 and Colombo in 1845. 'Well do I remember Mr Simeon saying that if I had been made Bishop of Calcutta merely to carry that measure', he once recalled, 'and were never to reach India, I should have done a great work.'[50] His Second Visitation was thus confined to the now restricted diocese of Calcutta and it was initiated by the delivery of a new Charge on July 6, 1838. He then embarked once more for Burma and Malay, and called at Penang and Malacca en route for Singapore where he consecrated the new church. On the return journey he met Judson at Moulmein and launched a new church fund at Chittagong. On January 1, 1839, back in Calcutta, he wrote: 'I would fain stand with my loins girded and my lamp burning, waiting for my Lord, my Master, my Love.'[51] News of a spiritual awakening in Mirzapore and Krishnagur soon drew him north to these scenes of labour, and he was thrilled by the promise of a golden harvest. 'What is all this? What is God about to do for us in India?' he exclaimed. 'Thousands of souls seem to be making their way up from the shadow of death to the fair light of Christ.'[52] On January 4, 1840, he reached Cawnpore, where he consecrated two new and beautiful churches; and on May 21, he reached Simla, where he spent five months in comparative rest and leisure. On October 26, he set out on the long return journey and, on April 3, 1841, he reached Calcutta with more than five thousand miles of travel to his credit.

His health had stood the strain quite well and he was soon contemplating a fresh Visitation. The Act of Parliament which had established the new Indian bishoprics was based on a plan for a tour of oversight by the Metropolitan at five-yearly intervals. Therefore his Third Visitation was metropolitical in character and it began with a Charge which he delivered at Calcutta on August 24, 1842. No pains were spared to make this new journey useful, or to secure unity of action in every see; thus he prepared a long minute with forty-two topics for discussion and arrangement with his brother bishops. He left Calcutta on the evening of August 24 for the Straits of Malacca and called once more at Moulmein, Penang, and Malacca en route for Singapore. Then he stretched across the Bay to Madras, where his visit was highly opportune after an interval of seven years. He found that the missions were much strengthened, but that caste was not yet destroyed; and once more he tried to insist upon the fact that the very life of the missions hinged upon the total abolition of caste within the Church. He then sailed for Ceylon and gave his Charge to the clergy in Colombo with a new clause to prohibit them from the management of coffee plantations! He paid his first visit to Tinnevelly and Palamcotta in January 1843, and then turned north to the Syrian Christians of Malabar and Travancore. He found that all his plans for help had been refused and the only course that remained was to set up an open mission. On February 17, he embarked once more and, on March 3, he reached Bombay; then he returned by sea to Calcutta and arrived on May 12 after a journey of eight thousand seven hundred miles in the course of which he had delivered no less than eighty sermons. On October 17, he set out for the interior of his great diocese with a significant entry in his journal: 'I seem to have been drifted away from my moorings, and carried out by the winds and tide. O blessed Jesus! Be Thou my heavenly Pilot! Bring back my shattered barque into safe water, and guide me to my desired haven!'[53] On June 1, 1844, he arrived at Simla where he laid the foundation stone for a new church and spent the summer months in preparing a volume of sermons for the press. On October 17, he left Simla; but as he came down from the hills he succumbed to fever and sank to the borders of death. His march was not resumed until December 17, but he reached Calcutta at length by easy stages on April 26, 1845.

The year 1839 had marked the conception of his plan for a new cathedral and all his energies had been given to this great scheme. 'Oh! if that glorious building should ever rise to the honour of my God and Saviour!' he had written on April 21, 1839; 'it will be the first Protestant cathedral ever erected in this land of idolatry and superstition.'[54] He soon obtained the grant of a handsome site and his heart soared with the vision splendid. 'But hush, my foolish heart!' he went on to add; 'all future things are with thy God and Saviour.'[55] On October 8, 1839, the first stone was laid and he began to save every rupee for the building. He had little hope that he would live to see it complete, but on each fresh return from his distant journeys his first delight was to mark its progress. Thus, in April 1841, he found the scaffold and framework well under way and, in July 1843, he found the walls of the tower going up. In April 1845, he saw the gilded arrow, nine feet long, on the summit of the spire; 'a pledge', he said 'of the arrow of the Lord's deliverance for India.'[56] It was nearly complete and he hailed the sight as the crown of more than twelve years of service for India. Every power of mind and body had been laid out for God throughout those years and the whole tone of piety had been raised throughout the length and breadth of the land. There were now three bishops on the field and the number of chaplains and clergy had been vastly increased. He had set on foot a spirit of church building throughout the East, and the relation of the bishop with the Government was far better understood than in the past. The Church Missions were full of life and promise, and the caste problem was at least on firm ground. He had been much spoken against in other days and had gone through evil report and good report; but the sound of strife had long died away and the character of his leadership was now recognized by all.

But he was a sick man and a visit to England was imperative. He was too weak to deliver his Fourth Charge in person and it had to be read for him. Then, on May 3, 1845, he set out on a voyage by the Red Sea for England, having laid a solemn charge on his two children not to speak against his intended return to India. On June 25, he was sheltered once more in his old home at Islington, worn and pale and thin, with hollow eyes sunk deep in his brow. He had planned to spend his time in quiet retreat, but he soon found that he was in great demand. He was soon in constant touch with Henry Venn of the Church Missionary Society, and his experience was invaluable as a guide to his friends at home. 'I have seen much of the Bishop of Calcutta,' Venn wrote, in July 1845; 'he is in great force of mind, and his whole soul is set upon the advance of the Gospel in all the simplicity and fullness with which he preached it at St. John's.'[57] One memorable incident took place in May 1846 when, for the second time, he preached the annual sermon for C.M.S. in St. Bride's. It required eighty-five minutes for the delivery; but it was a noble sermon and it sealed his testimony of twenty-nine years before. 'Brethren,' he said, as he drew to a close, 'I have done. I commend the sacred cause of Missions, and especially in India, to your prayers. I am re-embarking, if God permit, for the scene of my duties, baptized for the dead.'[58] His is the only name in the first one hundred years which occurs twice in the long and honoured list of those who preached this sermon. On August 31, 1846, in accordance with his pledge he sailed once more for the East. There was surely something of the self-devotion of an earlier and more heroic age in this second departure from home, and country, and kindred. The romance of India had long since passed away and he knew the afflictions which were bound to arise. He had felt the strife of tongues and he had known the scourge of fever. The love of children, the kindness of friends, the communion of the Church at home, had all to be relinquished at a time when life was waning; yet none of these things moved him.[59] Perhaps there is nothing finer than the way in which old missionaries unlearn the love of home, die to their native land, and wed their hearts to the peoples whom they have served and won. Daniel Wilson could not rest in England, but went back to lay his bones in the land where he had spent his strength. He was drawn by that grandest of all passions, the love of a Kingdom which has no frontiers and no favourites, the love of the Christ who had not where to lay His head.[60]

On December 14, 1846, he went ashore at Calcutta and drove at once to see his cathedral. Nine months later the building committee was dissolved and then reformed as the cathedral vestry. Then, on October 8, 1847, eight years to the day since the first stone had been laid, a long and solemn service was held for the consecration. It was like the fulfilment of a grand dream when at last the cathedral, in its seven acres of ground, rang with the songs of praise and worship. He had called it St. Paul's to mark both the doctrine and the spirit which it was his earnest desire to see upheld in its ministry. Seventy-five thousand pounds had been raised of which he had given no less than twenty thousand; the grand total was a sum which not only met the final cost of forty-five thousand pounds, but which also laid the basis of a cathedral endowment with thirty thousand pounds. Seldom perhaps is so great a design carried to such complete success, but the motive force had been the glory of God alone. 'Oh that Christ may condescend to fill the House with His glory,' he cried, 'and may a crowd of black converts hereafter sing in it, Thou art the King of Glory, O Christ!'[61] He knew that he could not toil so incessantly now as in times gone by, but he was quite prepared: 'I must go softly; I must take in sail.'[62] His next Visitation did not commence until November 3, 1848, when his Fifth Charge was delivered in Calcutta. He then embarked on a voyage to Madras and Bombay, and paid a fresh visit to Colombo and Cottayam. He tried to act at all times and in all places on the saying which was so often on his lips: 'We may err in a thousand ecclesiastical matters, but we cannot be doing wrong in preaching the Gospel.'[63] He was back in Calcutta by the March of 1849 and carried out certain local visitations in the next eighteen months. 'The good seed sown in these Visitations is of the last importance,' he said; 'I am satisfied a bishop does nothing more useful.'[64] Then, on November 11, 1850, he set sail once more for Burma and Malay and, at the request of the Bishop of London, for far-away Borneo!

He had to hitch his brig to a British warship to make the voyage from Singapore to Sarawak, but he reached his destination and a new church was consecrated in the domains of the English Rajah. He was back in Calcutta by March 1851, but he fell ill with a complaint which left him prone to dangerous seizure and in need of surgical relief for the rest of his life. His Sixth Charge was delivered in Calcutta on October 1, 1851, but he was too weak to carry out the Visitation of the upper provinces in person and Archdeacon Pratt was commissioned to go inland on his behalf. But though feeble of limb and weak in body, he still retained a vast amount of mental vigour and moral energy. He sat up for many hours each day at his desk engaged in writing or reading; but he kept no late hours and would retire at eleven o'clock. His last reading was always scriptural and devotional, but his active mind still gathered material from all quarters. Perhaps no one in India read so widely as he did and his pungent comments prove how well his reading was milled within. His love of flowers was the solace of his old age and a walk round the grounds with his

Malee a few steps behind was the ordinary termination of his morning drive. He bought botanical books of all kinds and his gardens were well supplied with the choicest plants. His voice had begun to fail him and he could not preach so often; but he still gave the most lucid expositions each morning and evening at prayers. He was growing mellow with age and trial, and the inner life of his soul was kept brightly burning. On March 3, 1850, he had recalled the March of 1796 when God first touched his heart and drew him to seek the good of his soul:

> I thank God with adoring gratitude for that call, but my evidences of adoption must be sought for in the habitual penitence, faith, love, and obedience of my heart and life. Christ must be to me all in all, my wisdom, righteousness, sanctification, and redemption. May He so be to me to my dying hour!'[65]

Again, in February 1854, we hear his well-known voice in the lament:

> The government of the thoughts is an especial difficulty with me. The association of ideas, the recurrence of old sins, the defilement of the fancy and imagination: these are my burden and grief. But the infinite atonement of the eternal Son of God is our refuge. There we hide our confusion of face and look to our heavenly Father with humble confidence.[66]

Daniel Wilson was a man of strong and decided views on most subjects and he was not afraid to avow them. He tried to walk in the old paths of Evangelical Truth and Church Order, and to stand in the gap as a rallying point for weaker brethren. When Evangelical Truth was not endangered, he would contend for Church Order; when Church Order was not imperilled he would contend for Evangelical Truth. Thus, in September 1837, we meet with an outburst from his pen which had been evoked by John Keble's Sermon on Tradition: 'Mark my words, if some of these men do not leave our Church and join the apostasy of

Rome!'[67] Newman's published remarks on the Reformers called forth a fresh outburst three months later

> Was ever anything so impudent as the condemnation he passes on Hooker, Jewell, and all the leaders of the Reformation till he comes down to Laud! My soul, come not thou into their secret; into their assembly, mine honour, be not thou united! No! If we cannot stand against the reproduction of these school subtleties, we are unworthy of the name of Protestants. If no one brother will unite with me, I am ready to protest alone![68]

He went on to voice a formal protest in his Charge of 1838, when he made it clear that the gravest menace to the peace of the Church then lay with the Tracts for the Times:

> It is to me a matter of surprise and shame that in the nineteenth century we should really have the fundamental position of the whole system of Popery virtually reasserted in the bosom of that very Church which was reformed so determinedly from this selfsame evil by the doctrine and labours and martyrdom of Cranmer and his noble fellow-sufferers.[69]

His Third Charge in 1842 was no less uncompromising in tone, but it took a wider range and condemned the whole Tractarian System as 'another Gospel': 'The moment the spell is burst, men will stand amazed that in a day like the present, and in the fairest of all the Protestant churches, a regular system, I had almost said conspiracy, to bring back Popery should be tolerated for a moment.'[70] Wilson was thus among the first to raise his voice against the new views in vogue at Oxford, and he spoke out plainly long before Tract XC raised a hue and cry in other quarters. He warned his clergy, fenced his missions, and strove without ceasing to preserve the Church of India in unity and purity. He could not check seeds of error which would come from England, but he saw to it that they took no root in his See. But this brought him into long and painful conflict with the

S.P.G., due to their appointment of a man of avowed Oxford views to Bishop's College in Calcutta. Wilson found that he was strongly opposed to all that he himself had been teaching and preaching for years. He tried hard to prevent pain or mischief but, in May 1841, he was forced to declare that he would not accept candidates for Orders in the future unless they could satisfy him in a minute inquiry on the Articles. He urged the S.P.G. to recall their man, but they declined to act; he grieved at what he saw, but could take no further step until his visit to England in 1845. Then he appeared before the Board of the S.P.G., with the Primate in the Chair, and with a hundred dignitaries of the Church as well as laymen of the highest repute ranged before him in order to present him with an Address of Welcome. He felt that he had to speak the truth in reply, painful though the task was, and he was heard to the end in blank and utter silence. When he sat down that dead silence still reigned, all outward expression of thought or feeling was suppressed, and not a voice was raised. The pause was long and marked; then the Primate rose and simply dismissed the Board with the Benediction. This breach with the S.P.G. slowly widened and their correspondence was broken off.[71] But had all who were then bishops in the Church of England spoken so promptly and acted so firmly, things might have turned out far better for the Church as a whole. The plain language and authoritative tone which had become habitual with him were never more manifest than in his Sixth Charge in 1851; it was as though he were more than ever resolved that the last notes of the trumpet should give no uncertain sound. 'All I have written and said against Popery and Tractarianism, I stand to,' he had exclaimed not long before; 'not a sentiment do I retract. With my dying breath do I proclaim the fatal seduction of what is called the Sacramental System.'[72]

Daniel Wilson belonged to the fourth generation of the Evangelical Revival and he proved himself a man of great moral courage in his outspoken loyalties. His Funeral Sermon on Dean Milner in 1820 and his character study on Charles Simeon in 1837 show how he had seized on the most salient elements in that system of truth and faith which they and he alike professed.[73] He had been great as a Churchman and preacher at Bedford Row and Islington; he was great, too, as a bishop and leader in Calcutta and India. He lived to reap of the harvest which he had sown with tears and toil, for it was his lot to see a change in the whole aspect of things throughout the East. He was endowed with grand energy and decision of mind and character, and this energy was felt in every phase of life. He had applied himself with keen industry and devotion to the cause of truth and righteousness, and this industry served him where genius might have served others. He might weary colleagues, but he grew not weary himself; when action was not required, then study might be indulged. This it was that made him learned, and holy, and useful, and few men toiled harder or to better purpose. Chaplains and missionaries were more than doubled in number and the churches of Bengal multiplied at least tenfold as a result of his exertions. Perhaps his most notable achievements were the erection of the cathedral in Calcutta and the suppression of the caste system in the native churches of South India. He thought that the cathedral would give a status to the Christian Faith which it had never before possessed; he thought that the caste system would work like poison in the Christian Church if it were not utterly repudiated. Alexander Duff bore witness to the fact that 'the evangelization of the world at large, and of India in particular, was ever uppermost in his heart.'[74] This was borne out by the way in which he toiled at Bengalee, Hindustani, and Sanskrit, that he might fit himself to deal with missionary problems. His half-expressed desire to lay down the pastoral staff of Calcutta and to take up that of Tanjore, was a true disclosure of his heart; he lived to toil, but all his toil was for the sake of souls.

He was far from faultless, but his faults all lay on the side of hasty impulse and sanguine temper. All who knew him felt these failings, but none were more conscious of them than the bishop himself. A sense of profound abasement and self-condemnation breaks out from every page of his journals. No one can read them through, with their humble confessions of guilt and their earnest entreaties for grace, without feeling that they were indeed written as in the very presence of God.[75] Hundreds of self-accusations strew his Letters as well as his journals, but no excuse is ever made. There is a marked resemblance in the tone and method of his private searchings of heart with those of the great Scot, Thomas Chalmers. He was not a man who excelled in the higher flights of Christian feeling; he was too conscious of the holiness of God and the corruption of his own heart to stand very high in joy or rapture. 'I never had much joy in believing; that was never in me,' he said while still desperately ill in 1844; 'it has been with me more a settled conviction and a hearty reception of the Gospel.'[76] But true piety was like a strand woven all round his heart and wrought into the whole fabric of his being, and it found an outlet with increasing freedom as life wore on. His strong and sensitive affections peep out from the reserve of his early manhood; his large and liberal offerings gave back to India all that he had ever received. He read through his Bible from Genesis to Revelation with Scott's Commentary year by year as long as he lived; he sought God's face in prayer in all the details of his life until in his latter years it took up almost half his time day by day. When at length he could not kneel as of old, he would bow down on the table with folded hands and tender eyes.[77] It would be difficult to sum up more happily than in the words of Sir John Kaye, as he recalled him in his account of Christianity in India: 'His strong devotional spirit, his self-forgetfulness in his Master's cause, his unstinting love towards his fellows, his earnestness of speech, his energy of action, had something of an almost apostolic greatness about them.'[78]

On October 2, 1855, his visit to Borneo had its sequel when he consecrated a bishop for Labuan in the cathedral at Calcutta; it was the first time that such a service had taken place for the Church of England outside the British Isles since the Reformation. Then, the very next day, he delivered his last charge in Calcutta, a Charge that was paternal, affectionate, and valedictory in tone; it bore the same relation to the six previous Charges that a calm and tranquil evening does to the early dawn and the summer day.[79] Then he embarked on his Seventh Visitation and sailed for Chittagong, Akyab, Rangoon, and Moulmein. It was his first visit to Rangoon and he travelled four hundred miles up the River Irrawaddy. 'Thus I dedicated Burma by faith to Christ our Lord as I did the Punjab,' he said; 'may the prayer be answered!'[80] On his return to Calcutta he set out for Madras and Ceylon, and then crossed the Bay of Bengal once more for Singapore, Malacca, and Penang. On April 17, 1856, he was back in Calcutta and his last extensive journey was over. But no one can read even this record of his final Visitation without a sense of wonder at his vigour and success in the seventy-eighth year of his life. While God gave health, he used it all in His service; thousands of miles and the call of a new country all came in the day's work. The year 1856 was chequered with many attacks of more or less severe illness, but was characterized by great activity and much success. His mind was fresh and alert, and he kept abreast of all the current literature. His love of home and England was as strong as ever, but his great and oft-expressed desire was that he might finish his course in the country of his adoption. 'Oh, that I may end well!' had been his *cri du coeur*; 'may my sun set without a cloud!'[81] But, in 1857, the Indian Mutiny burst like a thunder-clap on the land and he at once applied for the official appointment of a Day of Humiliation. This was refused, but he was still free to make his own arrangements. Therefore he gave notice of a special sermon to be delivered in the cathedral on July 24 at an hour when all could attend. It was his last sermon in the cathedral, his last public address to India, and it bore a memorable testimony to England's duty as God's trustee for India.

His strength began to fail from that day and he was absorbed for six long months in a struggle with increasing debility. On December 12, he set sail for the Sand Heads in an effort to recruit his strength, but it was too late to be of real benefit. As he made the return journey to Calcutta, weak and worn with fever, he said: 'I feel like a log on the water; I can neither read nor think.'[82] On December 26, he voiced his thoughts with a brightness and a freedom which he seldom indulged: 'I seem to be waiting for the instant coming of the Lord for whom I long, to whom alone I look for pardon and grace, and on whom only I rely for time and eternity.'[83] On his arrival in Calcutta on December 30 he felt as if he might slip out of life at any moment and, the next day, he wrote his last words in his journal: 'This morning at eight o'clock, Dr Webb pronounced my placid pulse much better; I would not for a moment change any one of the divine dealings with me.' A few trembling and illegible words followed, and then he closed his last entry with the Ascription: 'Blessed be God the Father, the Son, and the Holy Spirit, the God of Salvation, now and for ever. Amen!'[84] The pen was then laid down and no more was ever written. On January 1, 1858, the dark shadows of death were gathering round and he began to feel distress at the failure of mind and limbs. That night he talked long with Pratt, as though he would not let him go, and he spoke of himself in terms of the most affecting humility. Pratt voiced the assurance that the blood of Jesus Christ cleanseth us from all sin, and he seemed to take the comfort. But he replied with his old voice: 'Ah, my dear friend, we have talked of that before. You must take it with the context—it is for those who are walking in the light.'[85] At half-past five the next morning he fell into a doze; but as time passed on the servants were struck with his stillness. There was not a sound or movement as far as they could see; Pratt was called and found him lying as though he were unconscious. Doubtful whether what he saw was life or death, he knelt down and offered prayer as for a departing soul. Then he rose from his knees, kissed the pale, cold cheek, and sought for some lingering sign of life. There was none; without sound or struggle he had passed from that last earthly rest to the rest of the saints, in light. On January 2, 1858, the Master had fulfilled the prayer that His aged servant who was in the eightieth year of his life might end well!

Bibliography

Works by The Rev. Daniel Wilson, M.A.

The Evidences of Christianity (4th Ed., 1860).

An Introductory Essay to *A Practical View of Christianity* by William Wilberforce, Esq. (10th Ed., 1829).

'Recollections of the Rev. Charles Simeon', in *Memoirs of the Rev. Charles Simeon*, M.A. by William Carus (1837).

The Divine Authority and Perpetual Obligation of the Lord's Day, asserted in Seven Sermons (3rd Ed., 1840).

Expository Lectures on St. Paul's Epistle to the Colossians (1853)

Biographies Of Daniel Wilson And Other Works Quoted

Josiah Bateman, *The Life of Daniel Wilson* (1860).

William Carus, *Memoirs of the Life of Charles Simeon* (1847).

William Knight, *Memoir of Henry Venn* (1882).

Eugene Stock, *The History of the Church Missionary Society*, Vols. I-III (1899).

H. C. G. Moule, *The Evangelical School in the Church of England* (1901).

G. R. Balleine, *A History of the Evangelical Party* (New Ed., 1933).

Francis Warre Cornish, *The English Church in the Nineteenth Century* (1910).

Endnotes

Chapter 1 - George Whitefield

1 *Seventy-five Sermons*, Sermon lxxii, 754; cf. *Works*, Vol. V, Sermon ix, 130.
2 Balleine, 10.
3 See Balleine, 2.
4 Sermon at the Foundation of City Road Chapel, 1777; cf. Balleine, 5.
5 *A Short Account*, 21.
6 *Seventy-five Sermons*, Sermon lxxii, 755.
7 *A Short Account*, 28–9; cf. *Works*, Vol. I. Letter ccxxiv, 215.
8 Op. cit., 32.
9 Op. cit., 34.
10 Op. cit., 35.
11 *Works*, Vol V, Sermon ix, 130.
12 *A Short Account*, 37.
13 Op. cit., 38.
14 Op. cit., 26.
15 *Seventy-five Sermons*, Sermon lxxv, 787.
16 *A Short Account*, 44.
17 Op. cit., 47.
18 *Works*, Vol. I, Letter xvi, 19.
19 *Seventy-five Sermons*, Sermon lxxv, 788.
20 John Wesley, *Letters*, Vol. I, 204–5.
21 *A Further Account of God's Dealings*; cf. Tyerman, Vol I, 84.
22 Ryle, 36.
23 *A Further Account*; cf. Tyerman, Vol. I, 86.
24 *Works*, Vol. I, Letter xlii, 46.
25 Ryle, 37.
26 Tyerman, Vol. I, 180.
27 Manuscript, cf. Gillies, 31.
28 This letter was first published by Tyerman; cf. Vol. I, 193.
29 See Andrews, 65.
30 See Tyerman, Vol. I, 214.
31 See Gillies, 35.
32 See Andrews, 71.
33 See *Works*, Vol. V, Sermon xxiv, 364.

34 See Ryle, 39.
35 *Works,* Vol. V, Sermon xxiv, 371–2.
36 *Works*, Vol. I, Letter xcviii, 93.
37 *Works*, Vol. VI, Sermon xliii, 184.
38 *Seventy-five Sermons*, Sermon lxx, 736; cf. John Wesley to James Hervey: "I look upon all the world as my parish" (March 20, 1739)—Wesley, Letters, Vol. I, 286.
39 *Works*, Vol. I, Letter ccxxxv, 224.
40 Op. cit., Letters ccxxiii, 214; ccxli, 229.
41 Andrews, 126; cf. *Works*, Vol. I, Letter cclxxii, 256–7.
42 Gillies, 233.
43 *Works*, Vol. I, Letter cxcii, 181–2.
44 Op. cit., Letter cxcix, 189.
45 Op. cit., Letter ccxxi, 212.
46 Wesley, *Journals*, Vol. II, 439.
47 *Works*, Vol. I, Letter ccclxiii, 331.
48 *Works*, Vol. II, Letter dcxxii, 127.
49 Op. cit., Letter dccccxlviii, 363.
50 Gillies, 64.
51 *Works*, Vol. I, Letter cccxi, 384.
52 Op. cit., Letter ccccxi, 384, 386.
53 Op. cit., Letter ccccxxvii, 404; cf. 405, 409.
54 Op. cit., Letter ccccxlix, 429; cf. Letter ccclxvii, 334.
55 Op. cit., Letter ccccxlix, 429.
56 Cf. *Works*, Vol. II, Letter dvi, 12–13.
57 Tyerman, *The Oxford Methodists*, 223.
58 Henry Martyn, *Journals and Letters*, Vol. 1, 277.
59 *Works*, Vol. I, Letter cccxciv, 366.
60 *Works*, Vol. II, Letter dcxl, 144.
61 Op. cit., Letter dlxiv, 73–4.
62 Op. cit., Letter dlxxxv, 93.
63 Op. cit., Letter dxvii, 21.
64 Op. cit., Letter dxlviii, 54.
65 Sec Tyerman, Vol. I, 158.
66 See Tyerman, Vol. II, 37.
67 *Works*, Vol. II, Letter dclxvi, 164.
68 Op. cit., Letter dcxxxiv, 232; cf. Letter dccli, 252.
69 Op. cit., Letter dccxlv, 246.
70 Op. cit., Letter dcclxxi, 274–5.
71 Op. cit., Letter dcclxxxi, 285.
72 Op. cit., Letter dccxciv, 301.
73 Op. cit., Letter dccxcvi, 304.
74 Op. cit., Letter dcccxlii, 356.
75 Op. cit., Letter dccclxxi, 387.
76 Op. cit., Letter dcccciv, 421.
77 Op. cit., Letter dccccxxiii, 438.
78 Op. cit., Letter dccccxxx, 444.
79 Op. cit., Letter dccccxl, 453.
80 Op. cit., Letter dccccxliv, 458.
81 *Works*, Vol. III, Letter miv, 41.
82 *Works*, Vol. III, Letter mlxix, 111.
83 *The Life and Times of the Countess of Huntingdon,* Vol. I, 92.
84 *Works*, Vol. III, Letter mcxiv, 155; Letter mccclvii, 348.
85 *Works*, Vol. IV, 10.
86 *Works*, Vol. III, Letter mcxix, 160.
87 *Works*, Vol. IV, 128.
88 *Works*, Vol. IV, 337; cf. *Works*, Vol. III, Letter mcxxxviii, 181.
89 *Works*, Vol. III, Letter miv, 42; cf. Letter mccclxxxix, 372.
90 *Works*, Vol. II, Letter dcclxxxiii, 288.
91 Gillies, 89.
92 Op. cit., 179.
93 Tyerman, Vol. II, 82.
94 Op. cit., 232.
95 *Works*, Vol. III, 506.
96 Op. cit., Letter mcliii, 193.
97 *Works*, Vol. I, Letter ccccxi, 386.
98 Gillies, 265.
99 *Works*, Vol. III, Letter mccccxlix, 415.
100 Ryle, 45.
101 Andrews, 398.

102 Gillies, 265.
103 Gillies, 231.
104 Ryle, 31; cf. 45–9.
105 Cf. Buckland, xi.
106 Stephen, 394.
107 Cf. Drew, x.
108 Cf. Tyerman, Vol. II, 236.
109 Buckland, xvi.
110 Andrews, 432.
111 Tyerman, Vol. II, 511.
112 Ryle, 55.
113 *The Life and Times of the Countess of Huntingdon*, Vol. I, 92
114 *Life of Wilberforce*, Vol. II, 93.
115 See for illustration, *Works*, Vol. III, Letters dccccxcii, 30; mlxix, 111; mclxvii, 203.
116 Tyerman, Vol. I, 296-7, 304–5; Vol. II, 461, 512.
117 Ryle, 50-1, Newton, *Works*, Vol VI, 95.
118 *Works*, Vol. III, Letter mccccxl, 406.
119 Ryle, 51.
120 Stephen, 400.
121 *Works*, Vol. VI, Sermon xl, 135.
122 *Works*, Vol. II, Letter dccxciii, 300.
123 *Works*, Vol. VI, Sermon xxxviii, 101.
124 *Seventy-Five Sermons*, Sermon lxxiii, 767.
125 *A Further Account of God's Dealings*; cf. Tyerman, Vol. I, 84.
126 Mrs. Jonathan Edwards; cf. Tyerman, Vol. I, 428.
127 Balleine, 31.
128 Gillies, 223.
129 *Works*, Vol. II, Letter dcclxxvii, 280.
130 Ryle, 41.
131 *Works*, Vol. V, Sermon ii, 28.
132 Ryle, 56.
133 Ryle, 60.
134 Stephen, 392–3.
135 *Works*, Vol. III, Letter mcii, 144.
136 *Works*, Vol. III, Letter dccccclxxv, 14.
137 *Works*, Vol. II, Letter dcccii, 309.
138 Op. cit., Letter dccccxxvi, 440.
139 Stephen, 392; cf. Letters, dcxcviii; dccxlvii.
140 Tyerman, Vol. II, 616.
141 *Works*, Vol. III, Letter mcxli, 184.
142 *Works*, Vol. II, Letter dclxxxvi, 182.
143 Tyerman, *The Oxford Methodists*, 260.
144 Tyerman, Vol. II, 625.
145 Stephen, 401.
146 Wesley, *Journals*, Vol. V, 150.
147 *Works*, Vol. III, Letter mccclxix, 356.
148 Gillies, 216.
149 Tyerman, Vol. II, 596.
150 Tyerman, Vol. II, 596.
151 Tyerman, Vol. II, 598.

Chapter 2 - John Newton

1 *Letters to a Wife: Works*, Vol. V, 357.
2 *Narrative of Life*, 5.
3 Op. cit., 7.
4 *Letters to a Wife: Works*, Vol. V, 367.
5 *Narrative of Life*, 9.
6 Op. cit., 18.
7 Op. cit., 21.
8 Op. cit., 25.
9 *Letters to a Wife: Works*, Vol. V, 368.
10 *Narrative of Life*, 34.
11 Op. cit., 42.
12 Op. cit., 45
13 *Narrative of Life*, 50
14 Op. cit., 51.

15 Op. cit., 55.
16 Op. cit., 56.
17 *Letters to a Wife: Works*, Vol. V, 369.
18 *Narrative of Life*, 60.
19 Op. cit., 67.
20 *Omicron*, Letter xxxvi; *Works*, Vol. I, 386-7.
21 *Narrative of Life*, 72.
22 *Letters to a Wife: Works*, Vol. V, 385.
23 Op. cit., 486.
24 *Narrative of Life*, 76.
25 Preface to *Letters to a Wife: Works*, Vol. V, 307.
26 Bull, 37.
27 *Narrative of Life*, 86.
28 Op. cit., 87.
29 *Thoughts on the African Slave-Trade: Works*, Vol. VI, 544.
30 *Works*, Vol. V, 262-3.
31 Op. cit., 290.
32 *Works*, Vol. V, 291; Vol. VI, 541.
33 *Letters to a Wife: Works*, Vol. V, 407 n.; cf. Vol. VI, 523.
34 *Narrative of Life*, 87.
35 *Thoughts on the African Slave-Trade: Works*, Vol. VI, 548.
36 *Narrative of Life*, 90.
37 *Letters to a Wife: Works*, Vol. V, 502–3.
38 *Letters to a Wife: Works*, Vol. V, 503.
39 Op. cit., 506.
40 *Cardiphonia*, Letter i to Mr.—, Works, Vol. II, 44-6.
41 Bull, 97.
42 *Apologia: Works*, Vol. V, 19.
43 *Letters to a Wife: Works*, Vol. V, 533.
44 *Apologia: Works*, Vol. V, 56.
45 Cowper's Correspondence, Letter to Mrs. Unwin, November 18, 1782.
46 *Narrative of Life*, 107.
47 *Cardiphonia*, Letter i to the Rev. Mr B.—; *Works*, Vol. II, 94.
48 Bull, 139.
49 Moule, 162.
50 *Omicron*, Letter ii; *Works*, Vol. I, 145.
51 Tyerman, *Life of Whitefield*, Vol. II, 519.
52 Balleine, 106.
53 *Cardiphonia*, Letters to a Nobleman XIII; *Works*, Vol. I, 478.
54 *Omicron*, Letter XXIII; *Works*, Vol. I, 304.
55 *Narrative of Life*, 195.
56 *Omicron*, Letter II; *Works*, Vol. I, 145.
57 *Narrative of Life*, 163.
58 *Cardiphonia*, Letter III to Mr C.—; *Works*, Vol. II, 160.
59 *Cardiphonia*, Letter V to Mr.— ; *Works*, Vol. II, 58.
60 *Narrative of Life*, 154.
61 *Omicron*, Letter II; *Works*, Vol. I, 146.
62 *Narrative of Life*, 199.
63 "The Messiah", 1 Sermon; *Works*, Vol. IV, 582.
64 *Apologia: Works*, Vol. V, 10.
65 *Cardiphonia*, Letter V to the Rev. Mr Bull; *Works*, Vol. II, 241.
66 *Omicron*, Letter XIX; *Works*, Vol. I, 270.
67 *Narrative of Life*, 154.
68 *Olney Sermons*, xviii; *Works*, Vol. II, 558.
69 Bull, 158.
70 Moule, 155.
71 Bull, 185.
72 *Olney Hymns: Works*, Vol. III, 301.
73 *Olney Hymns: Works*, Vol. III, 302.
74 *Cardiphonia*, Letter I to the Rev. Mr Scott; *Works*, Vol. I, 562.
75 *Cardiphonia*, Letter III to the Rev. Mr Scott; *Works*, Vol. I, 572.

76 *Cardiphonia*, Letter V to the Rev. Mr Scott; *Works*, Vol. I, 585.
77 *Cardiphonia*, Letter VIII to the Rev. Mr Scott; *Works*, Vol. I, 618.
78 Bull, 215.
79 *The Force of Truth*, 31
80 Op. cit., 69.
81 Bull, 224.
82 *The Force of Truth*, 93.
83 Bull, 232.
84 Op. cit., 169.
85 Op. cit., 323.
86 Balleine, 107.
87 *Narrative of Life*, 159.
88 Preface to *Cardiphonia* 1911 Edition, 5.
89 Bull, 267.
90 *Cardiphonia*, Letter IV to Mrs.—; Works, Vol. II, 185.
91 *Cardiphonia*, Letter III to the Rev. Mr Bull; *Works*, Vol. II, 236.
92 *Works*, Vol. V, 135.
93 Bateman, *Life of Daniel Wilson*, Vol. I, 13.
94 F. J. Havey Dutton, *The Life and Times of Mrs. Sherwood*, 216-7.
95 *Narrative of Life*, 137.
96 *Letters to a Wife: Works*, Vol. V, 612.
97 *Letters to a Wife*,Appendix; *Works*, Vol. V, 620.
98 *The Life & Letters of Henry Venn*, 497.
99 *Life of Wilberforce*, Vol. I, 97.
100 *Life of Wilberforce* (One Volume Edition, 1868), 42.
101 See Bull, 306-8.
102 Bateman, *Life of Daniel Wilson*, Vol. I, 13-20.
103 Henry Martyn, *Journals and Letters*, Vol. I, 87, 247.
104 Moule, 164.
105 *Omicron*, Letter XI; *Works*, Vol I, 208.
106 *Cardiphonia*, Letter V to A Nobleman; *Works*, Vol. I, 444.
107 *Cardiphonia*, Letter I to the Rev. Mr O.—; *Works*, Vol. I, 658.
108 *Cardiphonia*, Letter IV to the Rev. Mr R.—; *Works*, Vol. I, 655.
109 *Omicron*, Letter XXXVII; *Works*, Vol. I, 398.
110 *Cardiphonia*, Letter II to Mr.—; *Works*, Vol. II, 49.
111 *Cardiphonia*, Letter I to—; *Works*, Vol. II, 141.
112 *Letters to a Wife*, Appendix; *Works*, Vol. V, 624.
113 *Cardiphonia*, Letter IV to Mrs.— ; *Works*, Vol. II, 19.
114 *Cardiphonia*, Letter I to Mrs. H.—; *Works*, Vol. II, 220.
115 *Cardiphonia*, Letter II to —; *Works*, Vol. II, 143.
116 W. E. H. Lecky, *History of England in the 18th Century*, Vol. III, 134.
117 Bateman, *Life of Daniel Wilson*, Vol. I, 13.
118 Scott, *Life of Thomas Scott*, 327.
119 Bull, 355.
120 *Life of Wilberforce*, Vol. III, 169.
121 *Narrative of Life*, 156.
122 *Narrative of Life*, 147.
123 Carus, *Life of Simeon*, 217.
124 Bull, 358. See also *The Autobiography of William Jay*, eds. George Redford and John Angell James. (Edinburgh: Banner of Truth, 1974), 279.
125 Bull, 359.
126 *Cardiphonia*, Letter III to Mrs.—; *Works*, Vol. II, 180.

Chapter 3 - Thomas Scott

1 John Scott, *Life of Thomas Scott*, 8.
2 Op. cit., 12.
3 *The Force of Truth*, 9.
4 John Scott, 19.
5 *The Force of Truth*, 11.
6 John Scott, 23.
7 *The Force of Truth*, 17.
8 John Scott, 31.
9 Op. cit., 35.
10 Op. cit., 36.
11 *The Force of Truth*, 18.
12 John Scott, 38.
13 *The Force of Truth*, 19.
14 John Scott, 55.
15 *The Force of Truth*, 20.
16 John Scott, 54.
17 *The Force of Truth*, 20.
18 Op. cit., 16.
19 *The Force of Truth*, 33.
20 John Scott, 63.
21 *The Force of Truth*, 24.
22 Bull, 210.
23 John Newton, *Cardiphonia*, 112.
24 Op. cit., 116.
25 Op. cit., 127.
26 Op. cit., 127.
27 Op. cit., 129.
28 Op. cit., 132.
29 Op. cit., 143.
30 Op. cit., 154.
31 Bull, 215.
32 John Scott, 79.
33 *The Force of Truth*, 36-7.
34 John Scott, 92.
35 Op. cit., 93.
36 Op. cit., 160.
37 *The Force of Truth*, 49.
38 Op. cit., 62.
39 Op. cit., 63.
40 Bull, 220.
41 *The Force of Truth*, 53.
42 Op. cit., 65.
43 *The Force of Truth*, 69.
44 Bull, 224.
45 Op. Cit., 225.
46 Op. cit., 227.
47 *The Force of Truth*, 73.
48 Op. cit., 74-5.
49 Op. cit., 95.
50 Bull, 232.
51 John Scott, 581-2.
52 *The Force of Truth*, 79–80.
53 *The Force of Truth*, 101.
54 *The Force of Truth*, 18.
55 John Scott, 393.
56 *The Force of Truth*, 113.
57 Bull, 228.
58 Op. cit., 230.
59 Op. cit., 232.
60 Op. cit., 233.
61 John Scott, 150.
62 Op. cit., 458.
63 Op. cit., 193.
64 Op. cit., 194.
65 Op. cit., 208.
66 Bull, 272.
67 John Scott, 212.
68 Op. cit., 216.
69 Op. cit., 167.
70 Op. cit., 173.
71 Op. cit., 173.
72 Op. cit., 218.
73 John Scott, 238.
74 Op. cit., 224.
75 *Life of Wilberforce*, Vol. I, 286.
76 Bull, 333.
77 John Scott, 237.
78 Op. cit., 236.
79 Abbey and Overton, *The English Church in the Eighteenth Century*.
80 John Scott, 287.
81 James Stephen, *Essays in Ecclesiastical Biography*, 428.

82 John Scott, 587.
83 James Stephen, 429.
84 Balleine, 120.
85 Bateman, *Life of Wilson*, Vol. II, 145.
86 Henry Venn, *Life & Letters*, 391.
87 John Scott, 344.
88 Downer, *Thomas Scott*, 95.
89 Balleine, 120.
90 John Scott, 598
91 John Scott, 439.
92 John Scott, 227.
93 Bateman, *Life of Wilson*, Vol. II, 436.
94 John Scott, 616.
95 *Life of Wilberforce*, Vol. I, 199, 253, 287, etc.
96 John Scott, 617.
97 Op. cit., 347.
98 Op. cit., 420.
99 *Life of Wilberforce*, Vol. II, 308.
100 Op. cit., Vol. V, 132.
101 Op. cit., 132.
102 John Scott, 262-3.
103 Op. cit., 264.
104 Op. cit., 266.
105 Op. cit., 266.
106 Op. cit., 267.
107 Op. cit., 268.
108 Op. cit., 387.
109 Op. cit., 654.
110 Knight, *Memoir of Henry Venn*, 390.
111 Op. cit., 391.
112 Eugene Stock, *History of C.M.S.*, Vol. I, 79; cf. Knight, 391.
113 Knight, 399; cf. John Scott, 316.
114 Eugene Stock, Vol. I, 76.
115 John Scott, 381-2.
116 John Scott, 384.
117 Op. cit., 317.
118 Op. cit., 503.
119 Bateman, Vol. I, 158.
120 John Scott, 388.
121 John Scott, 178.
122 John Scott, 590.
123 Op. cit., 139, 140.
124 Op. cit., 142.
125 Op. cit., 68.
126 Op. cit., 74.
127 Op. cit., 109.
128 Op. cit., 299.
129 Op. cit., 298.
130 Op. cit., 411.
131 Op. cit., 497.
132 See Downer, 81.
133 See Stephen, 433.
134 *Life of Wilberforce*, Vol. II, 308.
135 John Scott, 596.
136 Op. cit., 596.
137 Op. cit., 198.
138 Op. cit., 309.
139 Op. cit., 551.
140 Op. cit., 327.
141 Stephen, 433.
142 John Scott, 168.
143 Op. cit., 356.
144 Op. cit., 510.
145 Op. cit., 452.
146 Bateman, Vol. I, 158.
147 John Scott, 492.
148 Op. cit., 559.
149 Op. Cit., 562-3.

Chapter 4 - Richard Cecil

1 Daniel Wilson, Funeral Sermon on Richard Cecil; cf. *Original Thoughts*, 5.
2 See Seeley, 98.
3 Bateman, Vol. I, 39, 40.
4 *Remains*, 147.
5 Op. cit., 150.
6 Op. cit., 6.

7 Op. cit., 6.
8 Op. cit., 283.
9 Op. cit., 52.
10 Op. cit., 53.
11 Op. cit., 52.
12 Bateman, Vol. I, 41.
13 Seeley, 108.
14 *Remains*, 95.
15 Op. cit., 126.
16 Op. cit., 8.
17 Bull, 225.
18 *Remains*, 78.
19 *Remains*, 82.
20 Op. cit., 109.
21 Bateman, Vol. I, 174.
22 I. Morgan, *The Non-Conformity of Richard Baxter*, 250-1.
23 *Remains*, 13.
24 *Life of Wilberforce*, Vol. II, 279–80.
25 Overton and Relton, 236.
26 Bull, 328.
27 Henry Venn, *Life & Letters*, 435.
28 See Overton and Relton, 196.
29 See Balleine, 60.
30 *Life of Wilberforce*, Vol. II, 36.
31 Op. cit., 16.
32 Op. cit., 57.
33 Stock, Vol. I, 78.
34 Stock, Vol. I, 237.
35 Bateman, Vol. I, 44.
36 Op. cit., 39.
37 Op. cit., 39.
38 Op. cit., 74.
39 Bateman, Vol. II, 325.
40 Bateman, Vol. I, 75.
41 Op. cit., 484-5.
42 *Remains*, 56.
43 Op. cit., 57.
44 Op. cit., 25.
45 Op. cit., 22.
46 Op. cit., 22.
47 Op. cit., 66.
48 Op. cit., 266.
49 Op. cit., 24.
50 Op. cit., 284.
51 See *Original Thoughts*, viii.
52 *Remains*, 54.
53 Op cit., 275.
54 Op. cit., 259.
55 See *Original Thoughts*, vii.
56 *Remains*, 214.
57 Bateman, Vol. II, 277.
58 *Remains*, 112. See *Original Thoughts*, v; Bateman, Vol. I, 75.
59 *Remains*, 96.
60 Op. cit., 81.
61 Bateman, Vol. I, 83.
62 Henry Martyn, *Journals and Letters*, Vol. I, 243.
63 See Seeley, 118.
64 See Seeley, 119.
65 *Remains*, 54.
66 Op. cit., 63.
67 Op. cit., 71.
68 Op. cit., 180.
69 Op. cit., 220.
70 Op. cit., 256.
71 Bateman, Vol. II, 358.
72 Henry Martyn, *Journals and Letters*, Vol. I, 215.
73 Op. cit., 238.
74 Op. cit., 248.
75 Op. cit., 248.
76 Op. cit., 252.
77 Op. cit., 254.
78 Op. cit., 254.
79 Op. cit., 259.
80 Op. cit., 266.
81 Op. cit., 269.
82 Henry Venn, *Life & Letters*, 361-2.
83 Carus, 218.
84 Op. cit., 220.
85 Op. cit., 221.
86 Op. cit., 223.
87 See *Remains*, 163; Carus, 528.
88 *Remains*, 274; cf Carus, 600.
89 Stock, Vol. I, 43.
90 *Remains*, 106, 231.

91 Op. cit., 231, 273.
92 Op. cit., 42, 46.
93 Op. cit., 85.
94 Op. cit., 274.
95 Op. cit., 121.
96 Op. cit., 52.
97 Op. cit., 192.
98 Op. cit., 223.
99 Op. cit., 58.
100 Op. cit., 61.
101 Bateman, Vol. I, 128.
102 Op. cit., 129.
103 See *Remains*, 38, 39n.
104 Op. cit., 45.
105 Op. cit., 41 n.
106 Op. cit., 41 n.
107 Op. cit., 41 n.

Chapter 5 - Daniel Wilson

1 Bateman, Vol. I, 6.
2 Op. cit., 8.
3 Op. cit., 10.
4 Op. cit., 15.
5 Op. cit., 18.
6 Op. cit., 28.
7 Op. cit., 29.
8 Op. cit., 31
9 Op. cit., 33.
10 Op. cit., 44.
11 Balleine, 133.
12 Bateman, Vol. I, 68.
13 Op. cit., 80.
14 Op. cit., 86.
15 Op. cit., 111.
16 Op. cit., 112.
17 Op. cit., 129.
18 Op. cit., 132.
19 Op. cit., 123.
20 Knight, *Memoir of Henry Venn*, 404.
21 Bateman, 174-6.
22 Op. cit., 201.
23 Op. cit., 235.
24 Op. cit., 230.
25 Carus, 610-12.
26 Bateman,Vol. I, 272.
27 Op. cit., 96.
28 Op. cit., 97.
29 Op. cit., 100.
30 Op. cit., 261.
31 Op. cit., 106.
32 Op. cit., 107.
33 Op. cit., 108.
34 Op. cit., 221.
35 Op. cit., 279.
36 Op. cit., 280.
37 Carus, 701.
38 Bateman, Vol. I, 288.
39 Op. cit., 311.
40 Knight, 404.
41 Bateman, Vol. I, 321.
42 Bateman, Vol. I, 407.
43 Bateman, Vol. II, 13.
44 Op. cit., 18.
45 Bateman, Vol. I, 473.
46 Bateman, Vol. II, 47.
47 Carus, 764.
48 Bateman, Vol. II, 119.
49 Op. cit., 138.
50 Bateman, Vol. I, 358.
51 Bateman, Vol. II, 168.
52 Op. cit., 174.
53 Bateman, Vol. II, 227.
54 Op. cit., 171.
55 Op. cit., 172.
56 Op. cit., 243.
57 Knight, 119.
58 Stock, Vol. I, 426.
59 Bateman, Vol. II, 280.
60 P. T. Forsyth, *The Glorious Gospel*, 13.
61 Bateman, Vol. II, 297.
62 Op. cit., 283.

63 Bateman, Vol. I, 177.
64 Bateman, Vol. II, 328.
65 Bateman, Vol. II, 323.
66 Op. cit., 362.
67 Op. cit., 143.
68 Op. cit., 144.
69 Op. cit., 157.
70 Op. cit., 215.
71 Op. cit., 259-62.
72 Op. cit., 336.
73 *Life of Wilberforce*, Vol. V, 50; *Life of Simeon*, 833-48.
74 Bateman, Vol. II, 425.
75 Bateman, Vol. I, 271.
76 Op. cit., 236.
77 Op. cit., 435.
78 Stock, Vol. I, 292.
79 Bateman, Vol. II, 372.
80 Op. cit., 376.
81 Op. cit., 325.
82 Op. cit., 412
83 Op. cit., 412.
84 Op. cit., 410.
85 Op. cit., 426.